THE GWICH'IN CLIMATE REPORT

THE
GWICH'IN
CLIMATE
REPORT

A Regional 2005 Climate Impact Report from the Gwich'in
Athabascans of Fort Yukon, Venetie, and Arctic Village

A 2013 Gwich'in Elder and Youth Climate Solution
Statement to the World from Arctic Village

2020 Updated Climate Interviews

COMPILED AND EDITED BY MATT GILBERT

Interview Transcriptions by Pam Miller

UNIVERSITY OF ALASKA PRESS
Fairbanks

Published by University of Alaska Press
An imprint of University Press of Colorado
1624 Market Street, Suite 226
PMB 39883
Denver, Colorado 80202-1559

The University Press of Colorado is a proud member
of Association of University Presses.

The University Press of Colorado is a cooperative publishing enterprise supported, in part,
by Adams State University, Colorado State University, Fort Lewis College, Metropolitan State
University of Denver, University of Alaska Fairbanks, University of Colorado, University of
Denver, University of Northern Colorado, University of Wyoming, Utah State University, and
Western Colorado University.

∞ This paper meets the requirements of the ANSI/NISO Z39.48-1992 (Permanence of Paper).

ISBN: 978-1-64642-335-4 (paperback)
ISBN: 978-1-64642-336-1 (ebook)
https://doi.org/10.5876/9781646423361

Library of Congress Cataloging-in-Publication Data

Names: Gilbert, Matt, 1979– author, editor. | Miller, Pam (Transcriptionist), transcriber.
Title: The Gwich'in climate report / written & edited by Matt Gilbert ; interview transcriptions
   by Pam Miller.
Description: Fairbanks : University of Alaska Press, [2022] | Includes bibliographical references
   and index.
Identifiers: LCCN 2022014583 (print) | LCCN 2022014584 (ebook) | ISBN 9781646423354 (paper-
   back) | ISBN 9781646423361 (epub)
Subjects: LCSH: Climatic changes—Alaska—Fort Yukon. | Climatic changes—Alaska—Venetie.
   | Climatic changes—Alaska—Arctic Village. | Gwich'in Indians—Interviews. | Traditional
   ecological knowledge—Alaska—Yukon-Koyukuk Census Area. | Yukon-Koyukuk Census Area
   (Alaska)—Environmental conditions.
Classification: LCC QC903.2.U6 G55 2022 (print) | LCC QC903.2.U6 (ebook) | DDC
   304.2/5089972—dc23/eng20220621
LC record available at https://lccn.loc.gov/2022014583
LC ebook record available at https://lccn.loc.gov/2022014584

Made possible by funding from US Fish & Wildlife Service Arctic National Wildlife Refuge
Bureau of Indian Affairs Anchorage Office: ANCSA 14(h)1 Historical and Native Places Program
and private donors like you.

Cover illustration: 1917 Map of White Pass & Yukon Route and Connections, from David
Rumsey Historical Map Collection, image # 2384001.

Contents

THE GWICH'IN CLIMATE REPORT

A Regional 2005 Climate Impact Report from the Gwich'in Athabascans of Fort Yukon, Venetie, and Arctic Village

SUMMARY

This is an exhaustive research project on climate change done among the Gwich'in Athabascan people in the summer of 2005 and an updated study in 2020. This is the first publication in 17 years. Though it is 17 years old, the report is still the first of its kind and more relevant than ever. The report contains extraordinary insight into the intimate relationship Gwich'in Athabascans have had with the climate and land since time immemorial. The Gwich'in Elders had *so* much to share.

There are vast amounts of knowledge with which the Gwich'in entrusted me in this report.

The Gwich'in became the most vocal Alaska Natives on climate change, when the great effects were first being felt across the world in the early 2000s. Among the Athabascan groups in Interior Alaska, the Gwich'in were the first to speak out about it. They also offered solutions and their amazing knowledge of the ecosystem that stunned even senior scientists at the University of Alaska Fairbanks. They documented the drastic changes not only to their hunting lives but to their village lives as well.

Traditional Ecological Knowledge, or TEK as it's become known by, has become more and more relevant and important to climate change science and adaptation in general, especially to the remote areas of the world.

https://doi.org/10.5876/9781646423361.c001

The Arctic Climate Impact Assessment (ACIA) 2005 Report became the world-famous book on climate change, and it will be cited throughout this book. It recognizes TEK in the beginning: "Occasionally used and less frequently credited prior to and during most of the twentieth century, indigenous knowledge from the Arctic has received increasing attention over the past couple of decades" (AMAP, 2005, p. 64).

The main western scientific sources on climate change were used for cross-referencing the Elder knowledge in this book, but western science reports are hard to use for two reasons. First, western science is departmentalized and separated, whereas Native knowledge is wholistic and simple. Second, the vastness of the project is a problem. Almost every single thing Gwich'in people said could be cross-referenced, but I'm only one person, so I did not have the time nor the resources to accomplish such a momentous feat, and I also did not want the report to become too scientific, because there are already mountains of western science books on climate change.

Regarding Native knowledge, familiar with the Gwich'in in Arctic Village myself, I took the liberty of putting the thoughts together, categorized themes, stringed together discussion topics, combined testimonies for common themes, deconstructed the unique syntax of "Gwich'in English" for western readers, and broke down complicated Elder insights for better understanding.

I also drew pictures and graphs, designed diagrams, and connected small testimonies to show the ecological changes on the bigger scale. The main purpose of the summary is to consolidate common observations among the three main Gwich'in villages.

The knowledge of climate change proved very challenging to me in terms of sub-sectioning the knowledge into topics and categories. In my opinion, it weakens the integrity of the knowledge, but it was necessary for better understanding. The knowledge was also difficult to interpret and organize, because there were mountains and mountains of knowledge.

Villagers had their perspective of climate change and felt it to differing degrees, but the dire concern was the same. For example, in Arctic Village, where the terrain is rougher than Venetie and Fort Yukon, less snow in the fall made travel harder. Therefore, it proved a grave concern in Arctic Village for traditional seasonal fall hunting activities. Nevertheless, in Venetie, where the land is flatter and easier to travel upon, it was actually *helpful*. So, the extended benefits of summer conditions into winter months were helpful to some villages and detrimental for others. Gwich'in Elders' also knew chain reactions of climate impacts. Their awareness of region-wide changes includes Porcupine caribou herd migrations, runaway forestation of their tundra lands, and salmon migration changes as well as small changes such as migration timing of birds. Caribou have been the mainstay of the Gwich'in since the beginning, so changes to their migration routes and timing have been disconcerting.

The Elders mentioned they were fighting a two-front war: climate change and a disappearing culture. They feel their culture is their people's best chance of responding to climate change. As one Elder cleverly stated, "The world has to become like Gwich'in to resolve climate change." However, their very own youth has drifted away from this culture, and they fight a war to maintain it. They compete with the luxurious cultures of the modern world. The Gwich'in Elders know their culture will see them through the climate chaos to come.

The Gwich'in Elders and hunters wanted to give context by defining their old life first—a life before contact with the modern world, when Alaska was settled. With contact came the near extinction of hunting and fishing methods, decline of game, loss of language, foods, activities, social lives, and the health and happiness of their culture. "A hunting culture destroyed by food stamps," as the late Harry Thomas firmly stated.

It is from this standpoint that the Elders want people to know they are working from a broken system to respond to climate change, and it is important to fix that system first. The revival of culture and hunting and fishing practices is paramount and critical. It has to begin immediately.

THE 2005 REPORT

In April 2005, a month before graduating college, I won a National Student fellowship award from the National Wildlife Federation (NWF) to conduct climate impact studies among the Gwich'in. After graduation and moving home, I immediately began the region-wide research among the three main Gwich'in communities: Arctic Village, Venetie, and Fort Yukon.

The research started in June 2005, and I was lucky enough to find the best people to interview. I got the right help from the right villagers. I did my best to find the most traditional hunters, trappers, berry-pickers, and Elders in the villages. I wanted people who were always on the land. I interviewed twelve people in Arctic Village, five in Venetie, and eight in Fort Yukon.

After the research ended, I began writing the report for NWF. I found common patterns of climate impacts on wildlife and traditional land use and created a PowerPoint presentation, to display the documentation and present the key effects of climate change among the villages. I gave this presentation around the Interior. It was widely liked.

The climate impact materials got recognition from some organizations, but little else. I did not feel I was getting the support I deserved among the environmental groups in Anchorage and the local universities, so I quit and stored the project. I looked for work instead. I got back to my life.

The materials lay dormant for 15 years, until in spring 2019 the US Fish and Wildlife Service expressed strong interest in the research and funded the transcription and production of the formal report. I revived the long-dormant material and spent the summer of 2019 transcribing, illustrating, and writing the report.

The final product was The Gwich'in Climate Report: the most comprehensive Gwich'in climate research ever conducted. Elders, hunters, and gatherers who spent a lifetime on the land were interviewed. In the original 2005 report, there were twelve interviewees from Arctic Village, five from Venetie, and eight from Fort Yukon. Six of the Elders have since passed on, so it makes the report a lot more valuable. There are only a very few Gwich'in left with strong land knowledge.

Since I lost six, new Elders and hunters were chosen for the smaller 2020 updated report. In Venetie, Darrell Tritt was chosen as a new interviewee in place of Maggie Roberts. In Fort Yukon, Keith James was interviewed in place of the many Elders who passed since the 2005 report.

The Arctic National Wildlife Refuge issue took national stage again, when its legal protection was repealed by the Tax Act of 2017. President Trump rushed to open the area to oil and gas development, and the Alaska Delegation considered it Victory Day.

The Gwich'in nation have fought successfully for 40 years to keep the refuge closed to development. Hopefully, things will turn around.

The approach Gwich'in took in the climate report was different, because it was not one of advocacy but a statement. They were the voices of villagers who were not political, but everyday hunters, woodsmen, and fishermen, who are also women. They presented their knowledge of the environment and the drastic changes they are feeling and attempting to adapt to and allowing the world to make its own judgment. However, they do consistently advocate that society needs a new direction with energy.

Combined with the drawings to illustrate the sophisticated knowledge of the Elders, the climate report and interview transcripts are now available to the world. It was an honor and privilege to write the report, and I hope it will be valued and enjoyed for generations to come.

I hope this report can be a stepping-stone for others to do further research and implement management ideas in the report, improving collaboration between tribes and government agencies. This report is also open for edits by Gwich'in people. The US Fish and Wildlife funding completion of the report is a good first step, but more needs to be done.

The report includes 2013 interviews among the Gwich'in youth and Elders on climate solutions, and it concludes with 2020 updated climate interviews, requested by scientists at the University of Alaska Fairbanks (UAF) who were impressed with the report. Most of what the Gwich'in stated in this book can be confirmed by a report done by the International Arctic Research Center titled "Alaska's Changing Environment" in 2020 (Grabinski and McFarland 2020).

BRIEF INTRODUCTION: GWICH'IN ATHABASCANS

The Gwich'in are the northernmost tribe of the Athabascan people. There are 12 Athabascan groups. The Gwich'in lands stretch from the White Mountains up across the legendary Yukon River and the Flats to the foothills of the Brooks Range in Alaska and then east to Canada. In the US Geological Survey satellite map below, the thin red outline is Gwich'in land, although they did trade in the north and at the Arctic Ocean too.

Arctic Village is located in the Brooks Range mountains, Venetie at the foothills of the Brooks Range and Yukon Flats, and Fort Yukon is on the Yukon Flats and Yukon River.

Gwich'in Old Life

The Gwich'in Elders wanted to talk about the old life before broaching climate change so people could get a better idea of their culture first. In their lifetimes, they saw drastic changes like never before, as their people adopted the new modern world.

They described their old world, where "trash," as we know it, never existed. Overgrowth and forestation were unknown, the land was purer with tundra as far as the eye could see, skies unpolluted by airplanes, fire

Figure 1. Yukon Flats

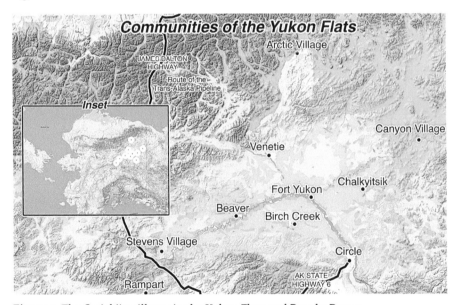

Figure 2. The Gwich'in villages in the Yukon Flats and Brooks Range

signals were used to communicate between villages with no obstructions, and the weather the next day was predictable. Although the Gwich'in always faced starvation and famine, they insisted that this life was healthier and cleaner.

This world of the past is now gone. The Gwich'in Elders face the modern world bringing with it extinction and climate change.

The most poignant statements came from Allen Tritt in Arctic Village, who clearly explained that the land is no longer the only place to obtain food. He added that the luxuries of the modern world in terms of food and entertainment discourages and disables Gwich'in children from hunting and fishing.

When I was a real kid, that time, it was really hard, we were always hungry, always hungry, always hungry—what we get, that's what we eat. That time old people [Elders], my grandfather and my grandmother and my dad, even my mom, said, "Yeendaa [in the future], there's going to be a lot of food and a lot of white man. There's going to be a lot of food. You guys are going to even walk on food."

Long ago, we had to go out hunting for food to survive. I remember my mother, Julia, telling me, "Go get rabbits!" I didn't want to, but she forced me to because I had so many brothers and sisters, I *had* to do it. The times are changing. There is a TV there, a telephone, and a movie there—who wants to work? That time (my childhood) we got no choice, we got to do it, that's the only way to eat.

What we aim at, we got to shoot him, but now when you go out hunting, you going to go out for fun. You going to have a candy bar in your pocket, or cracker. You're going to have soda on one side, and what do you worry about? When you go home, you know what you're going to eat. There's hot pocket and pizza here. When I was a kid, if a piece of candy was on the floor, I got to eat it—no choice. But now, if a cracker drops on the floor, we put it in the dog pot. Like no one hardly goes ice fishing because it's too easy to get food.

The late Stanley Jonas of Fort Yukon added his perspective about the food in these stories: "There's more food nowadays, but it seems like people are still hungry. Long ago, one fish wheel would feed five families."

Allen added that when you go out hunting today, you have a vehicle and a meal back home if you don't get anything, but in the old days, you *had* to get something or you would not eat. He says, "When you had a big family you had to be hunting *all* the time." Allen says the Gwich'in traditionally did not use bows and arrows, but "they knew what they had to do to get their food."

Stanley again added an interesting outlook on how hunting is not the same.

> Long ago, when kids were hungry, they called the council chief, they sent two to three [hunters] out with a canoe, there's no inboard [motor], that's all. Sure enough, they bring back moose, that's how animal is. Even close by you don't have to hunt very much to find them. Geez, my father worked for $2 a day, but I still felt rich!

William Flitt, another traditional Gwich'in in Fort Yukon, confirms this statement. "Long time ago, lots of moose on river. Nowadays, you hardly see any moose on river. You see tracks, but no moose." He emphasized that in his time, when you looked for it, you saw it and got it. He says that is not the case anymore.

Fort Yukon Elder Doris Ward gave her theory.

> They sell moose meat, that's why no moose. I got nobody to hunt for me. They got four moose for Christmas dinner, but we only saw one. They sold the rest. Seems like anything that moves, they kill it, that's why everything is disappearing.

Traditional chief of Arctic Village and the Tanana Chiefs Conference region, Trimble Gilbert, says,

> People in my time were good-spirited people. If they said one bad word, they would never forget it. It's not like that now, no one's like that anymore. If they steal, they tell everyone, but now, "I don't care" is the word.

The eldest Gwich'in Elder in Fort Yukon, Daniel Flitt, said, "Kids (nowadays) got a different mind."

Allen Tritt said the Elders of Old also paid attention to health. "Johnny Frank (Venetie) said, 'This is my body and I'm going to take care of it. I'm going to live 100 years.' He died when he was 98, so you see? He almost made it!" A famous Gwich'in trapper Raymond Tritt said, "Hunting made us exercise, buying food at the store, you don't exercise." Gwich'in Elder Gideon James in Arctic Village said hunting makes for a happy life. "When you harvest fish for dogs, it's good and makes for good fun for spring carnival racing." He says it helps the fish population too.

Gwich'in Land Management in the Old Days

The main way Gwich'in managed the land was through family areas. Gideon James explains the system:

> When we were kids, they harvested everything down to ducks. They knew when to harvest it, fall-time and springtime. This is how they controlled it. In order to make sure they covered a wide area, they assigned themselves an area by family. One family would be in this area, and another would be in this area. You got to have permission to go into another area.
>
> All around the Yukon it's like that. Even here right around this village and around the bend and all that stuff, it's your grandpa's area and we can't go there and shoot muskrat in his area. Yeah, it's a wide area, they have a muskrat camp, and they have a trapline in fall-time and they go fishing and stuff like that. They just do that on their own area.
>
> In order to cover a wide area, this is how they did it. All around the Yukon River and Porcupine River it's like that. Because that's what the family depend on, that particular area. They respect those kinds of tradition. They respect that traditional rule. It's like that all the way around the Yukon River and all up there everywhere! All over Alaska, actually, is like that.

David Russell explains that "this type of thing, down the state they have a farm. Instead of having a farm, they got traditional area; interesting the way they do it."

Gideon went on to explain that if everyone hunted in one area, it would get overpopulated, and the resources would be exhausted. This family system was a way to maintain efficiency and protect animal populations. "Just like Alice [Peter] got a fishing spot, same thing with Steven [Peter], they got a fishing spot in their land, and we got ours." He says the descendants know where their areas are too.

Asked why the system fell into disuse, Gideon said that everyone stopped harvesting muskrats because a lot of this family area system was related to muskrat camps. The families have a general idea of the location of their

Figure 3. Family areas in the Arctic Village Region (map designed by Matt Gilbert)

areas. Some of the families are protective of their area. Long ago, Gideon says one Elder shot at him when he tried to shoot a muskrat in his lake, demonstrating the stringent enforcement of this system.

Further research indicated family area systems in Venetie and Fort Yukon as well. Fort Yukon's family areas covered the entire land south of the Yukon to the White Mountains with fish wheels within the areas. Below is a rough sketch by traditional Gwich'in John Johnson of Fort Yukon, showing the multiple family areas. There were so many families in Fort Yukon that colors ran out and mixes were made to add more.

Within the green areas to the west laid the Kelly family, where they had five fish wheels extending to the far southwestern camps of White Eye Camp and Beaver. You can see the many other areas.

Along with family areas were countless trails all over Gwich'in land. "The walking trails covered the entire Gwich'in region like a giant web," says Norman Flitt of Fort Yukon. Trimble Gilbert explains the trails in detail:

> My grandpa Dehts'e'is a medicine man. He's the one that went up with hundreds of people, and they don't know the trail, but they made the trail. So, there's many lakes up that way, so Dehts'e', he just use the

Figure 4. USGS map with Gwich'in family areas
colored by John Johnson of Fort Yukon

medicine, sleep, and he knows where to go. He tells people where to go
and he makes a trail all the way up.

If you don't have a trail up that way, you're going to get lost. You're
going to spend more time going around big lakes, maybe taking you
one week to get up there. If you know that trail, it will take you maybe
one day.

The trails are extensive, complex, and long. They include trails to fishing
camps, hunting camps, lookout towers, and even trade routes to the south
at the Yukon and north to trading camps to trade with Inupiaqs.

The trails are local in that they lead to wooded areas, hunting areas, fish
camps, fishing spots, and lakes, all with the purpose of subsistence. There
are two trade routes. The north trade route goes to Double Mountain, a
traditional trading camp used by the Gwich'in to trade with the Inupiaq.
The south trade route goes to Porcupine River to Cadzow's Trading Post.[1]

The Gwich'in Elders mentioned that "brush cutting" was a land-
management practice, and there are studies that indicate Gwich'in also

---

1   I am publishing a Gwich'in geography book along with this climate report, in which I
    go into more detail on trails and ancient Gwich'in land use.

Figure 5. The many walking trails in Arctic Village alone with trade routes north and south (map designed by Matt Gilbert)

conducted controlled burns like most Native American tribes. "Cultural burning" refers to the Indigenous practice of "the intentional lighting of smaller, controlled fires to provide a desired cultural service, such as promoting the health of vegetation and animals that provide food, clothing, ceremonial items and more" (Roos, 2021).

Allen Tritt says, "Elders used to cut down brush for the caribou migration, because caribou don't like brush. They always thought about the lakes and fish in the lakes, they cut brush areas for fish and cleared out streams for fish flow too."

Allen says they allowed natural forest fires too, "because there wasn't much growth at that time." It's been proven that most of the Gwich'in land in the early twentieth century was tundra with hardly any trees, but climate change has spurred overgrowth and rapid forestation.

Animal population control was also another land-management practice by the Gwich'in. Gideon James explains, "Gwich'in harvest animals like fish and marten to control the populations and make populations good." Raymond Tritt of Arctic Village said when there was too much small game in the village, the "Elders hunted them (mostly ground squirrels) to eat as much as you can, keep it level." This was another form of animal population control.

Gideon James says that having dog teams encourages you to harvest a lot of fish in the lakes to feed your dogs, but it was also a way Gwich'in controlled fish populations to prevent them from getting too numerous.

Trimble Gilbert says the dogs have been ruined as well. "Dogs are not the same. These dogs are weak and unreliable. The new breeds ruined the normal working dog. Dogs nowadays are worthless." Stanley Jonas agreed with Trimble's statements with laughter. "That's right! Nobody's got a working dog, just those racing dogs, scrawny things. In 1946, I trapped at 20-Mile, above Chalkyitsik, with three dogs. Now three dogs can't even pull a sled, they have to have about 10 to 13 dogs."

The Gwich'in Elders also mentioned cleanliness as a paramount duty in the old days. Audrey Tritt is a Gwich'in fisherwoman who was raised by the Elders. She says:

> When they made a kill, they cleaned it in a certain area, not where they killed it. They leave the land clean. They don't even throw away fish scales and bones. Even cache poles, they neatly stack them, so animals won't trip over them.
>
> They didn't leave fish traps up, because animals could get tangled in them, they turned them over. They were that strict!

Throwing caribou skins away was unheard of but is done a lot today, she claims. "They used the [caribou] hair for dog beds and pound the bones into grease, everything was used."

Audrey Tritt and Raymond Tritt mentioned how when an ATV (four-wheeler) sits idle, it drains gas. They believe this could affect animal migrations. The Gwich'in in Venetie and Fort Yukon were more concerned about vehicles. Doris Ward of Fort Yukon and Robert Frank Sr. of Venetie said, "Vehicle exhaust turns the plants and trees brown." Stanley Jonas adds, "Everything is turning brown."

The Gwich'in Elders wanted their people to be aware of these polluting factors. Doris Ward says, "They [plants] have to have air to breathe. I pick lots of *neetsii* [berries]. I take the stems off and wash them good, then I cook it." Dr. Knut Kielland of the University of Alaska Fairbanks says, "All these paragraphs show how the Gwich'in were the first environmentalists" (Nelson, 1969).

Asked if the new generation could ever return to the old Gwich'in life, Raymond Tritt replied, "My generation and older can go back to the old life, but the younger generation grew up with TV, video games, all that, it would be hard for them."

The Disappearing Gwich'in Culture

The Gwich'in Elders' disappearing culture was just as important as the climate because they saw their culture as the best response to climate change. The Gwich'in Elders had a lot to say on the changing lifestyle and modern world replacing the culture that existed for millenniums. It would best be illustrated as a two-front war.

The Gwich'in Elders are taking the disappearance of their culture just as seriously as climate change. They consider it as serious as war. They know their culture is the best tool Gwich'in youth can have in order to adapt to

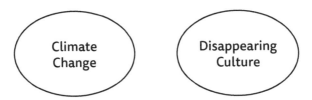

Figure 6. Gwich'in Elder War on two fronts

any ecological change in the future. I am sure they would agree that even the wider world would find their cultural way of thinking helpful too.

William Flitt says the Gwich'in youth *have* to carry on Gwich'in ways. "We have to start talking to our kids, they're raising themselves."

The effects of colonialism also have to be addressed, the treatment of intergenerational trauma, substance abuse, poor education, poverty, and institutional racism. The Gwich'in Elders war against the competing

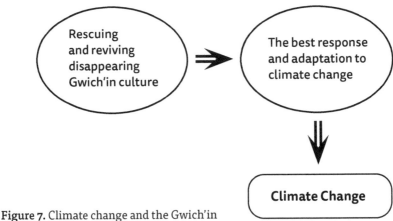

Figure 7. Climate change and the Gwich'in

modern world that makes living on the land unnecessary, and the only way the youth are going to learn their Gwich'in culture is on the land—not on a couch at home.

William Flitt of Fort Yukon says, "This new generation grew up with pop, chips, and microwavable food. They don't want to fry meat when they can microwave something in a few minutes." The late Elder Harry Thomas of Fort Yukon said the same thing. "Lots of times we make soup, and our grandkids will come, and we tell them to eat soup and they won't touch it. They want pizza."

Meaning, they have so many good-tasting food at their fingertips like chips and pizza, so it makes them reluctant to eat moose soup. Allen Tritt in Arctic Village said, "Why should they go through the trouble of hunting when they can get better food here in the village? It's a different world."

"No one want to hunt, just go to the liquor store and put music on full blast," William Flitt of Fort Yukon blatantly says. His words are hard but accurate when considering how much the hunting culture has died and time spent on the land reduced dramatically. Gwich'in have the option to live the Modern Life and not even have to hunt.

The Elders say hunting itself has changed among the youth. Flitt adds, "They hunt moose one day with 90 horsepower [motorboat engine], zoom out. 'I don't see moose,' then zoom back. They want to see it standing on the river. They don't want to go on the mainland." They want hunting to be easy.

Gideon James in Arctic Village had a perspective that strengthens Flitt's statement. "People nowadays are tender-footed. When they trap, they go a little way and one wrong thing, they turn around. We used to go all the way when I was a kid. We didn't turn around."

The late Harry Thomas does not agree with most of what the modern world offers the young Gwich'in. "I don't know how we can hunt with boat motors you can hear 10 miles away. Food stamps are ruining people." In so many words, Harry was saying food stamps destroy work ethic among his people and volunteering is extinct. Stanley Jonas says, "Store is too expensive anyways, $40–50 will buy you one meal."

Doris Ward summarized the topic by a chilling prediction. If Gwich'in continue to disrespect animals, and subsistence no longer becomes reliable and the store food is too expensive, Gwich'in might be reduced to depending on livestock. "Because they're not respecting animals or caring about the land, so animals are getting scarce."

Gwich'in Visions on Climate Change and Prophecies

In the lyrics of an old Gwich'in song, Trimble Gilbert says, "We were always aware of the ozone layer, we called it Zheh Vee Luu. And the old ones knew it was going to change and they even predicted the hole that was in it years ago."

From Arctic Village to Venetie to Fort Yukon, the Elders, hunters, and gatherers all heard the same prediction from their Elders too: "The weather is going to change."

The Elders all say they heard the Gwich'in prediction that the climate was going to get hot. They are now seeing it come to pass. William Flitt recalls the predictions of his Elders. "They said the world is going to change and it's going to be hot year-round, that is what they said long ago." Mildred Allen in Arctic Village made a similar statement. "The Elders said it's going to be warm in the future, no more 50 below," which the IARC Report has proven with studies and graphs (Grabinski and McFarland, 2020, p. 4).

Dr. Kielland confirms, "Sad to say, they are right, that's the forecast of the 2019 IPCC—Intergovernmental Panel on Climate Change" (http://www .ipcc.ch/2019/).

Allen Tritt says the main factor causing climate change is humans, which is also confirmed multiple times by the IPCC and ACIA. "The land changed because people changed," says Allen. Stanley Jonas had a similar statement, describing the chaotic climate. "Long ago, Elders looked out the window and they knew what kind of weather they would have tomorrow. It's not like that anymore. I turn my stove on in July, it's a crazy world. It rained in January too." Allen Tritt says he also doesn't know what will happen. "50 years from now, this whole village might cave in [into the river]."

The late Maggie Roberts of Venetie says the world could be entering another small ice age. "Long ago, we had two-winters, maybe it will be that way again." Doris Ward said, "It's going to turn back to the hot climate you heard about (Cretaceous Period), it can't stay the same. Slowly, the world is coming back to that. It rotates every day . . . slowly."

Trimble Gilbert says time itself has changed and is going faster. "Time is going faster and faster and so much is going on, you don't have time." Trimble also believes another factor causing global climate change is the oil being taken out of the ground. "The oil is like a refrigerator, it keeps the earth cool, that's the reason it's there. They replace it with water, but it won't work. It's warming the earth."

There is research that supports this statement by Trimble at the Phys.org website, https://phys.org/news/2019-08-fossil-fuel-drilling-contributing-climate.html.

GWICH'IN ON CLIMATE AND WEATHER

As mentioned already, Gwich'in Elders of old predicted the coming climate change and sensed it decades ago and knew it would get worse over time. In detail, the Gwich'in Elders tell how the weather and climate is changing before their eyes, "The weather changes too fast! The Elders predicted it," says Deena Tritt of Arctic Village.

Summer

First and foremost were the cold summers that many talked about in the report (Grabinski and McFarland, 2020, p. 5). Bobby Tritt in Venetie, Mike Lee in Arctic Village, and the late Harry Thomas in Fort Yukon agreed the summers are cold. Thomas says the summers are also very cloudy and only allows three to four days of sun, then a long period without it.

Thomas says, "Usually in July, its 70, 80, 90, it's not like that now [in 2005]. Three to four days now my wife had to build a fire [in the house]. It was so cold down at Elders Hall [Gwich'in Elder recreation center], I had to wear my jacket."

Harry's wife, Grace Thomas, added the health effects of cold summers. "People are getting sick from the weather. You go out and its 70 degrees, then in an hour it drops to 40 degrees." The Eldest man in Fort Yukon, Daniel Flitt, confirmed the odd weather. "Two days ago, it was cold. September weather and its July. We never had that kind of wind, maybe in early fall. Lots of different [differences in the world], even kids are different."

With climate change the summer weather varies in extremes, some summers are very hot instead of cold and some summers are cold. Mildred Allen of Arctic Village said, "Last year [2004] it went up to 90 degrees, all the trees were over-multiplying. If it stays 90 degrees, overgrowth will happen." Mildred added, "It's not even cold on mountaintops anymore."

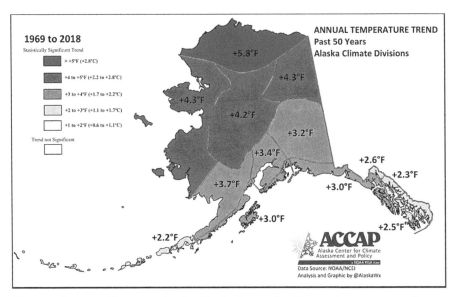

Figure 8. Increased heat map by the Alaska Center for Climate Assessment and Policy

Raymond Tritt of Arctic Village said, "The world is getting hotter and hotter" (Grabinski and McFarland, 2020, p. 4).

Robert Frank Sr. of Venetie said, "The sun is drying everything up, it's too hot." The late Dorothy John of Arctic Village added, "It's getting warmer and warmer." Gideon James says the sun rays are worse than before. "Long ago, it was sunny but you didn't feel it, now you do. It was hot but not burning hot like today. It didn't burn your skin like it does today, it's making the plants red too. I heard in Greenland sheep are even getting blind from these sun rays." Gideon implies that the sheep are a harbinger for humans.

Gideon indicates that UV rays can get so bad in the future that we will all need sunglasses every time we go out or we would go blind from the sun burning our eyes. The famous 2005 Arctic Climate Impact Assessment (ACIA) report supports Gideon's observation: "It has been repeatedly demonstrated that a decrease in total column ozone leads to an increase in UV radiation levels" (AMAP, 2005, p. 161).

Gideon's statement is also supported by a government study done by the National Library of Medicine: "For 30 years there has been concern that anthropogenic damage to the Earth's stratospheric ozone layer will lead to an increase of solar ultraviolet (UV) radiation reaching the Earth's surface, with a consequent adverse impact on human health, especially to the skin" (Diffey, 2004).

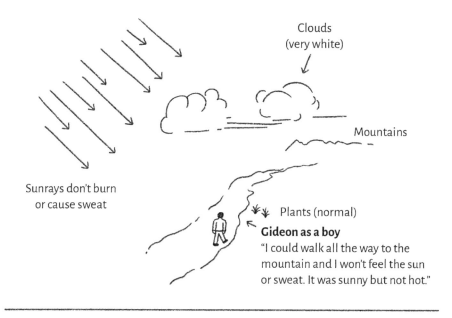

Clouds
(very white)

Mountains

Sunrays don't burn
or cause sweat

Plants (normal)

Gideon as a boy
"I could walk all the way to the
mountain and I won't feel the sun
or sweat. It was sunny but not hot."

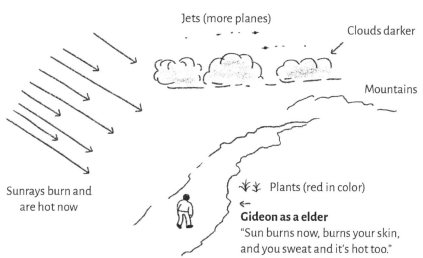

Jets (more planes)

Clouds darker

Mountains

Sunrays burn and
are hot now

Plants (red in color)

Gideon as a elder
"Sun burns now, burns your skin,
and you sweat and it's hot too."

Figure 9. Illustration by Matt Gilbert, redrawn by Lulu Kachele

Gideon also states that cloud formation has changed. "Long ago the clouds use to be puffy and round [strong], not anymore [weak and scattery]." Gideon's statement is supported by a study done by NASA which found, "Observations have shown, however, that warmer temperatures seem to create less dense, low-level clouds instead. The evidence we have so far suggests that this effect occurs because, as temperature increases, the air near the surface becomes drier, causing the cloud base to rise and reducing the cloud layer thickness" (ISCCP, 1999).

Gideon also implies the skies have become polluted by more air traffic. Allen Tritt confirms, "It's true, but right now so many motors are going on, generator, snow-go, outboard motor, airplane, truck, go back and forth to pipeline road. Jets fly over all over. That makes it seem like this." Gideon adds that the clouds today (2005) are "Ugly Clouds" and are black from the contamination.

William Flitt of Fort Yukon said that in the spring "snow just evaporates now in a week, one week no snow, second week ice, and third week water." Allen Tritt of Arctic Village also added that there hasn't been much rain. "No rain in 2004 and not much the last 10 years before that." In 2019, the opposite happened, with increased rains, showing varying extremes.

Fall

Harry Thomas of Fort Yukon said the falls are hot now, and Audrey Tritt of Arctic Village said, "There is no freeze-up in fall sometimes." Dr. Kielland confirms, "This is well documented by climate scientists" (http://www.ipcc.ch/2019/). The falls are heating up (Grabinski and McFarland, 2020, p. 5).

The natural cycle of fall, according to Gwich'in, is as follows: (1) freeze-up (ground hardens), (2) snow falls, then (3) winter sets in. However, "it doesn't freeze up, but it still snowed." Audrey explains. The cycle is disrupted.

In Arctic Village, Allen Tritt says the freeze-up came too early in mid-September 2004. Freeze-up shifted to summer months and exposed the frozen ground to more summer heat and thaws it again. So, climate change induces Indian summers, per se.

Then again, climate change creates longer freeze-ups sometimes too. Allen Tritt says, "The snow is late some years too (longer summers)."

Climate change enables freeze-up to speed up too. Richard Carroll in Fort Yukon says, "Freeze-up happens quick when there's low water. We've had low water [regularly]." Therefore, this regular low water speeds up the freeze-up almost every year now.

Mildred Allen of Arctic Village says a lack of freeze-up can be fatal to the animals. "When there's no snow [or freeze-up], there is no insulation for hibernating animals." Mildred says someone found a lot of dead mice under the ground when they lifted a bed of ground. She believes they might have frozen from an uninsulated frozen ground.

Kathy Tritt, a Gwich'in woman, says that rabbits are endangered from lack of snow too, because they hide under the snow. "If there is no snow, predators will get them easily."

Winter

The second-most common comment everyone had about the changing weather is the warming winters (Grabinski and McFarland, 2020, p. 5). Allen Tritt of Arctic Village and the late Stanley Jonas of Fort Yukon said, "Cold for two weeks [50-below temperatures] is gone, no more (Grabinski and McFarland, 2020, p. 4). Fifty-below now only lasts three to four days in the winter." This has been confirmed multiple times by all western arctic climate reports. In 2019, Raymond Tritt of Arctic Village said it used to get down to 70 below, but he says, "Those days are over now."

"Ice is not thick because it's too warm, no more 50 below. You can walk around in winter with just a jacket," Stanley Jonas adds. Richard Carroll Sr. of Fort Yukon also added, "There's not much snow to start with!" Many Elders in the villages interviewed confirmed Carroll's statement: "There is less snow" (AMAP, 2012, p. 10).

Mildred Allen of Arctic Village says they are getting winter rain too. "It was raining in the middle of November!"

The graph below is provided by the Alaska Center for Climate Assessment and Policy, depicting the extremes in weather to continue into the future. For example, as mentioned earlier, one summer may see no rainfall and extreme dryness, causing more forest fires, but another summer, like in 2012 and later in 2019 and 2020, heavy rainfall lasted all summer. In the 2020 update, heavy summer rainfall had become the norm for villages.

Western knowledge supporting the Gwich'in Elders is in the graph below, confirming the Elders' words that the coldest winters are a thing of the past and the entire climate is moving toward warmer winters and colder summers.

The Gwich'in Elders and traditional Gwich'in had a lot to say about spring and fall, too. Eddie Frank of Venetie says with a giggle, "Fall time, there is no snow. We're hauling wood with wagons and four-wheelers [ATV] in December!"

In other villages like Venetie, they are not seeing snow for long periods of time in fall.

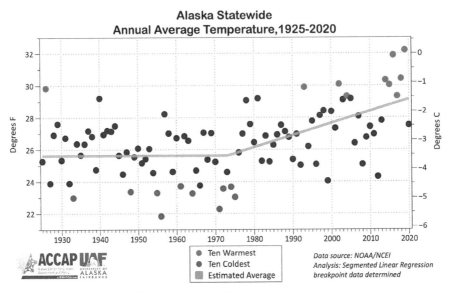

Figure 10. Alaska statewide average annual temperature, 1925–2020

The 2012 update to the Arctic Climate Impact Assessment 2005 Report says the entire cryosphere of the earth is changing (AMAP, 2012, pp. 6–9), and this would explain all these dramatic observations by the Elders.

Spring

The Elders' main comment about springtime was that it was coming too early and too fast, and the second most-stated comment was that the forests are hauntingly quiet. Dr. Knut Kielland confirms, "True—the growing season is now more than 50 percent longer than in the 1900s" (http://www .ipcc.ch/2019/).

Gideon James in Arctic Village said, "On June 5 there is green leaves, it's supposed to turn green June 10." Raymond Tritt of Arctic Village added, "Long ago, I remember we used to drive dogs [dog teams] June first and second." This statement by Mr. Tritt indicates how spring is coming earlier and earlier. Robert Frank in Venetie confirms, "Spring is coming too fast!"

Allen Tritt of Arctic Village said "things thaw out too fast in spring." He says the river thaws out in the beginning of May, and that's too early, because the normal time is the last week of May (Grabinski and McFarland, 2020, p. 3).

The biggest and most dramatic statement everyone made about the spring was the quietude of their forests. Traditional Chief Trimble Gilbert

Abnormalities in the Seasons

Winter		Spring			Summer			Fall			
Jan	Feb	March	April	May	June	July	Aug	Sept	Oct	Nov	Dec
Winter		Spring			Summer			Fall			Winter
1. Too warm 2. Two-week –50° below cold spells gone and reduced to 3–4 days 3. Occasional rain		1. Spring coming too early and too fast 2. Quiet with no animals making sounds 3. Break-up too early			1. Summer sometimes too cold or sometimes too hot 2. Cloudy and rainy 3. Too dry with too many forest fires			1. Too early 2. Too late 3. Not much snow 4. Freeze up does not occur			1. Too warm 2. Two-week –50° below cold spells gone and reduced to 3–4 days 3. Occasional rain

Figure 11. Season chart written by Matt Gilbert, based on Elder testimonies

says, "My mom said it was hard to sleep in spring because of so much noise [from animals], but now it's quiet."

Audrey Tritt of Arctic Village confirms Trimble's statement. "Ducks are coming in late, usually we seen ducks . . . not even seagulls. They're usually down there on Vashraii Koo [Arctic Village Creek mouth] making noise. You don't even hear that. They're usually all around. It's just quiet." Maggie Roberts of Venetie made a similar comment about Big Lake, north of Venetie. "Big Lake used to be noisy, not anymore."

Weather Effects on Individuals

Along with dramatic shifts in time and temperature, the climate and weather affect the Gwich'in on a personal level as well. Grace Thomas of Fort Yukon says that the rapidly shifting weather patterns are affecting people psychologically. "People are getting antsy and quarrelsome from the strange weather." Dr. Kielland from the University of Alaska Fairbanks confirms Grace's statement. "Yes, this is happening to people all over the northern countries."

Gideon James of Arctic Village added, "Lots of different diseases will appear because of weather and contaminants." Unfortunately, in 2020, Gideon James's prediction came true with the worldwide outbreak of the Coronavirus. Beginning in a tiny street market in Wuhan, China, the deadly virus swept the globe in a matter of weeks and killed millions of people. It caused businesses, governments, and schools to shut down for almost a year, an event unprecedented to most people in their lifetimes.

CLIMATE EFFECTS ON LAND, PLANTS, AND PERMAFROST

The main concern Elders had about climate impacts on land is the permafrost, because it is causing the lakes to drain out. The IARC's 2019 "Alaska's Changing Environment" Report confirms these accounts with drama. "Measurements of permafrost temperatures at depths of 30–65 feet, well below levels where the seasonal cycle is felt, show warming at essentially all monitoring sites in northern and interior Alaska" (Grabinski and McFarland, 2020, p. 11).

Gideon James of Arctic Village says, "The permafrost melts the ground deeper and deeper, and the ground splits open some places. The sun rays are melting it, that's why the lakes break out." Trimble Gilbert of Arctic Village adds, "There's big dips in the land from permafrost; that never happened long ago."

Dr. Kielland adds, "This is true for the Yukon Flats, on the Tanana Flats melting of the permafrost results in more wetlands/ponds, where there was previously dry land."

Bobby Tritt of Venetie talks about permafrost causing mudslides and runoffs from hills and mountains. "Big landslides off mountains and hills [melting the integrity of the permafrost]." Dr. Kielland again confirms this account with the IPCC 2019 Report. Mildred Allen of Arctic Village believes the hills and mountains will crumble.

Later in this report, the Elders explain how the melting permafrost drains out the lakes, because permafrost provides an underground basin for the water. "With no permafrost, the water percolates down and, combined with increased evaporation, can't be naturally resupplied" (AMAP, 2005, p. 382).

Overgrowth and Rapid Forestation

The second most discerning effect on land for the Gwich'in is overgrowth and rapid forestation, which got dramatically worse in the updated 2020 report. The late Dorothy John of Arctic Village said, "There was no trees or overgrowth when I was small." Audrey Tritt says the overgrowth is a huge change she is seeing too. Raymond Tritt adds, "It makes travel hard."

Daniel Flitt in Fort Yukon says, "Trees are growing fast. Willows are getting big and thick." Mildred Allen from Arctic Village adds, "Kii Vaataiin Lii [mountain in Arctic Village] is covered with willows—it never used to be."

In the early twentieth century, most of the land in the Interior was bare tundra desert. Allen Tritt confirms, "Most of the tundra was ice, so we didn't have forest fires. You could see a steamboat on the Yukon from Venetie." Descriptions in the book *Tundra* (1920) talk about open country between Beaver and Arctic Village. Franklin Tritt of Arctic Village said, "There were only a few trees around here, but now, everything grows up."

More Dryness

Most of the Gwich'in Elders talk about how dry the land is becoming and how it's leading to frequent and widespread forest fires (Turetsky et al., 2015). "The land is too dry!" Mildred Allen of Arctic Village says. "Our mud puddles in front of our house took a month to dry [normally], but now they dry in five days. It dries like nothing. We don't have to make a sawdust trail no more." She also states, "When we [with her late spouse] go out [into the woods to cut firewood], we can shake a dry tree and it cracks!"

Eddie Frank of Venetie gives a similar account. When Mr. Frank was out in his woodyard—a place in the woods where villagers gather firewood—he noticed trees uprooted (themselves) because they were so dry. The Gwich'in says the dryness is causing all the forest fires (Frank, 2021).

Trimble Gilbert of Arctic Village says there was no such thing as a threatening forest fire, because there was no forest just tundra. "There never used to be forest fires. They never fought fires." Many Gwich'in Elders say forest fires are a new phenomenon because their land was traditionally bare tundra. "We never had forest fires, because not many willows long ago," Audrey Tritt of Arctic Village added.

Other small observations in the lands are mosquitoes—the notorious bugs of Alaska. Like forest fires, mosquitoes were not as problematic for the Gwich'in long ago. "Mosquitoes were not as bad in the old days. There's going to be different insects." Trimble Gilbert says.

LAKES, RIVERS, AND CREEKS

The Gwich'in Elders and hunters rely just as much on fish for their subsistence as big game and have observed great changes in all their navigable waterways, whether they be lakes, creeks, or rivers.

The main concern about the rivers is that they are lowering everywhere, and this concerns the Gwich'in, because rivers are the most efficient means of travel during summers and for fishing.

Yukon River

The Yukon River has been the mainstay for the Gwicha Gwich'in for millenniums, along with moose and caribou long ago, and the legendary river has seen changes. Richard Carroll Sr., Harry Thomas, and William Flitt of Fort Yukon talked about climate effects on the Yukon River. Richard said the Yukon was low in 2005 and said the river and all the creeks are drying up. Flitt added, "You can't even go to certain places anymore, probably not even to Venetie. The river is too low!" Flitt also said break-up came early, and Harry Thomas said, "Two weeks early. It broke May 2 and it's supposed to be mid-May."

Harry Thomas claims the Yukon floods have become less frequent and the water levels have even lowered, based on his measurement of the water level in his garage. He showed me a water line marker at 3.5 to 4 feet off the ground and a second line 1 foot off the ground, indicating a drop in water levels of 2.5 to 3 feet.

Mr. Thomas did not indicate the time length he measured the 1-foot drop, but says Fort Yukon flooded in 1988, 1989, 1990, and 1991. The last big one was in 1982. Flitt says they even used to drink out of the Yukon, but they can't anymore.

Chandalar River

The Chandalar River is a river that feeds into the Yukon from the north and is a mainstay for Venetie, they had similar observations of their river. Tim Thumma of Venetie says the Chandalar River lowered too. "Chandalar was low, I didn't even drive most of July."

Eroison is another huge issue in Venetie, and it is caused by climate change. Robert Frank of Venetie made observations of the erosion: "Banks are eroding maybe 600 yards [in length] in some places."

East Fork River

The East Fork is the next river north that feeds into the Chandalar and has been a mainstay for Arctic Village, along with its tributary Vashraįį Kǫǫ.

Charlie Swaney, Mildred Allen, and Audrey Tritt of Arctic Village talked about climate effects on the East Fork River. Charlie Swaney is a resident of Arctic Village and has lived there for most his life. "I never saw that river that low in 30 years." Audrey Tritt confirms, "Rivers are low, but the ice is still moving." Mildred Allen adds, "Bob [her late spouse] had to drill four holes to reach water, no water under the ice [during winter]."

Mildred also made observations of erosion. "More and more of the bank is falling into the river chunk by chunk, and more channels are opening up." Allen Tritt says, "Rivers dried up and channels disappeared, so less places to go."

The smaller side creeks are disappearing as well. Gideon James says, "Creeks are drying up. When we were kids, [there was] water everywhere." Trimble Gilbert adds, "Bear Creek has dried up. Long ago, it used to run all the way to the river." Allen Tritt of Arctic Village says the East Fork and Vashraįi Koo (creek) was ten times higher than it is right now.

Allen confirms that lower rivers does limit travel to certain places.

Lakes

The next biggest climate phenomenon observed on the land by the Elders is the draining of their lakes, as was cited. Allen Tritt of Arctic Village says, "Lakes are dried out, it's all from vegetation, it sucks the water from the lakes." The late Dorothy John said, "I never see dried out lakes when I was little."

"There's going to be less fish," Robert Frank of Venetie said on account of the dried-out lakes. "When I was 6 or 7 years old the lakes around here used to be plum full, now they're all drained out. That's 55 years, see how short of a time [it took]?"

Mildred Allen of Arctic Village, as well as Stanley Jonas of Fort Yukon, says the permafrost melting below the lakes is causing it to drain out. The Gwich'in explained that permafrost acts like a bed to the lake and once the bed is gone, it bottoms out and the water drains into the ground. This was explained in the ACIA Report as well. Mildred says, "[The] lake dries out because no ice on the bottom to hold it, it bottoms out."

Stanley Jonas of Fort Yukon went into detail about the lakes and permafrost: "About 6 feet down now that everything is burned up and everything is thawed out. That's where all the water went, those lakes are just meadow

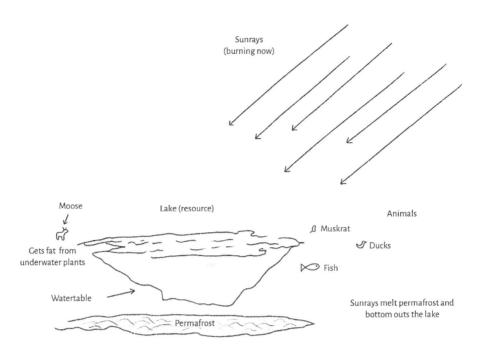

Figure 12. Gwich'in Elder knowledge of lake ecosystem changes (illustration by Matt Gilbert based on Elder testimonies, redrawn by Lulu Kachele)

now. I see it in lots of lakes that way up 20-Mile. Everything is just . . . that's where moose fat come from, the lakes, underwater plants. There's no more of that, so moose are not even fat as they used to be."

Mildred says the lake water is also changing because it is lower. "You can't drink the water because it's so thick [with vegetation]. You can't swim or you'll get a rash, and fish don't bite because [they've] got too much food!"

For Arctic Village, the most valuable lake lost to the changing climate was a lake named Choo tsik' klok. Gideon James and Trimble Gilbert of Arctic Village spoke volumes about the importance of the lake (Roach et al., 2013). It lies six or so miles north of Arctic Village.

Trimble Gilbert of Arctic Village says, "Choo tsik' klok was big, long ago, and rich. Lots of muskrats and whitefish, it was full of fish. We hunted ducks all the time on it. The lake is nothing but grass now. It's a good fishing place, that's why the old man built a cabin there." Gideon James adds, "It had special whitefish that's just rich, but it's all gone now. I asked US Fish & Wildlife Service to look into it, but nothing happened." This example shows how devastating the loss of lakes are to the Gwich'in.

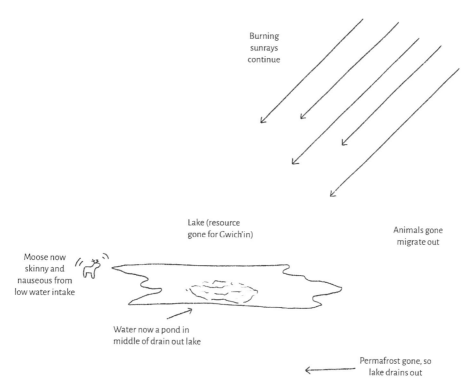

Burning
sunrays
continue

Lake (resource
gone for Gwich'in)

Animals gone
migrate out

Moose now
skinny and
nauseous from
low water intake

Water now a pond in
middle of drain out lake

Permafrost gone, so
lake drains out

Figure 13. Drawing by Matt Gilbert, redrawn by Lulu Kachele

Figure 14. Photograph of Choo' tsik klok Lake. Choo' tsik klok is the dried-out lake in the middle of the photograph. The outline of the original size is visible. (Picture by Matt Gilbert)

Another small observation of changes to the lakes is the thinning of the ice during winters. Trimble says, "The ice is thinning on lakes too. Old John Lake ice during winter used to be 7 feet thick, now it's only 3 [feet]."

CLIMATE IMPACTS ON HUNTING

Gwich'in Elders had a lot to say about climate effects on their hunting culture and the behavior of animals and migration changes.

The first observation was made on the changing habitat of animals. Robert Frank of Venetie says, "We have to go farther and farther out to hunt now. We used to have ducks around here, but now we have to go as far as 50 miles out now." In Venetie, the unusually cold summers had effects on drying fish as well. Bobby Tritt said, "My sister was trying to dry fish, but the fish were freezing at night. It was too cold to dry fish at night."

Some winters the Gwich'in have seen unusual amounts of snow. Allen Tritt of Arctic Village says, "Hard to hunt caribou because the snow gets deep so fast, we can't break trail with snow-go [snow machine]."

Accessibility

The biggest effect climate change is having on hunting is accessibility to hunting grounds. It was the most talked about subject among the Gwich'in hunters and Elders. Allen Tritt of Arctic Village explains, "Less snow is making hunting more difficult because of lost mobility. The terrain is rough, so hard to cross in less snow." Allen's daughter Audrey Tritt adds that the late fall freeze-ups make daily activities harder too.

Fort Yukon

William Flitt, the late Harry Thomas, and the late Stanley Jonas of Fort Yukon talked about climate effects on accessibility and travel. Flitt says, "People don't go hunting because the river is too low." Jonas talked about a recent hunting trip. "I went hunting with my son. We saw lots of moose and cows in one place. He really wanted to shoot them, but I told him no way! We couldn't reach it with the boat, the water was too low."

Harry Thomas adds, "In September it rains, and the river raises and you can go hunting, but it hasn't rained the last couple of years. I can't go up Black River for 2 to 3 years now. I didn't go out moose hunting in fall [water] too low. I don't want to tear up my motor."

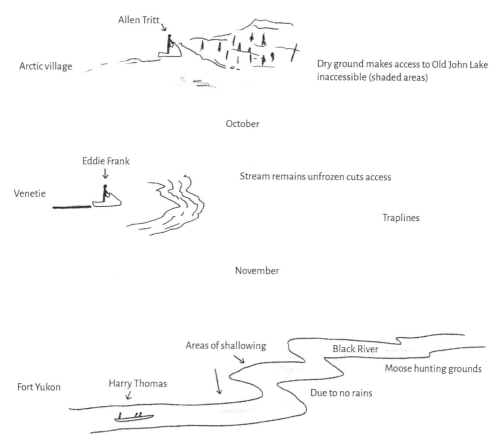

Figure 15. Climate change has created accessibility issues in all three Gwich'in villages (drawing by Matt Gilbert, redrawn by Lulu Kachele)

Venetie

Eddie Frank in Venetie talks about a stream that did not freeze when it was supposed to and how it cut his access to his trapline. "I can't go to my trapline because a stream that is supposed to be thawed by the end of November was still not thawed." It cut his access to his trapline.

Arctic Village

Allen Tritt of Arctic Village talks about how hard it has gotten traveling to Old John Lake, nearly 10 miles from the village across the mountains, "Hard to get to Old John Lake because [there's] no snow," in October when he goes up to fish.

Gas Prices

Harry Thomas of Fort Yukon mentioned how rising gas prices, combined with having to travel farther due to climate change, are affecting hunting. Harry says, "I don't know how people can afford it. Gas prices are inflating so it makes it hard. One hundred gallons to go where we hunt, so that's $400 plus oil, grub, wear and tear on my motor." The combined rising costs of fuel and food along with shifting animal habitats to farther places are making hunting very hard.

PORCUPINE CARIBOU HERD

The Gwich'in of Arctic Village have heavily relied upon and hunted the Porcupine caribou herd. It has been their main sustenance for millenniums. It is a giant herd of over 100,000 and winters in many areas, according to Trimble Gilbert. The herd has not been immune to all the changes. The most dramatic effect was the giant 2004 forest fire.

Forest Fire Impact on Caribou

After the record-size forest fire in 2004, Arctic Village saw its lowest numbers of caribou in memory. Almost everyone I interviewed in Arctic Village said that there were hardly any caribou harvested in fall 2004.

Charlie Swaney of Arctic Village surmised why the village had no caribou in 2004. "We had that big fire, and caribou don't like smoke, so they turned and make a bee line run to Canada, that's why we didn't get anything." He adds, "They were scarce the last five years, too."

The Porcupine caribou has fluctuated in migration patterns over the last 20 years or so, since this report was published; but climate change is effecting the herd with increased forest fires, weaker feeding grounds, stronger rivers at crossing, predatorial advantage from ecological change, and many more changes.

Caribou Farther from Arctic Village and Harder to Find

The Gwich'in believe a lot of animals are getting harder to find and are migrating farther away. Raymond Tritt, the late Dorothy John, and Gideon James of Arctic Village talk about how far from the village the caribou migration has shifted. Raymond said, "They are not as plentiful and not around the village like when I was a kid." Dorothy added, "They don't come around like old times." Gideon added, "You got to go long ways to get it."

According to the Arctic Climate Impact Assessment Report, animal habitats are shrinking: "Distribution ranges of many arctic habitats are likely to decrease with climate change and that this generally implies a reduction in overall extent of the habitat . . . though its mostly individualistic to the species" (AMAP, 2005, p. 570).

In 2005, Gwich'in spoke a lot of about the absence of caribou, but it's important to realize that this was the summer the caribou stayed away from Arctic Village because of the giant 2004 forest fire.

Allen Tritt of Arctic Village talks about the caribou. "Sometimes they sent one caribou to an area to gather food and he come back to them. Tell them where the food is and they go over there, that's what my grandmother told me, Sarah 'Ghoo' Tritt." Allen explains that you could always rely on finding caribou lying on glaciers below mountains, but that is no longer the case. "Always one caribou lying on glacier. [We] don't see that no more." Mountain glaciers are receding and melting all over the arctic (AMAP, 2012, p. 46).

The Porcupine caribou herd is becoming harder to find due to less snow, because their migrations are getting easier in the fall. The late hunter of Arctic Village Timothy Sam indicated how hard it got to find them. "I haven't gotten one the last 2 years." Gideon James of Arctic Village said, "They're moving too much and hard to hunt. Their feeding grounds are depleting and no snow, so they're moving more and more. That is one thing Fish and Wildlife never addressed."

At Gideon and Timothy's testimony of caribou being harder to find, Allen Tritt agreed, "This year we have a hard time getting caribou because, you're right, they're moving so fast."

Porcupine Caribou Herd Route Change

Everyone interviewed in Arctic Village agreed that the route of the Porcupine caribou herd has changed dramatically since the time of contact. They believe the herd's migration has shrunk in two areas: across the East Fork River and down south, toward Venetie.

After passing through Arctic Village, the Porcupine caribou herd makes a giant arc toward the Arctic National Wildlife Refuge, calves there in the highly controversial 1002 Area Trump has allowed drilling in, then migrates to Canada and then down to Old Crow, then back to Alaska toward Arctic Village again.

Eddie Frank and Maggie Roberts of Venetie can remember when the caribou used to come down near their village. Eddie explained, "We used to run into the caribou a lot out in the woods." Maggie adds, "In 1959 there was lots of caribou at Goldcamp, but no more." The last time the herd was seen in Venetie was 1995, but it is unknown if the herd has migrated down since 2005.

William Flitt in Fort Yukon says, "The caribou used to come down south below Circle long ago, and they could come from Venetie with dog teams to hunt them."

The herd now turns around at Brown Grass Lake halfway between Arctic Village and Venetie, and it does not cross the East Fork toward Arctic Village from the west anymore. All the Gwich'in Elders commonly said that vegetation controls the route of the herd. They don't like vegetation, because wolves hide in them.

The overgrowth and increased forestation disable them from migrating south, or, at least not as often as they used to.

Trimble Gilbert of Arctic Village believes they stopped crossing the East Fork in 1974 when they were building the Trans-Alaska Pipeline System (TAPS) because there was too much noise and activity, and the herd was so sensitive that they didn't want to cross the East Fork River—70 miles away from the TAPS construction activity. "The old caribou died, and the young ones don't know the routes on the other side, so they stopped crossing [East Fork River]."

"New research is clearly showing the importance of 'cultural memory' for caribou as to where they go to calve. With the loss of key caribou 'Elders' the herd go different places," Dr. Kielland states (Cameron et al., in review).

Figure 17 is an ArcGIS mapping software graph based on my own drawing, which was based on the testimonies of the Gwich'in Elders concerning the changing of the route over time.

I designed the map with the help of Patti Burns and Kim Streeter at the Alaska State Division of Geosurveys and Geography in Fairbanks.

Gideon James of Arctic Village says, when there is too much traffic on the Sheenjek, the herd gets deflected. The Gwich'in in Arctic Village don't see them during fall or spring. "Too many floaters on the Sheenjek disturbs the

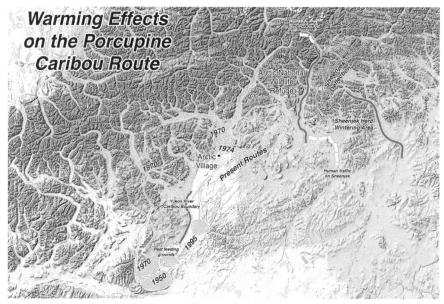

Figure 16. Map designed by Matt Gilbert with the Alaska State Division of Geosurvey and Geography

Figure 17. ArcGIS mapping based on Trimble Gilbert's drawings

herd and makes them turn around. Again, something I bring up to USFWS, but they never address it."

Caribou Bodies

The Gwich'in also say they have seen bodily changes to the animals of the Porcupine caribou herd. They say they are very skinny, and that their meat is not as rich or as tender and is less tasty. These observations vary by year, but the caribou are skinnier because they are finding it harder to find food, lichen. As Timothy Sam in Arctic Village said, they have to migrate more due to less snow, making predators more problematic. This increased mobility to find shifting feeding grounds and avoid predators, who are becoming more mobile themselves to less snow, causes their weight lost.

Dangers of the Porcupine River for the Herd

Trimble fears that when the Porcupine River thaws early, the calves will drown trying to swim across it.

In figure 17, the map is very rough and is not colored, but we were working with the best technology at the time. I did my best to draw the herd routes on the ArcGIS map just as the Gwich'in Elders drew it on the USGS-based maps. You can see how the Elders drew the route shrinking by decade and how it has inched northward.

Figure 18 was drawn by Trimble Gilbert and depicts a more specific route of the herd through the Arctic Village Valley, its original route before 1974, when Trimble says the herd stopped crossing the East Fork.

MOOSE

The Gwich'in indicate the moose have been affected by climate change as well, in many of the same ways the caribou have endured: less body fat, changes in habitat, and skewed migration patterns.

Venetie

Moose are the main sustenance for Venetie and Fort Yukon and the biggest game Gwich'in harvest on the Yukon Flats.

Moose were plentiful long ago, but not anymore, says Maggie Roberts of Venetie. Eddie Frank of Venetie believes they are migrating north, "The moose are moving northward because the growth [vegetation] is moving north" (Zhou et al., 2017). Dr. Kielland confirms, "This is well documented. I have a PhD student working on this."

Tim Thumma is a long-time resident and hunter of Venetie. "There was moose in a certain area below Bob Lake, but I haven't seen any there this winter [in 2005]."

Fort Yukon

William Flitt of Fort Yukon says hunting moose is getting more and more difficult, because they are becoming scarcer. "Long time ago, [there were] lots of moose on the river. Nowadays, you hardly see moose on the river. You see tracks, but no moose. You look for it but don't see it. It never used to be like that."

Arctic Village

Arctic Village is traditionally not a moose-hunting community because the complex hunting techniques found among the Yukon Flats Gwich'in and Koyukon Athabascans are not known among Arctic Village Gwich'in.

Early in the twentieth century, they started seeing a lot of moose. Traditional Chief Trimble Gilbert says they traditionally never had moose in the Arctic Village area and that just in the last hundred years, they started seeing them. Raymond Tritt of Arctic Village said, "More moose in the area." Raymond's brother Franklin Tritt agreed with him. "Yeah, there's more [moose], because lots of willows, that's why."

Body Conditions

Stanley Jonas of Fort Yukon says moose are not as fat as they used to be. "Moose don't have fat because [there are] no underwater plants, that's [where] they get their fat." The drained-out lakes have decimated the underwater plants, they claim. Elliot Johnson III of Fort Yukon said, "I saw a moose was wobbly. I think they're dizzy because they're drinking that thick shallow lake water with lots of vegetation."

Tim Thumma of Venetie says he notices changes in the moose's bodies too. "I tore the hair off and there were rings in the skin, that was unusual." The rings in the skin are something Gwich'in do not usually see.

SALMON AND ARCTIC VILLAGE FISH

Salmon

Along with moose, the main sustenance for Fort Yukon people is salmon. Changes in migration and quality of the salmon have been observed (Carothers et al., 2014; Wolfe et al., 2011). Stephen Klobucar, a postdoctoral research associate in fisheries at the University of Alaska Fairbanks attests to it.

William Flitt and Daniel Flitt of Fort Yukon agree that salmon are around a lot longer and arrive too early. Daniel says, "Yeah early, too early, middle of July and still running." Flitt adds, "Salmon used to run 10 days, now 2 months. They run all summer, it's funny for me."

After Fort Yukon, the salmon migrate up to Venetie, but traditionally, the fish's meat and teeth get poor by the time they reach Venetie. This was due to the fish "aging" or the quality of its health declining by the time it made it to Venetie, but this has changed.

Tim Thumma of Venetie says, "I caught so much salmon. Salmon increase has spiked." Thumma exclaimed with excitement, "The last five years, I see more dog salmon and others."

Eddie Frank of Venetie says the quality of meat from the dog salmon is good now. The late Maggie Roberts of Venetie said, "Dog salmon was not good when it got up here, but now, the dog salmon coming up are good quality, like Yukon salmon."

Venetie residents were seeing more king salmon, due to climate change allowing easier migrations to their northern village—something different from the past. Eddie Frank adds, "Their teeth are not poor anymore." Thumma further adds, "We rarely catch salmon that we could eat, but now it's changed. I hear this summer some people got up to 40 salmon. The usual intake is four or five if you're lucky, and they're poor [but now they're not]."

Fisheries' scientists have long known that water temperature affects salmon (e.g., Mauger et al., 2017), and Gideon James affirmed it with his statement, "Water temperature is important for fish. The sunrays are affecting the fish now because it's different, it burns you."

A lot of these accounts of the salmon and Yukon River by the Gwich'in are confirmed in science reports such as the *Subsistence and personal use salmon harvests in the Alaska portion of the Yukon River drainage, 2012* (Fisheries Data Series No. 1528) (Jallen et al., 2015).

The ACIA 2005 Report states it much better. "The ability of fish to adapt to changing environments is species-specific. In the case of rapid temperature increases associated with climate change, there are three possible outcomes for any species: local extinction due to thermal stress, a northward shift in geographic range where dispersive pathways and other biotic and abiotic conditions allow, and genetic change within the limits of heredity through rapid natural selection. All three are likely to occur, depending on species" (p. 406).

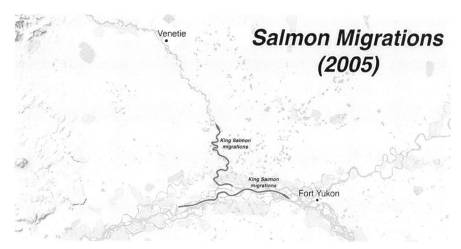

Figure 18. Salmon migration route from Yukon up Chandalar River to Venetie

Arctic Village Fish

The Gwich'in name for Arctic Village is Vashraii Koo (mouth of slough) because the slough runs along the base of the village and empties out into the East Fork River, as a tributary.

Audrey Tritt in Arctic Village sets a fish net every spring at the slough below the village. She noticed a lot of changes, but the first was that the fish were late. The second change she noticed mirrors the observation in Fort Yukon, that the fish's runs are longer. The Arctic Village slough yields mostly whitefish, grayling, and sometimes catfish. "I'm catching fish all summer, but usually it's only spring and fall," Audrey explains.

The late traditional hunter and fisherman Timothy Sam of Arctic Village said, "I'm catching less fish at Old John Lake [in 2005]."

In some areas, the fish are more plentiful, like in Audrey's net. In other areas, Gwich'in are seeing dramatic drops in their numbers. Trimble Gilbert of Arctic Village recalls when there were a lot more in the East Fork. "Up at *Neetsii ddhaa* (30 miles north of Arctic Village), you will see clear water and fish jumping, you don't see that no more."

Raymond Tritt of Arctic Village said the same thing about the mouth of Arctic Village slough (Vashraii Koo), "Long ago, you go down to the slough and you can always catch 30 [grayling], but not no more. You'll catch two or three if you're lucky now." Trimble adds, "You used to catch lots [at] every bend and used to see them from the bank, no more."

Mildred Allen of Arctic Village says things have changed with ice fishing in the spring for grayling, too. "You used to catch lots of fish between ice cracks, not like that anymore." Stephen Klobucar from UAF Fisheries confirms this, "Yeah this would make sense because you get more warmth from the sun in those ice cracks, and they chase temperature."

DUCKS

Venetie

Ducks/waterfowl has been affected by climate change like every other animal in the arctic, especially for Venetie—a Gwich'in community centered in wetlands. The popular account in Venetie is ducks are shifting flying routes and habitats. This has been confirmed by the ACIA: "Changes in freshwater and estuarine habitat will result in altered routes and timing of migration. Emigration of aquatic mammals and waterfowl is likely to extend northward as more temperate ecosystems and habitats develop at higher latitudes" (AMAP, 2005, p. 418).

Venetie is in the wetlands, and one Venetie resident jokingly remarked, "We're swamp Gwich'in." It may stand to reason, then, why ducks are a resource heavily depended upon by Venetie residents. They have noticed changes in the physiology of ducks, but like the caribou in Arctic Village, the ducks are moving farther away from Venetie and growing scarcer. Robert Frank of Venetie says, "Just like ducks, we used to have all kinds of ducks around here. They got to go down 50-Mile to get ducks now."

The late Maggie Roberts of Venetie remembers Big Lake long ago and said it used to be noisy with ducks. Tim Thumma noticed the drop in duck population too. "We have to go back and forth to [the lakes] to get the same numbers we used to. The surf scooter and mallard numbers are down. I usually get 40 to 70 black ducks too, but not now."

Robert Frank Sr. says ducks used to migrate to Venetie from the east, but now come in from the west. In 2005, he says the 2004 fire forced the ducks 50 miles away, and the hunters had to go all the way down there to hunt them, as indicated on the map in figure 20.

Fort Yukon

The Gwich'in of Fort Yukon are duck hunters as well as fishermen and noticed changes, too. William Flitt says, "Geese don't make a sound when

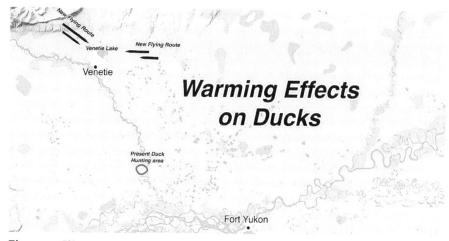

Figure 19. Warming effects on ducks (map designed by Matt Gilbert)

they come in, too." The late Harry Thomas saw changes in the geese migrating south early. "First week of August, geese are ready to fly, their heads turn black like the old ones. We were fooling around one day [in the woods], and we saw their heads turning black already and it was July 21!"

Body Conditions

William Flitt says geese have changed physiologically, too. "You used to boil geese to pluck it, but you don't have to anymore. Now it just plucks."

Arctic Village

Mike Lee of Arctic Village hunted ducks his whole life and says they're getting scarce in Arctic Village. Gwich'in Elder Allen Tritt confirms this: "The river [East Fork] used to be full of ducks, it's not like that anymore." Allen says he doesn't see geese flying in V formations in the sky anymore either. "Sometimes you'll see little ones, but no big ones anymore." Allen also says that the ducks are coming later, too.

Allen also noticed that loons no longer cry on lakes. "Loons don't make noise no more." Allen says the springs in Arctic Village used to be filled with the sounds of ducks. "My mom said she can't hear nothing [because there was] so much noise, it's not like that anymore."

BERRIES

The Gwich'in in all the villages noticed a scarcity in their berries as well (Economic Times, 2021). Deena Tritt of Arctic Village has been a berry-picker her whole life, and picks gallons of berries every fall in Arctic Village. She noticed dramatic changes with blueberries. "They're scattered now. They used to be a big batch together, and you could sit there all day and pick, but not anymore. They're smaller, scattered, and not ripe anymore, they pop easy," Deena explains. She says it's the same with the cranberries as well.

Gideon James of Arctic Village confirms Deena's account of berries being scarce. "It seems like they're only on the mountains now." Mildred Allen reaffirms both their statements. "We used to not worry about them because [there were] lots all over, but now they're only a small batch and last a very short while. We have to run out there and pick them in a rush now!" She laughs.

Mildred says Gwich'in boil cranberries to make cranberry juice, but she says it takes longer to boil them now.

Raymond Tritt said he saw no salmon berries on the mountain in 2005. They have since returned but were absent for 2005—the year following the 2004 fire. Trimble Gilbert says during the 2004 fire, there were no berries at all, and the smoke likely stunted their growth, killing them. Grace Thomas of Fort Yukon stated she couldn't grow anything in her garden the summer of 2004 too.

The berries that are very scarce and hard to find for Gwich'in gatherers and hunters are: Arctic Village: blueberries, blackberries (argued by one Elder to be totally extinct), salmon berries, and cranberries; Venetie: Tim Thumma says berries of all types are becoming scarce and smaller in size in Venetie, although he did not specify which ones; and Fort Yukon: The late Harry Thomas said, "Blueberries ripened two weeks early, supposed to be end of July, but they ripened a week ago."

ANIMAL BEHAVIORAL AND MIGRATION CHANGES

The Gwich'in have noticed changes in all animals, but the ones within this report were specifically mentioned. I have divided them here by village.

Arctic Village

GRIZZLY BEAR

Gideon James of Arctic Village claims there is an increase in grizzly bear nuisance (invading camps and coming into villages) and attributes it to the disappearance of blackberries. "Grizzly bears bother camps because maybe no berries, that's why! They have a diet they have to fulfill. I hope US Fish and Wildlife Service look into it!"

Trimble Gilbert of Arctic Village has an interesting theory on the grizzly bear nuisance. "They feed them from the camp in the 1970s and now they come into camps all the time." That is to say, they have gotten addicted to western foods. There are no known studies to confirm this statement, but it would be interesting to find out if bears really are "addicted" to western foods.

MUSKRAT

Deena Tritt of Arctic Village used to skin and cook muskrats for Elders but, she states, now the "Muskrat is skinny. Elders don't want to eat it, so I had to throw it out." In 2019, Trimble Gilbert said he hardly sees muskrats anymore. So, climate change has made them scarce and sickly.

MARTEN AND LYNX

In 2005, following the giant fire, Trimble Gilbert says he was very perturbed by the recent accounts of marten in the Arctic Village area, which is not their usual territory. They have traditionally inhabited lands farther south. He believes the 2004 fire forced them north. But as of 2020, they have migrated back.

In 2005, Raymond Tritt of Arctic Village, a lifelong trapper, says he saw lynx in the Arctic Village area and thought that was very strange. "Lynx aren't in Arctic Village, it's usually in Christian Village or Venetie area [90 miles south]." But in 2020, the lynx had migrated back south.

ANIMALS IN SCARCITY

Trimble Gilbert gave a list of animals that were once plentiful but have dramatically dropped in population and are "hard to find." He believes the porcupine is utterly extinct.

Wolverine	Sheep
Fox	Ptarmigan
Muskrats	Porcupine (extinct)
Beaver	

Trimble says ptarmigan used to be plentiful in the immediate area of the village but can only be found in the mountains now.

Venetie

Bobby Tritt in Venetie predicted that rabbits [snowshoe hare] and small animals would migrate elsewhere after the 2004 fire, and most of them had. The late Maggie Roberts noticed a scarcity in rabbits in summer 2005.

Fort Yukon

In Fort Yukon, Richard Carroll Sr. noticed a lot more rabbits in Fort Yukon and they perhaps escaped the 2004 fire and gathered in Fort Yukon. Arctic Village saw an increase in rabbits too.

BIRDS

The Gwich'in had a lot to say about the birds in their villages. The common theme in all three villages was the scarcity of birds and their quietude. Mildred Allen of Arctic Village said, "Lots of birds when I was small, noisy, now it's quiet."

Daniel Flitt of Fort Yukon, one of the eldest Gwich'in alive at the time of this report, said, "[There were] all kinds of birds [long ago], [and now] there's nothing, just a few." Traditional Chief Trimble Gilbert believes that because the spring comes early, the birds migrate in early.

The birds and waterfowl listed here are completely absent from the villages in this report and are suspected by the Elders to be extinct or migrated elsewhere:

Arctic Village
- Snipe/Yellowtail (Dil')
- Kah'ee trah' (English name unknown)
- Blackbirds

- Bank swallows
- Mudhouse swallows
- Brownhead swallows
- Dah'stil (English name unknown)
- Grouse
- Stalvik (English name unknown)
- Nootsik (hill-diver duck)

Venetie
- Snipe/Yellowtail (Dil')
- Swallows (one or two species)
- Phalarope

Fort Yukon
- Snipe/Yellowtail (Dil')
- Blackbird
- Solitary sandpiper

The following are birds the Gwich'in still get in their villages but that have dropped dramatically in numbers.

Arctic Village
- Seagulls
- Arctic terns
- Robins
- Hawks
- Ptarmigan (migrated to mountains)
- Swans

Venetie
- Robins
- Mudhouse swallows

Venetie
- Mud swallows
- Swallows (all species)

Fort Yukon
- There were no comments by the Elders on bird population decreases in Fort Yukon, but they most likely see the same patterns.

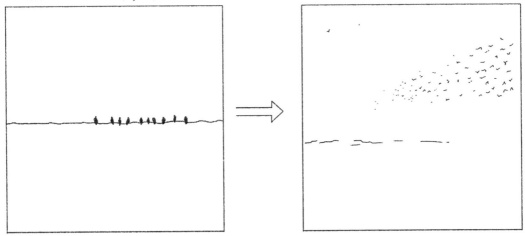

Swallows typically gather on telephone lines at the end of July before migrating south, observed one week earlier than normal in July 2005.

After sitting on the telephone lines 3-4 days, the swallows migrate south.

Figure 20. Harry Thomas's observation of swallows in Fort Yukon, 2005 (illustration by Matt Gilbert, summer 2019, redrawn by Lulu Kachele)

Birds' Changed Behavior

In all three villages, the Gwich'in Elders said the birds no longer sing, and the ones that still do come migrate in weeks early. Elders in Venetie and Arctic Village say they no longer see birds sitting on the telephone wires.

The late Harry Thomas and his wife Grace Thomas talked about how the migration of swallows has shifted. Harry explained, "The swallows were ready to leave, and it wasn't even August yet—too early." His wife Grace added, "They come when ice breaks up and it broke 2 weeks early."

Harry mentioned robins too. "Robins should fly out now or end of July, but they flew 2 weeks ago. By the end of July, we might not have birds!" The robins are supposed to still be in Fort Yukon the whole month of July, but they left 2 weeks early, which was very strange to Harry.

He explained the migration process for swallows in Fort Yukon that he witnesses outside his house. "End of July, swallows sit on telephone wires, it means they gave birth already and are ready to fly. They sit on the wire 3 to 4 days, then fly [in early August]. They're already sitting on the lines and its July 21!"

INVASIVE ANIMALS AND INSECTS

The Gwich'in people have not only witnessed the absence of their animals, but also the introduction of new ones. Mildred Allen of Arctic Village says she expects more and more insects coming into Arctic Village. Here is a list of new animal species and insects beginning to appear in Gwich'in villages:

Arctic Village
Magpie
Polar bear (seen more and more)

Venetie
Brant (goose)
Wood duck
Eider (duck)

Fort Yukon
There were no comments by the Elders on new species appearing in Fort Yukon, but again, it more than likely follows the same patterns.

In Venetie, Robert Frank told a story of witnessing a type of bird he had never seen before. "I was sitting on my couch one morning, when outside my window I saw a strange bird. It had a red body and a blue stripe down its back and its head. I thought someone's pet got loose."

In 2019, Arctic Village saw new white birds that sat on the branches of spruce trees. Their swallows were never seen on spruce branches.

GWICH'IN MANAGEMENT
PROPOSALS AND IDEAS

The Gwich'in did not want to only give impact information, so I encouraged exploring solutions. The main solution that came up from most of them is co-management. The ACIA 2005 states: "Meeting the goals of sustainability requires that resource managers, local communities, and other parties cooperate in resource management. These management functions typically include ecological monitoring and impact assessment, research, communication between parties, policy-making, and enforcement" (p. 613).

They had a lot of ideas for the US Fish and Wildlife Service, all public land agencies, the world, and themselves. First, Allen Tritt of Arctic Village said the Gwich'in can't manage the land like the old days because it would conflict with the current western land management in place. "That land is hard to take care of nowadays with too many laws to it," Allen says. Robert Frank Sr. of Venetie added, "Fish and Game (and USFWS) should be doing what you're doing right now, climate interviews." Trimble Gilbert in Arctic Village (himself a former US Fish and Wildlife Officer) agreed with this statement in 2019. "They should be speaking to us about all these changes."

Bobby Tritt in Venetie stressed the longtime unemployment issue in villages and believes giving Native people more management responsibilities would create more jobs. For example, he proposed that "they should have predator-control programs to put Native hunters to work."

Bobby says another responsibility for Natives would be to "pay us to do harvest reports. It will be helpful to help fish population if we need too. Hire villagers to count fish."

Bobby pitched a huge management and employment project for Venetie and the US Fish and Wildlife. "They need to open up that creek by Big Lake." He believes this would revive the old Gwich'in management practice of clearing sediments from creeks to open them for fish flow.

Robert Frank also stresses the government agencies extending more management jobs to villages. "When prices are low [for fur], trappers don't make income and can't provide for families; Fish and Wildlife should help us."

Robert Frank also says testing meat every year could be a job for Native people too, allowing them to keep track of any pollutants [in animals].

Throughout this entire report, Gideon James had the most ideas and comments for the US Fish and Wildlife Service, but his main concern was for the Porcupine caribou herd. "I told them to put notices up about the traffic on the Sheenjek [river] deflecting the herd, but they didn't do it. I don't think they care."

I hope government agencies such as the Refuge Offices of the US Fish and Wildlife Services and the Alaska Department of Fish and Game do care and will review this report. It is common knowledge that most Alaskan government agencies are understaffed, but wildlife services can improve and assist the Gwich'in more and create co-management.

Gwich'in Land Management Ideas

The Gwich'in management programs the Gwich'in in this report want to implement with the US Fish and Wildlife Service are:

BRUSH CUTTING

Benefits
- Prevents overgrowth
- Prevents forest fires
- Assists animal migrations (as practiced in the old days)
- Protects villages from forest fires

PREDATOR CONTROL PROGRAMS

Benefits
- Decreases wolf overpopulation when they are threatening other animals
- Decreases bear overpopulation when they are threatening other animals

CREEK CONTROL PROGRAMS

Benefits
- Opening up creeks for lakes and rivers
- Clearing clogged-up creeks for fish passage

PARTING STATEMENTS

Concerning more solutions to the climate crisis, Mildred Allen of Arctic Village says, "The Gwich'in people know what's wrong, waking up the whole world about the environmental change we're going through." Robert Frank of Venetie suggested more partnerships for Gwich'in among Indigenous peoples, such as "intertribal business ventures and partnerships with other Indigenous peoples." He wants more international Indigenous partnerships with climate.

CONCLUSION

This report is self-explanatory in its depth and illustrations of how climate is impacting the communities. This is an intimate look at climate change by the Gwich'in and can be used to better understand it. The American Climate Science Community has popularly said Alaska is the canary in the coal mine, and the effects of climate change are happening in Alaska first.

The Gwich'in outlook, sustainable lifestyle, and sense of management over their land to adapt to the climate crisis can be a solution to climate change worldwide. The climate impacts are being felt first in Alaska, and the solutions can come from Alaska as well.

Thank you very much (*Mahsi cho*).

Project Director,

Matt Gilbert

BIBLIOGRAPHY

AMAP. (2005). Arctic Climate Impact Assessment. ACIA Overview report. Arctic Monitoring and Assessment Programme (AMAP), Cambridge University Press. 1020 pp.

AMAP. (2012). Arctic Climate Issues 2011: Changes in Arctic Snow, Water, Ice and Permafrost. SWIPA 2011 Overview Report. Arctic Monitoring and Assessment Programme (AMAP), Oslo. xi + 97 pp.

Cameron, M. K., Joly, G. A. Breed, Mulder, C. P. H., & Kielland, K. (in review) Calving site locations of caribou: Selection driven by best forage or good memories? *Ecological Applications*.

Carothers, C., Brown, C., Moerlein, K. J., López, J., Andersen, D. B., & Retherford, B. (2014). Measuring perceptions of climate change in northern Alaska: Pairing ethnography with cultural consensus analysis. *Ecology and Society*, 19(4), 27.

Diffey, B. (2004 Jan. 7). Climate change, ozone depletion and the impact on ultraviolet exposure of human skin. *Phys Med Biol.*, 49(1), R1–11. doi: 10.1088/0031-9155/49/1/r01. PMID: 14971768. Website Source: Climate change, ozone depletion and the impact on ultraviolet exposure of human skin-PubMed (nih.gov).

Economic Times. (2021 June 7). Your precious blueberries may go missing from smoothies due to climate change. *The Economic Times*. Retrieved June 3, 2022. https://economictimes.indiatimes.com/magazines/panache/your-precious -blueberries-may-go-missing-from-smoothies-due-to-climate-change/ articleshow/83302548.cms.

Frank, Thomas. (2021 June 29). Extremely dry U.S. West is ripe for wildfires. *Scientific American*. https://www.scientificamerican.com/article/extremely-dry-u-s-west-is -ripe-for-wildfires.

Jallen, D. M., Decker, S. K. S., & Hamazaki, T. (2015, September). *Subsistence and personal use salmon harvests in the Alaska portion of the Yukon River drainage, 2012* (Fisheries Data Series No. 15-28). Alaska Department of Fish and Game.

ISCCP (International Satellite Cloud Climatology Project). (1999). "Cloud Climatology: Simple Early Views of Clouds." *NASA*, ISCCP: Cloud Climatology (nasa.gov).

Mauger, S., Shaftel, R., Leppi, J. C., & Rinella, D. J. (2016, September 27). Summer temperature regimes in southcentral Alaska streams: Watershed drivers of variation and potential implications for Pacific salmon, NRC Research Press. *Canadian Journal of Fisheries and Aquatic Sciences*, 74(5), 702–715.

Nelson, R. K. *Hunters of the Northern Forest*. Chicago: University of Chicago Press, 1969.

Roach, J. K., Griffith, B., & Verbyla, D. (2013, March 27). Landscape influences on climate-related lake shrinkage at high latitudes. *Global Change Biology*, 19(7), 2276–2284. https://doi.org/10.1111/gcb.12196.

Roos, Dave. (2021). Native Americans Used Fire to Protect and Cultivate Land. Indigenous people routinely burned land to drive, prey, clear underbrush and provide pastures. https://www.history.com/news/native-american-wildfire.

Turetsky, M. R., Benscoter, B. W., Page, S., Rein, G., van der Werf, G. R., & Watts, A. C. (2015). Global vulnerability of peatlands to fire and carbon loss. *Nature Geoscience*, 8, 11–14.

Grabinski, Z., and H. R. McFarland. 2020. "Alaska's Changing Wildfire Environment." Outreach booklet. Alaska Fire Science Consortium, International Arctic Research Center, University of Alaska Fairbanks.

Zhou, J., Prugh, L., Tape, K. D., Kofinas, G., & Kielland, K. (2017). The role of vegetation structure in controlling distributions of vertebrate herbivores in Arctic Alaska. *Arctic, Antarctic, and Alpine Research*, 49(2), 291–304. https://doi.org/10.1657/AAAR0016-058.

ARCTIC VILLAGE CLIMATE CHANGE TRANSCRIPTS

Deena Tritt | 05/10/05 | Time: 10:00

» *Berries*

When I was a little girl, it was all over, and they're big and they're more juicy, but now they don't ripen. It's small it's not juicy. There are certain spots where they're around the village now. It's hard not to find a bunch together. We just sometimes bumped into a little batch of berries that's not even ripe, it's supposed to be ripe, big, blue. It's not, most of the time it's green. If you're lucky you'll find big ones, but now they're just small. They pop easy, they don't usually do that.

Cranberries are the same, really hard, same size, you have to boil it more to make cranberry source. [Note: They used to be soft.]

Plants are gold brown, didn't grow out good from last year. The village is swamp area, plants like blueberry, cranberry. I thought they would grow good, but you have to go far away to find cranberry or blueberry. It used to be in one big batch, it's not like that anymore.

» *Blueberry vegetation zones are farther away, so it increases mobility and thus it is harder to pick blueberries.*

All four of us had to go to one place because there would be a lot of blueberries in one place, but now we have to scatter.

Animals are skinny.

2005 summer had more sunshine, so more berry.

There used to be one big batch in one place, you spent half a day picking berries in that one place. Now it's not like that. You go there, and in 2 minutes you drive to another area, sometime there's nothing good to pick, because they pop easy. They're small or too dry.

When I was little, they were big, and their leaves were real green, it was more juicy. There used to be lots in one area. You could walk across from my house, you can see a whole bunch all over. It is a swamp area, it should've grown good, but it don't. They are small and pop easy. There is not a whole bunch anymore. I hardly picked last year because I had to shift areas too many times. [Note: This makes it harder because you are burning more energy for less berries.] Hard to pick now because you have to move around more.

Caribou are skinny. There was an Elder who wanted to eat a muskrat, but I had to throw it out because it was too skinny.

Animals are very skinny in the last year.

Berry picking last summer in 2004:

High bushes and trees are all brown.

Leaves are orange and brown.

Weather changes fast; one minute it's sunshine, next minute it's going to rain.

Elders say: Alice, Abros, Lena Albert said, "Things are going to change."

How did they deal with it? They feel sorry for us, for our kids.

The more sunshine the better, [so] the berries [can] grow

Mike Lee | 05/10/05 | Time: 5:00

Last few years, winters are warmer, summers colder.

Summers are pretty chilly.

Lakes dry, permafrost melting farther down, eroding the soil so lakes are dried.

I heard there used to be flocks of ducks on every lake, now there are hardly any. That is what the Elders told me.

1988 to 1997: Not much of a change. Caribou would migrate through, not much change in that time span. Each year the same.

It did not seem like there were many changes that I have seen.

1998 to 2005: We started seeing a rapid decline.

1998 to 1999: The caribou did showed up, but the amount was a lot less.

I don't know if that had to do with the weather or it had to do with hunters way out there. I don't know what caused it to do that.

But one thing I've noticed was that there were more outside hunters in this area than before. It could have been that they disturbed them as they were migrating down and coming through here.

It also could be that, huh . . . at that time the weather really started changing too. It could be the weather that drove a lot of the herd somewhere else. At that time, it's hard to say, but we really seen an effect on it, because there wasn't as much caribou showing through here as normal.

1999 to 2001: In winter, it really really disturbed the caribou. That first year they had record snowfalls. The cows didn't make it up to the calving grounds because the snow is just too deep. They had their calves while down, while mainly at the time in Canada, in the Old Crow area or below where they had the calves. Still, even after they were willing to make it to the calving areas, they still went up there. That next year, I remember it was a bad fire season. There was a lot of smoke that came in here. I think that was what really disturbed the caribou. We didn't see that many during that time. Another thing I forgot to mention, too: After 1997 there was more people going up into the refuge. That could have been a disturbance. Change in their routes, a reason why not as many are coming down this way. But after 2000, it was getting to the point, it was outrageous, so many people going up there. It may not just be the people disturbing them, but its human waste and stuff like that. Its right through at where they migrate. I know that is what is part of what is affecting them.

After those two record snowfalls, we didn't see hardly any caribou at all on the mountains here for 2 years straight. Hardly any.

The summer of 2001 to 2002: [n/a]

Summer 2003: Caribou showed up in August. Small bulls, there was also cows and calves. Only young bulls showed up.

In 2003, there was hardly any 3- and 4- and 5-year-old bulls.

I think it was because of how many years back, how many calves died. We saw the effect of it. Climate change.

During that, fatality rate was so high. I lived in Alaska all my life and I have never seen that much snow before.

1999 to 2000: June 1, 2000: We were still driving snow-gos. I lived in Alaska all my life, and I've never driven a snow-go on June 1.

Summer 2004: Worst summer for caribou since I've been here. During that whole summer span there was only one caribou taken. One caribou taken! And that was right at the mouth of Junjik. We were hunting like crazy because Marjoree's wedding was coming up. I don't know how many times we went out.

That was it. That was it. Fall-time, no caribou, nothing, no sign, nothing.

In all the years I've been in Arctic Village, I'd say that was the worst year.

Last year we had a record fire season. Just when that fire season was taking off, it showed on the computer with the satellite collar project, that the caribou were coming down towards Arctic Village. When the smoke came in, it was around June 8, I believe, that the caribou just took a sharp turn and made a beeline straight to Canada. I'm almost positive that that had to do with the smoke, I mean there was so much smoke in this village all summer, I don't think they had a season like that here before with so much smoke. I mean they had in the past, but not like last year. I'm almost positive that's what happened to the caribou last summer.

Winter 2000: Quite a few caribou showed up here starting in December. From December up until April, we had caribou all over here. I think that had to do with weather, where they were at that time, there was a lot more snow in Canada at that time. When they got over here, there wasn't as much snow. It was a little easier for them.

Winter 2001: Not very many caribou here.

Winter 2003: Caribou showed up from the southeast. Which means they went over to Canada and took a turn and started coming over this way, and showing up downriver, on the mountain. That was in October and from October all the way until April we had caribou, lots of caribou through here all winter long. I don't know why they went way down and then came over and up this way. I don't know why. You say, they come from the north, east coming through, that's what older folks told me, that's what happened in the past.

Winter 2004: Caribou showed up in the east, which is normal. But during that time, the caribou didn't stay in one place. They were always on the move. They were in good shape. Most of the caribou that were harvested were in good shape. The thing is, they wouldn't stay in one place.

They would be constantly moving to another place, and then to another place, and another place. There was a lot of caribou then. I think the reason they did that is that in October after the ground started freezing, the lakes were freezing and everything. We had a warm front come through and we even had rain. Which I've never seen before. There was snow on the ground.

The reason they didn't stay in one place is because of that rain, the top layer of the ground. The moss and all that they eat was all frozen. It froze because of that rain. Therefore, it was harder for them to get their food. And I think they were trying to look for areas where it was easier for them to dig up their food.

Winter 2004 to 2005: They came from the east, which is normal. They stuck around here all winter long, but they were all skinny. Most of them were all skinny. And I think that had to do with there was so many wolves with them; I mean, hundreds of wolves were with this caribou herd. They weren't able to settle down in one place to eat good. The wolves kept them moving all the time, all winter long. And I think that's why most of the caribou we got were skinny. One more thing with the caribou, up north around Junjik area, a lot of the central herd showed up. In the past, they've been known to do that, sometimes in the hundreds, but this winter it was in the thousands. And, huh . . . a long, long time ago that happened a few times, but that was a long time ago, back in the '50s. Fifty-five years later, it's happened again. Fish and Wildlife don't know why. Something is happening in the slope that is driving them down. They're changing their path; a lot of those caribou are joining in with the PCH [Porcupine caribou herd]. Even that herd, is the same shape as the PCH, hardly any fat.

Summer 2005; predictions: If the smoke doesn't show up like it did last summer, I'm pretty sure the caribou will show up here. The smoke was so heavy and so thick. The reason why they don't like the smoke is they can't smell [anything else]. And that's their main sense of how they sense danger and stuff like that, is smell. They took off towards Canada, thinking they could get away from the smoke.

» *Will the fire effect the route?*

Yes. At the end of April, first part of May, they already have forest fires. It's starting early. One different from this winter, compared to last winter, last winter there was hardly any snow. This year is a lot more snow than last winter. That could be on the positive side for the ground drying up later on, like last summer.

Very, very little rain last summer. Two or three big rains here, but they only lasted one day. They would have little showers here and there, but the longest the rain lasted was 14 hours.

Allen was telling me he hadn't seen that river that low for 30 years. Lack of rain. It could be that the smoke affected the weather fronts coming in because it was so thick.

2004 to 2005: Snow depth OK, a little bit deeper than normal.

2003 to 2004: Way less snow, which made it a lot harder going hunting because it's a lot, huh, rough, the terrain is more rough because of lack of snow.

Winter 1999 to 2000: Most difficult years I had of going out hunting and going out getting wood. It was just, the amount of snow, it was just . . . unbelievable. Especially the winter of '99–'00. In the springtime, even in March, if you wanted to make another wood trail or something? You go off your trail, 5 feet later you're stuck. Some places, I get off my snow-go, I sink up to my chest! Here I'm 6 feet tall. I know in those 2 years it was extremely difficult for animals.

End of January, a couple of weeks, in February 2005: A 3-week span, the weather was 55 to 65 below for about 3 weeks. I remember that one morning I woke up, its 67 below. That's something we hadn't seen in a long time. That made it difficult for everybody. Still, we did it.

Since those two record-snowfall years the winters were normal.

Back in '93, it was only 3 days when it was cold like that, compared to 3 weeks this January.

Summer 2004: Very little ground squirrels; back in their house, their grass in all that? With all that rain, it wet part of their house.

That ice, it was good, 2 inches of ice on the lakes at that time, after the rain was done, most of the lakes were thawed out.

Summer 2003: Lots of weasels on the mountain. Eat baby ground squirrels. The next summer, the ground squirrel population is very low.

Each year, there is more moose here each year.

There wasn't much brush here, there wasn't as many trees, the trees weren't as tall. Especially the brush.

Nowadays, it's thriving out there. The vegetation out there is thriving. There's more vegetation now than there ever was, and that's one [thing] that's bringing up the moose population in this area. Since the summer of 2000 till now, even in the wintertime, I see more and more moose. Last 10 years, I go out farther than anybody getting firewood, so I notice things like that.

The smoke drives them farther up, and also, it drives them farther up on the mountainsides too. They rely on the smell. But it's a little different, because moose are much bigger, they can defend themselves.

The brush is getting so high, so thick, and all that. Long time ago the caribou used to migrate through this valley upriver, it's not like that now. I think it has to do with all this vegetation just thriving.

» *The bushes change the caribou route?*

Yeah, it changed their route

Winter 2005: Down past, about 40 miles down, when we went down there, I've seen moose tracks everywhere, I know that had to do with that fire.

One kind of animal is the bears, last summer we had bears everywhere, I know it had to do with that fire. They even had to kill bears here in the village.

Almost every trip, we went upriver we see two, three bears.

This winter, there was a lot more martens around here, I think that largely had to do with that fire too.

I did notice a little decline in ptarmigan. A year ago, there was even ptarmigan down here [*pointing to the bottom of his house*].

Especially bears.

» *Water level*

Summer 2004: I noticed a huge change.

It was in summer of '99, there was a big change too. Most of the summers I've been here the waters have pretty much been normal. In the summer of '99, it was the highest I had ever seen that river. It was almost over the road.

We were building that new post office. The road to Lorraine's, it was over that road. We had a record snowfall that winter.

Fall 2002: September 8–10: Three days straight was rain. The river got high, that is the highest I had ever seen it. Allen said he hasn't seen the river that high in quite a while.

Last time I saw the river this low was back in the 50s.

There were some places upriver you could walk across.

Last fall we could've made it upriver without a jet unit.

We would've had to get out of the boat a lot of places and push it.

We had to go quite a ways up there to get moose.

Even with a jet unit we hit bottom [of the river].

The vegetation is sucking the lakes dry.

Lakes have receded up to 40 feet in the last 10 years.

That hill [marked on map] up here is mountain area, that hill is nothing but brush. It wasn't like that before, 10 years ago? It wasn't like that.

Fort Yukon to Venetie, how many lakes are drying out down there? I'm almost sure it's because of all the vegetation thriving right now.

In the last 10 years, the change in how much vegetation is growing, I mean, it's unreal. I haven't seen vegetation thrive like that, in such a short time.

» *Is that why the central herd is coming down?*

It could be that too. It could be that too.

The reason that the Central herd is coming is because they're getting tired of it.

Central herd: We're not just talking about hundreds, or thousands, everyone that's gone up that way saw them.

Difference between Central and Porcupine is that the Central herd is light color, Porcupine is darker.

There's times we had the Central herd here, but they're in small groups of 15 to 20. That Central herd, that one time we went up there, on the side of the mountain there, above Tsii'vii'tit'. There was 300–400 there, I mean it was covered. That's one big change. They said it happened a few times, but that was before pipeline, though. It's turning out that they haven't gone back. Maybe they're starting to migrate where the Porcupine is migrating.

This is the fastest I've seen the snow melt. Record warm weather we're having right now. The weather we're having right now during the day, its usually June weather. You see how fast, just a week ago, this whole mountain, all these mountains it's all white. Look at it now [very little snow on mountain]. That's another thing I forgot to mention, I don't think I ever seen the snow melt so fast.

» *Ice conditions*

Two-year record snowfall, the ice went out fast.

Ten to twelve miles down Cat Trail, I go down to get wood. The thing I notice, there's an overflow where I've never seen it before.

» *Ice fish*

Fall 2004: Tsiivii'tit, we were catching bigger whitefish than normal. The whitefish come from the lakes, they all came out into the river, the water never raised up last summer; therefore, all those big fish were still in the river. The water was never high last summer.

The water goes up and they go into different lakes, but the water never raised up all summer, therefore all those big fish were still in the river. The water was never high last summer. Last year [2004] was the worst year for that river.

Twenty years from now, most of these lakes around here, especially ponds, unless there are creeks running through them, are going to dry out.

» **What will happen if the lakes continue to dry out for the next 10 years?**

It will have a huge impact on fish, because the water is going to be warming up, especially with salmon.

Salmon are going way up the Yukon. Where their spawning grounds are. What's happening now is the water is warming and they're trying to get out of that Yukon River as fast as they can, and therefore, they're going into fresh water faster than normal. Back in 2003, down in Venetie, they said they'd never seen so many salmon coming through there than that year. I think what they're trying to do is get out of the Yukon as fast as possible, because the water is warming up. That's having to do with global warming.

These glaciers are melting at a tremendous speed, and it has to do with global warming.

Tell you the truth, I'm scared to see how it's going to be 10 years from now. Tell you the truth, I've been out in the woods all my life. I've seen more changes now than I ever did in my life. The world is changing, the earth is changing.

Audrey Tritt | 05/12/05 | Time: 1:10

» *Snowfall changes, during spring and fall*

What I noticed this fall [2005], it was . . . it didn't freeze up and it snowed. What I mean by that is it usually gets really cold before the snow really stays. Right now, its springtime, its thawing out fast, right now the river is already ready to go out and it's the 12th of May. The river don't usually go out till the last week of May. I think that has to do with not freezing the ground.

» *Springtime*

Thaw out fast, the earth is not freezing this fall.
The river is breaking up real fast.
The fish was even late.

» *When it snows, when the ground isn't frozen in the fall-time, how does that affect hunting and fishing?*

It gets really muddy and slushy, and, um . . . in the fall-time, cause it's not freezing and we're trying to do things and it's not frozen. Usually it's frozen, it's easier.

» *Access to hunting areas are harder?*

Yeah, hard to get to, and hard on the vehicles, and its kinda hard to get the animals because they seem to know, um . . . the areas where it's real muddy, and they'll hang out there and we can't get to it.

» *Springtime . . . when the river goes out fast, does it shorten the fishing season?*

This springtime it did shorten our fishing, because we usually make the fishing holes in April, and we go up there and go fishing, but we don't catching nothing till the first week of May. First week of May there's water already coming up and the ice is already running, and we couldn't get to the place where we fish, because there's already too much water.

» *Muddy and slushy where?*

Duch'chan'lee, the main roads that we go on, usually its frozen solid and we could just get anywhere, but with the ground not frozen, we can't get anywhere. The four-wheelers will get stuck, and, huh . . . we have to walk a distance, 'cause its muddy.

» *Porcupine caribou herd migration changes*

Ten years, we never seen caribou for the last 5 years. Finally, within the last 5 years we finally see caribou actually hanging around in this area. Right now, there's still caribou hanging around up on the mountain. I haven't seen that in years, since I was 11. How much is hanging in this area, I think it has to do with global warming.

» *Global warming?*

The animals travel when it's cold at night. With it warm like this, it's probably relaxing more. Because when it's cold, that's when it travels. To keep the flies and bugs away because it's cold and that's when they move.

» *Meat texture*

No difference.

» *Moose*

No difference. We see a lot of moose around this year, I'm thinking maybe because of that forest fire. We see a lot of marten tracks too, never see marten tracks like that around here before. Lot of wolves too, lots. By Old John Lake, we put in nets up there. I mean the marten tracks were tons of it. Even saw where a wolf had a caribou down. All winter long there was caribou around; moose too.

I put in the net in the fall-time. Go up there and check the net, that was in November. Seen wolverine tracks, two of them, hanging around. That was up towards past the Airport Lake. Wolverine tracks, fox tracks, just a few of them, but marten, that's the first time I seen marten tracks around here.

Ducks are coming in late, usually we seen ducks . . . not even few seagulls, they're usually down there on Vashrąįi Kǫǫ (creek below Arctic Village) making noise, you don't even hear that, they're usually all around. It's just quiet.

» *First year [2005] seagulls were in the area?*

Yeah, this is the first time I see the birds and stuff, I mean it's late this year, just a few seagulls flying around.

The bees are huge, I never see those bees that big, ever. I mean they're really big. They're usually small, little tiny bees.

» *Texture of fish meat*

I notice the whitefish I'm catching is really rich, and, um . . . it's from the river. It's usually not that rich. They're probably just hanging closeby other lakes or where they're settling all winter.

I don't know if anyone had any nets on the river. Last summer, they had nets in all summer, they were catching fish all summer, that's not normal. Usually, you put in nets and there's hardly any catch. We just don't put in nets all summer, I don't know, we just put it in springtime, fall-time, that's what was taught to me.

» *Blueberries*

There's not that much. There's not that many blueberries. They don't get as big, they're just small. There's usually a lot of berries, but there's not that many. They just drop real fast. Two weeks into July, next thing you know blueberries are all starting to ripen, we're waiting for it to ripen, next thing you know they're just dropping. Too dry, maybe all the lakes are drying out, because of the growth, there's more trees out there now, there used to be no trees and willows in this tundra. Used to be just rocks, now there's [all] kinds of trees.

» *Looking over the map of Charlie's marks of bush growths*

A lot of lakes are drying out. And it is from a lot of trees. We used to [go] a long ways to get wood, now it's not even that far. Back when it's normal, we had to go way far to get dry wood, we had to go on the Fort Yukon, long ways, this winter trail, but now it's all over. Lot of good, dry wood. We don't even have to go that far. Just certain areas we had to go for dry wood, now it's all over.

» *How does that affect the animals?*

The food it eats, the trees are getting more of the water and stuff for those willows and stuff? Pussywillows aren't even out, that's usually out before Easter. We used to pick them and put them in church. It's just now starting to do that. Everything is just late.

» *Bush growth affects animals*

So much growth, they don't migrate right there, 'cause they can't get through

They used to even cut down willows just to keep the migration going, the Elders, as they trail along with the herd.

» *Cranberries*

They're about right.

Blueberries just drop real fast, it ripens real fast and drops.

» *Wetter and warmer winters*

Right now, the trees and stuff is growing real fast. There's just so much of it. There's a lot of trees now.

» *Water levels*

It seems like its real shallow, and the ice is going out real fast. The river is already going out. Usually the water is really high, but the water is really low and ice is still moving.

The dried lakes is because of the growth. It just seems like there's more growth closer to the village and that one lake is drying out really fast. Right by the airport, that goes behind here, this creek.

» *Rains*

It hardly rained last summer, it was just really dry.

» *Last 5 to 10 years rain?*

Not much rain.

» *When you were growing up?*

Yeah, it always rained. Man, always just soaked.

» *What will these changes mean for Arctic Village?*

I'm just concerned about the fish and the animals. If there's too much growth it's going to change the migration. And if there's too much growth a lot of lakes are going to start drying out, and there won't be enough fish in the lakes. We'll probably have to go way out, farther out, because, um . . . all these lakes are connected to this river, and if its all drying out, if all the streams are drying out, it can't do its migration to the fish, in the springtime it goes up into the lakes, in the fall-time it comes back down. And if it's too shallow it won't be in the lakes, and it's going to change its migration. It's going to spawn somewhere else, but somewhere else, but if it spawns where, um . . . a different place, if it doesn't have its food. It's not going to survive, because of some lakes, they don't have the same growth as the lakes drying out, it's all different.

» *Forest fires in the old days*

They let it burn, because [in] the old days, there wasn't that much growth, there was more gravel, there was hardly any willows around here. 'Cause we came up here [in] '73 or '74. I was 5 or 6 years old, it was flat, nothing but little willows. Now its 2005, nothing but trees.

» *What would the old ones think of too much growth?*

They were more concerned for the lakes, because of the migration of the fish, they use the lakes, certain lakes, they'll go cut down areas by the creek, so it will be easier for them to feed their subsistence. There's areas where they had to walk up to the first tower, second tower, they walk up in that area right now. And move their family, and they'll cut out by the creek and they'll get ready to put in their nets or their Lush hooks. All the stuff that they'll need, they'll prepare it and they'll walk up with a dog pack. They used a lot of dogs in those days, today is four-wheelers, and that's polluting the land, because the four-wheeler, when it sits, it idles, and sometimes there's oil drainage or gas. And it leaves the spot, even the animals change the migration because they smell it. The Elders didn't know. We don't have to [work hard] no more, and so they started using them.

But now I started realizing because when I go up, we used to walk from here to that Old John Lake, it was clean, now when they came up with soda, chips, four-wheelers. We go up that way, we see piles of that stuff where people used to camp, we didn't see that when we were kids, no way! Even where we cut up fish or cut up meat, we had to dig a hole, we had to put even its scales, the bones [in the hole]. We had to bury everything, there was a certain area we had to cut it out, cut out a moss wherever we're camping.

We can't leave the earth dirty, so we had to put everything in there and then cover it back up. Even the cash poles we put one place, it had to be neatly stocked and it can't be in the way, because if animals go through they won't trip over it. They were real strict. Even with the fish trap, when we used to Dun'an lee, we had to turn that over, make sure there's a branch by there, they use that screen when that screen came out, so animals won't get caught in it.

» *The big question: How did Elders get used to the changing world? Something strange happened*

If they learn it, they will, but if not, they move on.

Communities all stick together and help each other out, that's how they survive.

Another thing, is where global warming is coming from . . . the big thing I'm thinking about . . . is oil . . . oil and natural gas. And I think it's important, because of what they supplement it when they take the natural out, and they use salt water. And it is very important because that's what's causing global warming. 'Cause they're taking mother nature out and supplementing it with salt water. I think it's got a lot to do with the global warming.

They have to do more studies on what they are using for supplementing.

If you put salt on the ice, you dissolve it. That is why on the coast there's big chunks of ice just falling off, because it's heating up. Where they're putting the oil and natural gas out there, it's thawing out. That's the main concern!

The other parts of Alaska is starting to grow more, where they're not touching mother nature.

This is mostly what the Elders were telling me is that they were living off the land until they started doing the fur trade. That's when they started working, and they still did their subsistence because that was their life. Even myself, if I don't eat Native food, I'm just hungry until I have it. I can't just live off of store-bought stuff, my body will just feel weak, my attitude will even change. Cause I'm not used to that kind of food all the time. It works both ways too, if I eat too much Native food, I crave store-bought food, so now it's like, have a little of everything, just got used to it.

» *Scientists realize the Natives know the environment best*

If they're going to do anything in Alaska, they need to get with the community because they know the community more than bringing outsiders in and doing the job, that's why they want local hiring. That's why we're being strong at doing local hiring. It's just like, if I go to the city, look for work and don't know the environment, I'll just figure a way to do it, but I might mess up somewhere. It works the same out here.

Like, it don't get 65 below, only coldest it get is in the 50s. [*This winter, 2004–2005*] No! 54, yeah! 40. Usually we have a cold spell for 2 weeks, we don't even see that. It'll just be cold for like a week, couple of days, and its just warm. What I mean by warm, when I was a child, it's like 60–50 below for a whole two weeks. Now it's only 3 or 4 days or 1 week, and it'll warm up. Then, next thing you know, it'll just be cold again. That's climate change!

» How did the Elders see forest fires?

Some places they let it burn, because they wanted it to grow, because there wasn't that much growth. Today it's the opposite. It's growing more. We have more growth than before. As a matter of fact, too much growth, because the lakes are drying out.

» Christian Village? Of fish camps Arctic used to migrate to?

The soil is better for growing. Even Venetie is like that. Up in Arctic Village area it's mostly meat and fish. Christian Village was trapping, they set traplines. Venetie, they used to grow carrots, potatoes. And they got all this natural growth they go out and use too.

» Settlement in Arctic Village? They went to fish camps because there were lots of fish there, right?

They used to go because there was no stores, no TVs, no four-wheelers. They used to go and go where . . . where they used to . . . get all the stuff to survive with for that summer.

We used to go to Old John in May; April, they'll take all our stuff over there with a snow machine and then we'll stay there for 2 months. And then we'll come back, and then go back in the fall, July, August, September. And then we'll come back 'cause we got to go to school. We have to walk from here to over there. Even right now, if we try to walk over that way it's all growing, lot of willows, lot of trees. The only good trails is when we're driving with snow machines 'cause it could take us anywhere.

» You think it was like this thousands of years ago?

No! No! It wasn't like this. To begin with, Alaska was just a big chunk of ice. Now it's all just growing. And all these right here that's growing, its seeds that blow across. That wind, it blows it over, it settles, the ground is changing, and it's starting to grow.

The people, they even go here to Old Crow. They even walk that far because that's where the caribou goes, and then they go down by Beaver area and then back up this way, that's what was told to me.

» That is why they were able to do that for hundreds of years, because there was no bush growth and trees.

Yeah, it's easier to move, and they made caribou fences in certain areas because if there's a whole bunch of them they'll just settle there and they'll make this fence, even that right there, have to be clean. You can't just shoot it right there and skin it, they have a certain area where you just gut it, clean it. They don't do it right where they get the animal, they move it away, so the animal will come.

The big thing they were really strict with is how to keep the land clean and make sure they make use of the animals, even the berries, whatever they survive with, they make sure to prepare it well. They won't just throw anything away either, they'll even save it. Cause it was so hard, really, just like, on their own with a big family, and there's a family of 14 to 16. I'm not just talking one. Yeah . . . the oldest one is just like the mother, too, most of the time. Have to stay in and take care of each other. The oldest one is the one responsible for the other ones.

» *Looking at whitefish*
It's just real rich [describing the guts].

» *It [fish guts] hasn't been that rich in a long time?*
Uh-huh. Not for a long time. I haven't seen it like that.

» *Since you were a teenager?*
Yeah, probably teenager 'cause we used to go upriver and see it like that and they were bigger. But the ones we catch down here, they're just small and not so rich the last couple years. But this year, I just noticed it's really rich. 'Cause I've been fishing down there for the last how many years . . .

» *You think there'll be a big forest fire this season?*
I don't know if it's really true, but they were saying Tok area, they had smog going on all winter. 'Cause it was burning underneath.

» *If we were back in the old days and saw that forest fire, we would've had to move, huh?*
We would've had to move the village. Or better yet, we might not have even been right there because there's not caribou around there. But it's hard to say because we go there for fishing too. Go to Venetie landing, though.

» *If the migration shifted north, we would have to, too?*
Yeah, we have to.
They'll probably set it up where they'll make a line where the fire won't jump through. That's what they did in Venetie, they made a fire line

around the village. They had to take the Elders out because the smoke was too strong for them.

» *Did they make fire lines in the old days?*

Yeah! They didn't just let it come and destroy what they have. It's not easy to make a bow and arrow, the kind they made.

There wasn't that much bugs too. They [the Elders] said it was not much mosquitoes. Not as bad. Man! Today it's like that swarms of it.

Even the bumblebees are bigger. I wonder how the butterflies are going to be if we see the bumblebees like that. There's going to be a lot of fire bugs because of all that burnt area. There's going to be a lot of different insects.

Everything is connected one way or another.

Even right now. That marten, they used to hang around in that area, they [the Elders] all moved up here. But I don't know which way they went. But they say they do that. They have a weird migration.

» *What is the way the Elders say it'll be different for you?*

That we have to hang onto our culture, and teach our subsistence way to our children, because they're not going to be around to show them. But it's really hard to get their attention or get their interest because, like me, I had to live out there. They don't want to leave their modern . . . what I mean by that is their enjoyment. Like me, I enjoy to be out in the woods, but today the children they have to stay in school.

» *Caribou skin, babbich?*

A lot of people don't really do those, not as much as the Elders used to. But I see a lot of skin just being thrown away.

» *They wouldn't do that in the old days?*

No way! No way, man! They wouldn't even throw a skin away, they save the hair for bedding for the dogs in the winter, they even pound the bones to get grease. Everything that you can think of, they use it. They had no choice, no store.

» *I wonder what they would say if they saw all the waste.*

We won't hear the end of it. We'd get spanked for wasting all that good food. They were strict, you did wrong, you talked back, you got spanked.

» The more disciplined the society, the more they follow their culture ways, and the more they follow their culture ways, the more they preserve the environment?

Yep! You got it! Goes right along with the animals.

» Animals are same way?

Yeah! You mess with mother nature, what [do] they do? They change the migration. They go somewhere else where they won't be bothered.

» Elders and ancestors understood nature?

They were the nature! That's how they lived was off the nature, cause they're the nature. They even use that tree for medicine, they even got wild lid ii muskat off the willows. They know how to . . . everything . . . they even use caribou parts for certain bowls, uh, they make pitchers. I mean dipper from the caribou. They even use the skin of the caribou heart to make a bag. They use the caribou leg skin to make the boots. There's all the ways.

» How are we different from other Indigenous peoples all over the world?

Well, we're real different because we had cold weather. We had to prepare ourselves for that, that's a major one, because a lot of different nationalities don't deal with the cold. That's one thing that makes us different, is adjusting with the climate.

Like them, they're just too hot, the heat. If we're going to go over, how are we going to hike in the heat? That's one difference. The other difference is how we use the animals for clothing. I mean, its like, caribou skin, we use that for a parka. They didn't have no way of wasting anything because that's what they used to survive with.

» Caribou skin, [what] other things [do] we make out of it?

Pants, boots, they even use the baby caribou just for the baby clothes. They don't even tan it, they have to turn the fur inside out and make a jacket. They don't even skin it, too, I mean, all the way. They just skin the caribou right out, and pull it right off and let it dry that way, and put the kid in there. They use the backstrap for thread, of the caribou, backstrap? That's the string they sew with. They use certain kinds of bone for the needle. I can't really think of anything else.

» *How many caribou you got this year?*

Nothing, not even one in the last 2 years.

» *Did it start getting less and less for the past 5 years?*

Average about 2 every year.

» *Is it coming around on time?*

They come in different time.

» *Nothing to do with climate?*

No, I don't think so. They go by their own time when they're going to have a calf, the kind of mosquitos do in summertime.

» *Moose?*

OK. Nobody got sick over eating meat of fish.

» *Small game?*

Rabbit, very few around. I hardly heard anybody getting them. Too much snow this winter, so they hardly travel.

» *Fishing?*

Old John Lake, they catch fewer than they used to. I don't know what happened there. They die off, too, after so many years.

» *People say the summers are drier now.*

It depends on thunder that comes in, if it don't come in May, then we won't have much rain this summer. Usually comes May, June. August, that's when they come through here, that's the main forecast of raining.

» *Dried lakes*

There are few washed out, it's not a major problem, 'cause we got so many lakes we don't know what to do with them.

» *Weather*

It's all controlled by the nature. Where it usually needs its rain. To me, it rains one day, sunshine tomorrow.

» *Spring thaw-up? Earlier or later?*

Last year, this time of year, now it's all melt out. It comes in. Got to do with sunshine. More sunshine we got this spring, so it all thawed out already.

» *Nothing strange that is going on in nature right now?*

Just like these trees turn out green earlier than last year and, uh . . . just like, uh, see willows, we already had them, but they're just starting to come out now. Don't know what the problem is.

All that oil and natural gas pumped out of North Slope, something's got to give out in the state of Alaska. And that's what's happening now, natural gas burning 24 hours, and that gives out a lot of heat. Bad for the ozone layer.

» *What about that big forest fire?*

It's happening in the past, in the present, and it's going to happen in the future, 'cause nature takes care of itself. Just like these willows, moose ate it all, it's going to burn one time or another and new plants will come out. That's what happened in Venetie.

» *Did that happen before?*

Thirty to forty years ago the whole place was burned and it burned again. Even Christian Village area, Fort Yukon. Just part of nature.

. . . .

Mildred Allen | 05/15/05 | Time: 15:00

. . . .

» *Caribou/moose meat difference?*

Caribou is more tender and tastier. Moose, the one they got a few weeks ago was pretty good, but the moose they gave me last winter was tough. The taste in moose is not much taste in it.

» *Small game?*

Less. Maybe they moved to another area. We see less rabbit tracks when we go out, there's few, few ptarmigans, they come in flocks, but they move around. I think they're mostly in the mountain area.

» *Invasive species?*

Last year they seen a magpie.

» *Fishing season shorter because of thinning of ice?*

Less water, when the ice moves, in the old days, we always caught a lot of grayling. Stand out there on the ice, catch a lot of fish between the cracks. Nowadays we don't see that anymore. Hardly any fish. The one day I only caught four. Yeah, I think they just move past here and down to Venetie area. That's where it ends up.

» *Different from previous years?*

Yeah, different. 'Cause they hardly ever see our fish down in Venetie. Big grayling? All they get is a small, tiny one, and all of a sudden, our fish! Fish from this area, they're popping up in where they fish. Maybe it just goes right through here. I don't know what causes that, no water. Bob had to dig four holes to get to the water in March, middle of March, I think. Finally hit water.

Probably small channel in the middle somewhere, huh?

Creeks, lakes drying up.

» *Blueberries*

Last two years, we had early spring, like now? Like I told you the other day, flowers are blooming out on June 10th, berries are coming early. By end of June, there's blueberries, way too early. A month early, I think. Now it's happening something again.

Kiddy said it's going to be cold again this summer because of this early summer weather.

Cranberries didn't have a chance to grow 'cause it burnt up. No rain and too much sun and smoke. It just started to come out and all of a sudden it's so smoky it just burned up. From the heat, yeah, even the cranberry plants look different, brownish. So there went our berries.

» *Less berries: have to move around?*

You got to move all over. We go all over this area here. Practically all around this village where all the patches are. We don't get very much, no berries. Last year it stayed for about 5 days? Boy! Everybody rushes out there and pick what they can.

There's usually a lot of berries across here. I always pick berries here. But it's all dry now, no berries. There's only a few last year. Like you said, we walk from this little patch, and we have to walk across to find another little patch here and there. Barely got half a can, bad!

» *Dry summers—how does it affect plants?*

Dry up, it don't blossom and it's not good for the small animals, so animals have to move on, a different area, huh? To get their food, supply for the winter.

» *Change the habitat?*

It's a cycle.

» *Warmer winters*

Fast change, the animals don't even know what to do, huh? One day it's raining, one day it's snowing. They move by their senses. They say there's still caribou around here, it's supposed to move up north, but it's still around. Messing up their route, their migration route.

» *Caribou migration route changes—is it changing?*

Due to the climate change, huh? Sometimes it snows with hail or something? They don't know what to do, huh? Whether they should go this way or stay. Last year it was so smoky they all stayed in one place over there for a long time, and they end up going to Old Crow 'cause they can't see, huh?

» *So they didn't come near the village, huh? Nobody got any?*

No. No caribou, it's too far out.

» *Dried lakes?*

Permafrost thawing out, and it just go down, huh? There's no ice on there to hold it. And all the creeks are drying up. There used to be a lot of water back here, it's even hard to cross, where people go duck hunting? It's even hard to fish, because there's so many weeds growing? There's more plants down there too. It's so thick you can't even drink the water, its bad, you can't even swim in it, you get a rash. Yeah. Too many plants, water plants. The fish don't even bite, 'cause they got all their food there. Why they want to take our hook when they got all the food there [*laughs*]. Pike it just playing with my hook.

» *Where is this at? This plant growth?*

All over. At the bottom of the lake. You can just feel it. It never used to be like that. When we would go swimming, we just walk on bare rocks and dirt, now it's all plants. Kids used to swim down there, they can't even swim no more. And it's so swampy, you just sink in when you try to get out there. It's bad!

More snails in these lakes. Lot of little water bugs. Thawing out, huh? Down past the airport, Dinjik Van? Where kids always swim? That water used to be way up there, now it's farther out. Just like little round area, that's all they swim in. The trees around there are drying up, more willows are growing. Maybe the willow just drinks up the water. Permafrost. Thawing out.

Overgrowth, too much vegetation nowadays. And the trees are brown.

» More vegetation = more animals

Drier, more plants, it's just rich with lichen. That's why more caribou are around. Somebody said they took a layer of ground and tore it out and there was lots of little dead mice under there. You think they starve? Overpopulated? I wonder what caused it. No food. Cause all the berries, they don't get a chance to grow, I don't know.

Hardly see any birds too, huh? No birds. [When we were] growing up there was lots of birds around. All the lakes just make a lot of noise, now it's just quiet.

» River level?

Right now its high, huh? Last year or the year before, it went up high when it wasn't supposed to, so they said that was pretty funny.

» Rain pattern?

Way up till November, it rains. Even in middle of November it was raining last year. Last night it was sprinkling.

Last year it rained up till the end of June, and from there it just dried up. 'Cause of that forest fire.

» Forest fire?

Too dry.

» Do you think that will happened again this summer?

Looks like it, 'cause early spring it's already dry. So that might happen again, it'll be the third year in a row. It's too dry.

I was looking at this puddle outside, it sat there three days and it was gone, usually it sits there like a month. Before that little puddle goes away. Five years ago we put sawdust on there, we put gravel in it, to cover it up, now it's just gone in 3 days. Boards over it. Trying to build a trench so we can drain it out. Every way we can we try to cover it up [*laughs*]. We don't have problem with it anymore, it just sinks. You think that's good for the trees, too dry, huh? Maybe that's why they turn brownish.

We haul wood up there by Steven Vahan stii', Bob and I, it's just dry. The tree, sometimes I just shake it and it just cracks. Dry one. Lots of dry trees.

» *Forest fires emit CO2, thus perpetuating global warming*

We live in it. We feel the changes.

» *Spring thaw-up*

Last year it evaporated. It didn't even get muddy or nothing, it's just all gone, evaporated. It got so hot, didn't have a chance to melt that snow, it just . . .

Fall is Indian summer, huh. All the way into middle of October. By then it's kinda chilly. That's not good for small game. They should be going under the snow for hibernation. Or underground, and snow covers them like a blanket, but no snow.

There's a lot of ground squirrels up there, and they come out. We drive around and see lots of ground squirrels out and about.

» *Bush growth?*

I read in one of the old stories from the Elders [that] they don't move towards Venetie 'cause there's too many willows down that way. Caribou, it's hard for them to move into the willows. So they just turn around down there by Brown Grass Lake. So now we're getting that problem up this way, huh? Too many willows, more willows than ever before. You see these old pictures, bare, huh, bare all over.

Va'shri' Jujik, they did a permafrost test, it went way down.

The bank is going into the river. Chunk by chunk. That river still looks the same though. More channels. It's worse down that way. No water, nothing but rocks.

» *I bet it [would] be hard to get to Venetie?*

Yeah! Danger.

» *Insects*

They're overpopulated. Too many insects! They're all over all the time. Ants, an ant hill.

» *Was it like this when you were growing up?*

No. Uh-huh.

Last November after it snowed, I was walking down towards school, a big spider was walking across the road, on top of the snow and I asked somebody and they said it's going to be warm for a while.

We see flies flying around during winter, they say its going to warm up.

Yeah they said a long time ago it's in the future, it's going to be like this. How much they know, huh? It's going to be warm in the future, they said. Everything is going to be thawing out. No more 50 below.

» *They said its going to be warm in the future?*

Like Florida area, our weather is going to be like that. And they're going to have our weather. So now they're saying it's snowing down that way.

In a way it's good, too. I hear a lot of people say that. Eventually it just goes with the changes. Last year it got so hot, it went up to 90 degrees. You see all these cones? You go outside you're going to see all my trees all the cones just flourish. Over multiply. On top of each other, it was just growing fast. And all of a sudden hot weather just turn back to 50–60 and it just stopped. Just imagine if we stayed at 90, one week everything would just be over—full of growth. Cold weather just keeps it where it's at.

» *Permafrost is bad for housing?*

They got to keep leveling, keep working on it. Unless you're on good ground. Last year Bob had to level this house, been here 8 years, it's just crooked. We have to level it out. He say it was permafrost.

» *What do Elders think of forest fires?*

The land has to replenish itself. That's how it's supposed to be. Just a cycle.

» *What do you think they would do now?*

Advise us to be prepared. They'd have all the answers for us.

» *What should we do about this?*

Go with the flow, I guess. Be neutral. Take only what you need from the land. Nourish your body with plants, plants like Hudson Bay tea. I pick that almost every year and give it to our Elders. And other plants we might use for our health. So that's how we're suppose to be. Like our grandparents. Take care of the land, when I pick berries I always pick up trash, bring it back into the village, and throw it into trash can. We burnt up our trash too, before we took it to the dump. The Gwich'in people know that's wrong, wake up the whole world about the environmental change we're going through. We are caribou people, we're trying to save our caribou, now they're all scattering out, 'cause of climate change, global warming. Sometimes they don't know which way to go because they're mixing up with other herds too. And then they bother them with airplanes too much, just flying over, scaring them. They're peaceful animals. Spook real easy.

I remember when we were kids we'd sit way on top of the mountain. Build a fire and watch them. Slowing moving around. We'd watch them in morning time, we get up, we go down and catch one caribou, we cook it and dry it. Watch them and felt good, 5,000 caribou covered.

They used to come this way too [*gesturing to the south*].

Last year one caribou ran through here, behind the house. Wintertime, April. The area across is full of lichen, rich.

All these hills, erosion, all crumbling, hills and mountains.

We climbed Kii vaataiin Lii over 15 years ago. There weren't many willows, nowadays it's just thick, there's even plants growing on top.

» *There were never plants growing on top*

No. Bare ground.

It was cold nonstop. Whoh! Got to wear a parka to be on top. Now we just run up there with our shirts.

Raymond Tritt | 06/01/05 | Time: 30:00

» *Harvest intake*

I didn't get any caribou last year. Just some people got some caribou, that's about it.

About 20 years ago, when I was a small kid, I remember, there were a lot of caribou. There's even a lot of caribou behind the mission, Maggie Lake? Every springtime, always caribou go there. Up this way [Chinlee], August you go up there, couple [river] bend, you run into caribou. Now, recently, hardly any caribou even you go up the mountain, you go up river you don't see any caribou. You have to go way up. Sometimes you run into them, sometimes you have to wait for them. Just quite a few going by, that's about it.

It's changing, they probably might change their route too. They usually come up here and go around the mountain. They'll probably go farther back.

» *Why would they go farther back?*

The weather.

This world is really changing. This time of the year, most of the snow, big snow starts melting way back in the 60s. It's already summer!

Way back in the 60s, we [were] still driving dogs. Ahhh . . . the world is getting hotter and hotter, I guess.

Spring is coming earlier.

In 2005, fall-time, this year it was pretty good snow.

This year it's [caribou] really skinny.

Moose is all right.

» *Is it true there are more coming up here?*

Yeah, it's true.

Back in 60s you see only five that time all winter, but now, almost every place you go you see moose. See there's getting [to be] a lot of animals coming. [*Note: Moose migrated into the Arctic Village area a century ago, so more than one moose is a lot. With climate impacts, the population has dwindled.*]

» *Why do you think there are a lot of animals coming around?*

Too many people around, this valley here, it's the only place that is quiet, wild. People hardly come around, but all the way around us, just people around us. There's hunters up there [*pointing to the east*] hikers up there [*pointing to the north*].

» *We can't go back to the old life, huh?*

Like me, or your grandpa. They could go back to the old times, but not those younger generations. They [grow] up with TV, games, and all that. It's going to be hard for them. They'll probably live without it too. But it's going to be boring for them for a while, till they get used to it.

» *Small game?*

Ptarmigan, there's hardly any ptarmigan, but [when] I go up the mountain I run into them.

» *New species?*

Those lynx, they usually down Christian Village area or Venetie area, y'know, they don't usually come up this way. But you see back in 4 or 5 years ago, we saw tracks down [by the] airport, lynx tracks. When I was hauling wood, it was in my wood trail. We never see lynx tracks up this way, ever since, I was . . . I remember. Even your grandpa Allen, look at, said it's lynx, what the heck is that lynx doing way up here. That's because of the weather change I guess, or there's probably more food down that way. All the marten move up this way too.

» *Will the displaced species stay?*

They'll probably head back down.

Long time ago, we caught a lot of fish, we go down in the morning, y'know, we can catch 20 to 25, or 30 sometimes, in the morning. But now you can't do that, you catch like 2 or 3 early in the morning, if you get really lucky you get more, but . . .

» *A long time ago you could always depend on catching 30?*

Yes, early morning, right. That was a long time ago.

» *Not many berries?*

Last summer I went up and looked at it. It's usually big, but now it's just small. It's just hardly growing too. So we're just blaming it on the weather. Salmon berries is always growing up, covering the mountain. One time I went up there. Went to see. Just like a flower, all over the place, like flowers. A couple years back, I went back up there in fall-time, there's nothing. Little bunch here and there, but last fall we were up there, and there was a whole bunch all over the place.

Sometimes summertime is good, sometimes it's bad, stuff like that, up and down.

» *Winter?*

No answer.

» *Dried lakes?*

There's one good lake up here, we looked at it, permafrost, it thawed out, under the ground. I don't know how, it probably got warmer. Drain the lake out—Noah Lake. Good lake, too. That's really sad. Ducks, fish [went with it].

[*Looking over map: Arctic B-3 Quad*]

» *Bush growth*

Down by the old church, when I was small, there used to be grass there. We used to play around there. Now you could see those willows, they're just thick, like bush.

Trees behind the clinic, when I was small those trees were really small. Jee, they're growing fast. Might be a bush like Venetie, Fort Yukon.

» *Good or bad?*

Well, good. In a way, there could be a lot of animals. I think it's going to be good, but it's going to be hard to get wood, though. [You] can't drive anyplace unless you go up the mountain, you could drive anyplace.

» *Rain pattern?*

No.

» *Bank erosion?*

Ice moves, springtime, the ice moves, mud and all that bank.

» *What would the Elders do about the many animals we are seeing around the village?*

Eat as much as you can, keep it level.

David Peter did not like forest fires, because it took a long time for them to grow back. Animals don't have much to eat, so they're just burning them up.

» *Raymond's advice*

Mountain calving area, keep it very clean.

When you pour gas in a four-wheeler, make sure you don't spill it.

You put oil in the snow-go, make sure you don't spill oil, camping ground, or that trail, the path of the caribou.

» *Wildlife and Environmental Management in the old days?*

They never stay in one place, even in wintertime they travel. That's a long time ago.

» *The work was hard in the old days, so everyone was in shape?*

Yeah.

White people only buy food in the store.

[Note: *Raymond means hunting and fishing keeps Gwich'in people in shape, as opposed to only walking to the store and buying food and getting no exercise. It was a generalization, but he was trying to prove an underlying point.*]

Global warming is going to affect all the animals, all the human beings too.

» *Moose?*

Only a few moose around here nowadays, there used to be lots of them, but now there's only a few, there's not that much like it use to be.

» *Small game?*

Hardly any nowadays. Quite a few rabbits, but not those foxes or other animals, we don't see them very much anymore.

» *Caribou meat*

Nothing changed.
The lakes shouldn't be doing that [drying out].
It's going to affect all the fish and everything. All the fish will be dead in the lake, no water.

» *Rain pattern*

I think they're different every year. Like last, it was real hot last year, year 2004, real hot summer. This summer we have cloudy and kinda cool, and rain, that's all we had, this summer [2005].
Summer 2003: It was pretty good.

» *Past 10 years*

Nothing changed.

» *Spring thaw-up*

No change.

» *Fall freeze-up*

Sometimes we get early fall, sometimes we get late fall.
No change.

» *Bush growth*

There were only a few trees around here, but now, everything grows up. All these trees, they grow.

» *Good or bad?*

I think that is good for that, huh . . . for animals. All these willows? That's the one that moose eat, that willow. So I think its good for them, the animals, to have things grow like that.

» *Humans?*

I think we need trees, Yeah! It's good.

» *2000–1999 record snowfall*

I don't remember.

» *2004—worst caribou season?*

That's true.

» *Winter 2002–2003, caribou came up from the south*

Yeah, came from the south. Lots of wolves out there, lots of caribou this winter.

» *2003–2004 snow depth low*

Yeah, that was true.

» *What do you see that is not right?*

It gets cold, then it gets warm, stuff like that, it's been doing [that] lately. Wintertime, it gets the same way. It gets warm, than it gets cold. It gets real cold, and then it gets real winter. The other winters. Sometimes it gets really cold, sometimes it gets really warm. Last two winters it was like that I know of.

» *When did you first start noticing these changes?*

Since last year.

» *Global warming?*

It's going to be a disaster in the future.

» *2004 forest fire?*

All the animals moved somewhere else. That's what hurt that Venetie. Hardly any moose down Venetie, since the forest fire. Bad for the people.

» *Store food expenses?*

Sky high.

» *Elder's words?*

In the future, like they had that depression way back in 1929? They're going to have the same thing again in the future, depression, starvation, and all the stuff, is going to happen in the future. People have to be prepared for that. Depression we're facing, starvation, people have to prepare for that one, y'know?

» *Water level?*

No change.

» *January cold?*

40–50 below.

» *Elders saying another depression?*

In the future, there will be another depression and starvation. Everything looks the same to me. I can tell real easy if something changes. Maybe next 10 years from now, maybe it'll start changing.

Gideon James | 06/05/03 | Time: 1:45

» *1995–1999 harvest intake?*

Since its not migrating directly through here anymore, it's pretty hard to tell how much. Sometimes people have to go long ways to get it.

I think the vegetation is getting thicker up in a certain place on the mountain. That may be one of the reasons, because 40–50 years ago caribou go all the way down to Venetie, even cross the river there. I really think that vegetation gets thicker and caribou just don't go to those kinds of areas. When you go up on the mountain, you walk certain areas, those willows, [intertwined] you walk through there it's intertwined together like that, so I guess maybe that has something to do with it. Y'know, coming down this far in the season in the summer, really.

» *Were the willows like that when you were young?*

No. Not that I remember. Up on the higher ground there's hardly any form of water. Animals, you know, they depend on water that'd maybe be the reason why, but I don't really know that.

I noticed, as soon as hot weather gets here, many of these creeks, they dry up. When we were kids, we had lots of water all the time.

» *When did these streams started drying up?*

I'd say about 10 years now.

» *Shallower than before?*

Especially up towards the headwater, Chandalar, hardly any water. Below the mountain creeks, you know, in the summertime, y'know, hardly see any water in that creek. Until you go farther down the base of the mountain than you see some water, but not up high.

» *How are the summers?*

It seems like the berry plants, plants, they turn different colors nowadays, lot of reddish color instead of green, it's got kind of a reddish color to it. Lots of berries disappear, like blackberries, that disappeared. Hardly any of them grow anymore. When I was a kid there was a lot of them, a lot of berries around, those blackberries that grow on top of that sometimes they grow on top of that niggerheads [tussucks], stuff like that. There's lots of them around. I see the plants alright, but no berries on them.

So I think lot of things to do with that different kind of heat. Y'know, nowadays we have heat when the sun comes out, comes out between the clouds, the heat just hits you right there and hits you hard. When we were kids [it was] not like that. Sunshine, it'd be all day we could be walking up the mountain and we don't hardly feel it. It was just sunshine, that's it. It's not hot, it's not burning hot like it is today.

The plants that I was talking about, some berry plants, that's getting burned up. Lot of years there's no berries. Eventually it just doesn't grow anymore. Just like I talked about, that blackberries, it just doesn't grow in certain places anymore.

» *When did you notice the heat?*

You know, in the last 5 years that I noticed that the heat really is different, rays y'know. Something like there's no blockage, there's just direct rays. A long time ago, when we were kids, there was nothing like that. No. It was sunshine. Sunshine and hot, but it just doesn't burn your skin like that. Yeah.

Fish too have that kind of effect, because fish, you know, stay in that deep water all winter and when that warm weather comes a lot of times they go to the shallow water. When a sun like that hits the water and warms, it's no good for the fishes—cold-blooded species. Hot rays like that, it's no good for them.

» *Winters in the last 5 years*

I noticed in the winters it gets cold quicker. 'Bout middle of September it starts to freeze. In middle of September, the river starts to freeze and that's too early. Even last year, I know the river froze around middle of September, and that's too early.

Back in 1997 when we went moose hunting on September 16–17, it was still warm. It was still warm. We went up there for one week and we came back and we don't see no ice on the river coming back. Like last year even before [September] 15, the river just froze over, it came early, it's been coming early.

» *You think that's bad?*

Without hardly any snow, freezing like this early is really bad for the caribou 'cause they got to have water. Not only them, the rabbits and other species that depend on water, they got to have water.

» *What about spring thaw-out?*

It comes much earlier, early, I would say about 2 weeks it's been happening. When we were kids back in the late 40s, we would be up muskrat camp, but we don't come back down until June 5, and today is June 5. Look out there [gesturing to window], the green leaves out there, back in those days those green leaves don't appear until around 10th of June or something like that. The climate change you're talking about, it's really happening. It thaws out too early, the shift, it gets cold early and then it thaws out too early. Yeah, like in 1971, we drove a snow machine on May 17, that's a couple weeks ago, we drove a snow machine, lots of snow. It's true that it melts too early.

» *Rain pattern*

And then you would have 1 or 2 days of hot weather and then here, this cloud, dark clouds come around and start to rain here and there all the time. It's been happening for the last 4 or 5 years, that I know. We hardly have good weather, mostly its wind and rain. I would think that . . . the clouds too. When you look at these clouds, you look out there, you see a lot of dark color in it. When we were kids all this other white stuff, that's all we had is the white clouds like that. None of that little black one like that, y'know, it's a completely different kind of cloud that we have today, an indication that there is some contamination that is happening.

» *Contamination, huh?*

Yeah. It is, it's pretty ugly clouds that we have today. Us, long time ago, we just have white clouds. Nowadays there's a lot of darkness in it.

» *It's been raining during winter recently, huh?*

It doesn't stay cold. And, huh . . . I'm telling you, this kind of climate, it keeps melting the ground, y'know, deeper and deeper, y'know, deeper and deeper, it keeps melting the ground deeper and deeper and in the process it melts the permafrost. Lots of times, those lakes that close to the river, it breaks out. It breaks out into the river. And all the fish go with it in the lakes. Right up here around the [river] bend. There's four lakes up towards the river that were lined up, it all broke out. There's no more fish over there, there's no more fish in that big lake. Your grandfather used to fish in that lake Choo'tsik'klok, now it's gone.

» *Looking over map*

[*Indicating on map where they broke up where the lakes that dried up.*] All these little lakes got water dropped. They're connected under the ground.

When this one broke out, all of them did that [too]. The lake where they go swimming? Water dropped 5 feet. Lots of that stuff is happening. That ray is like that, it melts the permafrost and these lakes it breaks out.

Daazraii Van broke out into this creek [*gesturing*]. Right now when you walk up that way, this lake and that lake are same level now, we used to have a summer trail that goes across here, now you can't go across here.

So all that stuff is happening, this happens in middle of winter, it just split open like that, those things are happening around here, y'know because the ground is melting.

» *How shallow are these lakes?*

One of these lakes is way down there. One of these little lakes [*gesturing*]. Good water too right here [*gesturing*], at these lakes?

Looking for a well? They should drill a well right here, I bet you anything they will hit water.

These two lakes, they're connected under the ground, all these are like that, they're connected under the ground all the way down that way. I noticed it, I've been watching it for years. When this broke out, all this happened, a lot of that stuff is happening because of melting.

» *Bush growth*

It's not that much, but up on the mountain it does. Up on the mountain they got a little more brush, thicker.

» *More moose?*

No. I don't think so, it's just that another thing you notice in wintertime when the caribou are here is they tend to move around quite a bit. There's a bunch of herds over there by Old John Lake, that's about 10,000 caribou, and they move all the way up to Junjik River and they stayed up there for 2 months. Some of them, they come around the other side, stuff like that. They move like that in wintertime. Generally, they don't move like that in the wintertime, they stay in one general area. That's normal, that's what they do. In [wintertime] they just don't move in the middle of the winter, go to different [places] like that, they don't do that, even ask your grandpa. They don't migrate in wintertime. . . . They feed in the area and then in the springtime they move, but not during the wintertime. I fear that their feeding is depleting their food; there might not be enough food for them. Timothy was telling me he followed the caribou and it took him all day and never caught them up. That's what they are. They keep going and going.

They smell that stuff through the snow, they just put their nose on the snow and they smell it. They know where their feeding is, they're not dumb. Their feeding is depleting their food, that's one thing the Fish and Wildlife never address is how much food is available for them [caribou] around this area. Not only this area but different areas, that place where it burned too, down there by Venetie, there's lots of it now, it's burned up now.

» *Disaster relief for Venetie forest fire?*

Sure.

» *Increase caribou mobility*

A couple of Elders told me that wolves kept that other species healthy when it kills the animals, everything down to mice feed on it. Blaming wolves for killing too much caribou, I don't think that's right. I even asked your grandpa James, I ran across 1/3 of a moose, eaten, and was left right there. There were not tracks around it. There were old tracks, but it was still there. I asked him, "Why do they do that?" One of the answers he gave me was, "Those wolves will have young ones in the springtime and they will go back and get it."

They think moose leave a lot of meat behind to go to waste, it's not. They go back and get it when they have young ones. I think blaming wolves for too many kills I don't think that's right, that's just a white man story.

» *2002–2003 caribou came up from the southeast*

Lots of times those caribou when they travel most likely they stick closely to the ridge. I think what happened was that there's a ridge between here and Christian River, so they went to the end of the ridge and came up this way. They stick strictly to the mountain range. The mountain ridge, that's how they travel, so I believe that's exactly what happened.

» *Why did they go to the end of the ridge though?*

That's how they travel, like a long time ago they used to go right across, right across Canada. Too much brush and stuff like that, maybe that could be the reason. They used to, a lot of people live halfway from here by Brown Grass Lake over towards the river. There's a cabin on the river there, that's where the animal goes across. Sometimes they do go across and they'll go to the other side, I think that's what happened this winter down towards Gold Camp.

» *Cabin?*

[*Points out on map.*] They don't cross there no more.

» *Did the smoke make the caribou go straight to Canada?*

Yeah, the smoke was blowing this way, moose and all. Yeah, cause last fall when we went up farther up this way [north, up East Fork River]. Usually around here, you see moose around this area [below *Neetsiidhaa*], no tracks all the way up. We drove the boat way up there. That's when we shot caribou. I was up there overnight, one walked up to me. Next day, I climbed up on top of the hill, I saw three more and then when they came down they saw three more.

» *Charlie said 2004 [was the] worst caribou season he remembers*

Yeah, uh-huh. This got a lot of historical places, because long time ago there's lot of people that live around here all the time in wintertime. In this area, your grandpa will probably tell you that too. Right where this cabin is, right in this area. A lot of times they turn around this way [*point-*

ing to halfway to the cabin], sometimes they do go down here. When there's not enough snow they just keep traveling.

That smoke really chased them [the moose mentioned earlier] up there.

» *Charlie said 2004 [there was] one caribou taken?*

Yeah.

Another thing too is, write it down, is human activity migration route, we don't know, a lot of times they turn around the other side of Sheenjik River. There might be lot of traffic along the Sheenjik River to cause it to turn around.

» *Ever put a notice up?*

What we can do is work with Fish and Wildlife, Arctic Refuge, and submit a proposal to them to let us at least monitor the caribou migration route. Have people out there in different places make sure that when they come through there they don't get disturbed and they go on the right route. I think [the way] animals wanted to do their normal travel is that they want to go certain places, [but] when they get disturbed, they get directed different ways. They're not lost but their normal migration does not happen that way. I think one time we need to talk to Fish and Wildlife to see if we need to do the monitoring ourselves.

» *Small game since the fire?*

Since the big fire we get to see more marten tracks around here.

Another thing too is when we talk about harvest, when we talk about quantity of species. In my experience, we have to harvest to keep it healthy. Same thing with fish, we just can't assume fish will be healthy if we don't harvest [it]. You got to take some, we have to take some. Same thing with different species just like marten, we have to harvest it, because if we don't, it gets overpopulated and depletes their food. That's what happened to muskrat, they depleted their food, and they died out, because we quit harvesting them. Lots of these species need to be harvested, if we don't, it disappears, it's just overpopulated, that's what I fear with Old John Lake is that you get too many fish in there it might, the fish might die out; it happened. It will happen. That's what I try to address to the Fish and Wildlife, but they don't get it.

There's a lot of fish in there, I know because I fish over there every year. Like last year, holy cats there's lot of fish! The technology is available, they should count how many fish are in there, estimate, anyway. If there was a 10,000 or maybe even 100,000 in that lake we should be able to take 10 percent of it, 10,000 fish. What we going to do with it? Let's find a market for it, sell it. In the fall-time, when that ice freezes over you put a net under there, every other day you check it you pull three hundred fish out. That's a lot of fish, throwing them on the ice it freezes it, talk about preserving it, it's right there.

» *One of my goals is to create partnerships*

My point is some of these species need to be harvested, that's right! Just like those lakes that break out, what happens to that fish? Just like that Choo tsik' klok is a special fish, that big whitefish it's just rich. It's all gone now, no more of that stuff.

» *What happened to it?*

I dunno. I tried to ask that question to Fish and Wildlife and they couldn't answer it. I don't think they care, I just don't think that they care, the way they've been reacting to my concern. They have a set budget, a yearly budget, a set budget, they just get a salary, they just work on small projects. Today, I see Fish and Wildlife airplane down [at the] airport. I open the door and that guy come up and said, "How's the weather this year?" I replied, "It's been raining!" He asked about if I see any musk ox. I said, "No one went out yet." See? Stuff like that! They just waste money on unnecessary stuff! I've been to their office over there and a lot of these people sit around and do nothing, BIA [Bureau of Indian Affairs] does the same thing.

» *Global warming will make it worse for populations of animals?*

Yeah, for fish, it's really critical the temperature of the water, if it gets too hot they can't stand it, that's why I brought up shallow water. After winter season they come up on the shallow water. Normal for them, they stay down deep all winter. When they do they run to that warm water like that. They can't take it.

» *Spawning areas not good anymore?*

Yeah, fish spawn in wintertime and then little ones start coming now. You look in the water you see little fish. History of over Greenland, over in Lapland the sheep that they have over there, I think there's a couple of incidences that those sheep went blind because of those [sun] rays. I heard it.

» *Plants are red?*

Those plants are actually burned up. I think it just burns because it changes color on the leaves and everything. You can tell, reddest color is from heat.

» *Marten around the village? How will that affect local animals?*

They don't hang around where humans are around, they mostly take care of themselves out there. I think marten, they migrate too, they do migrate.

» *Grizzly bears? Anything different about them?*

A lot of times they complain about bears coming into the camp and stuff like that? They have a diet just like any other animals one of them is they have diet. They got to have, they eat roots certain times of the year, they eat berries in certain times of the year, and they eat fish certain times of the year, they got a diet like that. That's another thing Fish and Game don't study, they don't study those things. A year that had a bad time for berries, berries don't come out. Bears like that they seek, that's why they come to the cabin and look for stuff like that. I really think so. When we were small there was nothing like that.

The reason they come to the cabin is that they seek that kind of a diet.

» *Berries scarce?*

Yeah, that's true, even across the river the whole back end of that, across the river. Lots of it, every year, we didn't have to go very far to pick berries. Last year, the only place they could grow was up on the mountain, yeah I noticed last year.

» *How do these changes relate to the whole world?*

Even now there's prediction of more hurricanes and tornados and stuff like that, it's all related to global warming, because these contaminants are blocking the sun, you have moisture down here just like a greenhouse.

If you go inside a greenhouse it's just damp in there, in that condition it's more liable to create hurricanes and tornados, so that's what's been happening. Even this year they predict more hurricanes than last year and that doesn't sound very good, and it causes flooding, all that contamination, all that is caused by global warming, by climate change. This contaminant that goes into the air, polluting, stuff like that, it's not going to go away, just like a tree. Normally when that tree is green they just leave it alone, that's normal.

They only take half-dry, but the green ones they leave alone. Those are the ones that purify the air, [repeated]. If you cut down one of those green rainforests and all that, it's more liable for more contamination to happen, that's what caused a lot of this contamination to be there. Green forests are the ones that purify the air and they cut those down and you're not helping the mother earth by doing that. It's just got too much, it just, it wouldn't maintain the balance, its already tipped the contamination, that's why. Next 20 years, there's going to be another fight, another battle over water. The United States doesn't have clean water no more.

Lots of these farm lands have been contaminated now 'cause of that chemical they use to grow [crops]. If you use too much chemical on the land that have too much sand, you contaminate that area, a lot of that farming happens that way. This country is not helping anything as far as improving environmental measures. They just kept destroying, they just [make a] habit of contamination and polluting, that's all they're doing. United States is the worst one. They complain Russia is doing that, but Russians have regulations, they keep those things under wraps, because they don't have a big company like Exxon and other companies that do all these things, which in this country, that we do. Those are the people that are doing the most contamination.

» *What should the world do about these [global warming] changes?*

I think don't think the world is going to do anything, I think the world is going to realize they made the biggest mistake by designing some of those things that are hazards to the environment. I don't think Arctic Village is going to be healthy, but the rest of the world is going have to realize they just can't go on like this no more. Like tornados, and the end of the season there's going to be more damage, billions and billions of dollars in damage. One of these days they're going to have to realize it.

» *Permafrost?*

I think the permafrost is slowly going to melt. It's only going to happen near the water.

» *What would the Elders do?*

Y'know, all they're talking about, how these animals change their behavior, change the pattern of migration, they always talk about that.

» *What did they say about that?*

We are part of things to blame, part of the ways. Like I mentioned about the harvesting, we can't just depend on the white man all the time. We just listen to them all the time, we just can't do that! People think I'm crazy, I have bunch of dogs, but that's the way people used to do it a long time ago, to use things that are available around this area like fish and some meat.

» *Lots of dogs to control the fish population?*

Not only that, our people are happy when they go to a gathering or carnival. They're happy they're having a good time, even more happy when their own people participate in these activities. I've been there and I know what I'm talking about it.

» *What did Elders think of forest fires in the old days?*

That's what I told you about white people taking advantage of us and brainwashing us, "this is good for you" and all that stuff. Now we are in this kind of condition and they're going to have to realize it.

Just like these two guys that came in yesterday, they're going to put in equipment on the runway that's going to be safer for airplanes to land. That's their way of life. Fifty years that I know we have [had] airplanes around here, no accidents have ever happened. Why do we need all this up-to-date equipment? There's been no major accident except that guy that overloaded his airplane and crashed. I hate to be talking that way, but that's the way I look at it.

It's really a sad thing to see when people don't realize what's actually happening. If you live in a hurricane-prone area like Florida, you better make up your mind, why these things are happening? Find out! That's stupid people, they just think they're going to rebuild and nothing is going to go wrong again. Things like these are going to happen again.

The center of this earth is really hot, some of those bubbles find their way to the top and that's why they have earthquakes. They have plates all over the world, I see that one time, sometimes those plates move. Just like volcanos, that mountain over there made by a volcano, lots of these things are made by volcanos. A lot of these sharp edges that you see is made by a volcano. Lots of places are like that, it's made by a volcano.

» *Politics of it? Partnerships with wildlife groups and environmental groups?*

You got to have a national issue, address a national issue in such a way that you bring back history that this thing happened, [it's] getting worse the last 30 years. Lots of different diseases will appear.

» *Why more diseases?*

Because of weather, contaminants. When you go to Walmart you walk in there and just look around and see how many different stuff that they have on the shelf, thousands of different little parts, things that they sell. All those things, it takes energy, it takes some type of energy to make these things. Lots of those little stuff you don't even need. That's where most of the pollution comes from is making those things, y'know? Like you go to Washington, D.C. and some of the big cities, you go into the mall, they make it so good you're amazed of how these kinds of architecture are being done that way. They blow the fresh air in there so you won't feel any kind of mood, that's all they do.

To convince you that this is what needed all this stuff, you see the big building and air conditioning and the big windows and all that stuff, that's what pollutes the air.

» *They throw air in there to make it feel like its natural?*

When you go outside it just hits you right in the face, they want you to stay inside.

» *Gwich'in never made things they didn't need? That's why the land is clean?*

Just like we're talking, me and Timothy, since when we were kids, there was not such a thing as trash. Florence said, "Oh! I know what used to be trash at that time, those catalogues. Several catalogues we ordered stuff from, its about four different kinds, those used to be trash." We laugh about it. There's no can to throw away. Anything can try to make something else out of it.

» *Like chairs or something, huh?*

Yeah, uh-huh, like a gasoline can, we make a water bucket out of it. In the wooden box it comes in, we make either shelf or chair out of it. This modern-day stuff, I don't agree with it, that's why I make all the stuff in my house, I don't buy anything. I even got stuff from my mom, [she] gave me those things. I can't buy furniture, I just make it. I just make stuff on my own. I disagree with all that stuff. I don't throw pop cans away, I tell those kids you don't throw pop cans away. You don't throw plastic bags away. You put it over there in a bag and then I reuse it again, I catch fish, I freeze it. Meat, I put meat in there and freeze it.

» *Is there anything being done about the dump?*

[*Shows a drawing depicting covering the trash with dirt and planting grass on top of it.*]

» *Animals will not be affected by this setup?*

No, unless they dig down. Oneida, they have a reservation. Years later, they found out that part of that reservation used to be a dumpsite. They sued the state, so they got a big land after that.

But this is our responsibility, our responsibility to do this. That's what I tried to do with that old stuff up there, I tried to push dirt over it. We need to take control over what they throw away. Over the years, we tried to make an awareness program over those things, but people just keep throwing pop cans away. I don't throw plastic bags away, unless it's just no good. Even those brown bags like that, I don't throw them away.

The main thing is that nobody took our land away. A lot of our younger generation is well-informed about what has happened. The Alaska Land Claim Bill (Alaska Native Land Claims Settlement Act 1971) really messed everything up; lucky thing that we were not part of it. We would never have this land, Doyon would have it. We'd never build that airport, they won't give us that land to build an airport on. Chalkyitsik, they have money to build an airport and they wouldn't give them land.

» *Will global warming get kids to pay more attention to it?*

Yeah, it would push [the idea that] a traditional way of life would be a way to go. Earlier in the spring I was feeding dogs and a lot of dog defecation around and I told them [the kids], "Oh heck, this is nothing. There is nothing wrong with this, no different than horse and cow manure." [*Inaudible*]. You need to learn how to control that. I put it in a box in wintertime, it just airs out. The one I put out there last year, it's almost like ground now. Nothing wrong with it, just throw it back on the ground. Lots of things the white man tells us is wrong.

When we were kids they harvested everything down to ducks. They knew when to harvest it: fall-time and springtime. They know when to harvest it, that's how they control it.

In order to make sure they cover a wide area, they assign themselves areas, one family would be in this area, and another family would be in this area. If one family had this area and another family had this [area], you got to have permission to go into another area. All around Yukon is like that. Even here, right around this village and around the [river]bend and all that stuff, it's your grandpa's [land]. We can't go out there and shoot muskrat, it's his area.

» *He diagrams the family areas on the map*

That's who controls all that stuff. If everyone used this one little area right here, there would be nobody to come around to this area. In order to cover a wide area, this is how they did it.

» *Why don't they do that now?*

I always bring it up.

All around Yukon River, Porcupine River, it's all like that.

Yeah, it's a wide area, they have muskrat camp and they have trapline in fall-time, and they go fishing and stuff like that. They just do that on their own, own area.

» *Why can't you go into their area?*

Because that's what the family depends on, that particular area is where the family depends on. They respect that kind of tradition, they respect that traditional rule. It's alike all the way around the Yukon River and all up there everywhere! All over Alaska actually is like that. David Russell explained it just like this type of thing, down the state they have a farm. Instead of having a farm they got a traditional area.

» *It's not like that now, huh?*

No. Just like your grandpa camps up there. Generally, that's where all your family, they still go there, like Gregory and those guys. Us too, up there Junjik Van [Lake], we go there all the time.

» *Where is the John family area?*

Up around Tsiivii tit, all around there, interesting the way they do it. [*Outlining the area on a GPS map.*]

» *If everyone hunts in one area?*

The other area will probably get overpopulated. Just like Alice [Peter], they got a fishing spot, same thing with Steven [Peter], they got a fishing spot in their land. They got a fishing spot on our land. Same thing with

Issac Tritt, that's why he fished around that [river] bend up there, that's his area.

» *Why don't they follow that anymore?*

They stopped harvesting muskrats, a lot of that was related to muskrat camps and stuff like that and they quit doing that, and that's when everything didn't go that way anymore. But they still do have a general idea of where their area is, even the younger ones, just like McGarrett and them guys, they know where their area is.

» *Something in them tells them?*

Uh-huh.

» *Do you pass it on to your kids so they just know?*

They just know it. Down the line Galen will know, Curtis will know, those kids will know. Some of them are protective, they think it's their area and they protect it.

Kias [Peter Sr.] knows all of that. If you point all that on the Porcupine [River], he knows who uses the area and everything. Him and Christian Tritt, when they were teenagers, they left their parents, they had to go out and work with somebody. They got to be helpers to somebody and they went to a lot of places like that. That's how he managed to go to a lot of places when he was young.

» *Even though they had their own area, they still shared the caribou?*

Yeah, they know when it's going to come in. They do! Yeah.

One time it just came over Thah' eetsii' 1950, there was no airport down there then. Lots come across lots of meat [emphasized].

» *Because the airport is there, their route shifted this way?*

Uh-huh.

» *With population growth, will their route shrink?*

I don't think so, when they see a big lake they swim across. In those days we [could] see their trail. They left a trail there for years. You can still see those around here.

» *Our trails?*

We got trails up that way, I can't follow it [knowledge of its location]. Kias can.

» *What was that route for?*

When muskrat season was over they come back over the land with a dog pack. A lot of times I walk back from Tsiivii tit. All those little drainage, high water, build a little bridge to go across, a lot of water too, a lot of water in springtime. Yeah, I remember we come back here June 5 and 10.

» *The trails should be re-marked*

I got stuck and I couldn't find it again. We need to trace it again. I remember that one area, it goes between those two lakes, narrow strip of land between two lakes. Talk about family having areas, me and my dad were going over land carrying a canoe, David Ole was there, we stopped and ate. Then that lake opened up so we can paddle (across), before that we had to carry it. We got to Daazraii Van, there's a lot of muskrats, but I can't shoot [them] because it's David Ole's territory. Early in the morning, David Ole was in his tent ready to go to sleep. At the end of Daazraii Van, so many muskrats, I shot at one. I missed. After I missed, somebody shot from the shore. The bullet hit about not too far from me. David Ole yelled at me, scared me, I thought he was going to shoot me. I didn't tell my dad though, if I told him he would ball me out.

Dorothy John | 06/08/05 | Time: 15:00

» *Notice anything different about the winters?*
Weather changes fast, that's all I notice.

» *Summertime?*
Same thing.
There's lot of change in the past, but I can't point out what it is.

» *Springtime/fall-time, same thing?*
It just seems like its getting warmer and warmer up here.

» *Water, river level?*
Going down. There used to be a lot of water in springtime, but now hardly any water rise.

» *Dried lakes?*

Never happened when you were young?

No. Just a few. Never seen that lake before.

» *Why do you think its like that?*

Thaw. What you call it the ground froze under? [*Permafrost.*] Yeah, that's why I think.

» *Do you think that will be bad for the village?*

Yeah sure, there'll be less fish.

» *Bushes and trees?*

They're growing, they're really growing good.

» *I bet when you were young this place was clear?*

Yeah. It's not like this.

» *Do you think that's good?*

It's good. I like it, anyway. More animals, you know? Used to have no rabbit around here, but we got rabbit now. Lots of animals we don't have, its up here.

» *Ice conditions? Thinner? River thaw out faster?*

Yeah it seems like it, I don't know.

» *Caribou? Anything different?*

They come around, but not like old times.

» *I bet when you were young there were lots?*

Uh-huh. They come around on the mountain, a whole bunch of them come around, I don't know why they stopped doing that. They go another way, y'know. I guess every year, or every so many years they change direction I think, they go a different way. They do that for 2 to 3 years, then they start going another way.

» *Moose?*

Yeah, always. When I was little there was moose around here.

» *Blueberries?*

Last year, no berries, it dries up, I think. We haven't had a rainfall [all of] June/July, we don't have no rain, just hot, I guess that's why it dries out. We don't have any last year, no berries.

» *You just feel like something is not right?*

Yeah.

» *Someone told me they used to see a lot of animals around during springtime, springtime is noisy. Do you agree?*

Yeah, it's true, you know? I don't know how come less is coming around. It's all died off or . . . that's true.

It's different every year, because not enough snow in the winter. I guess less water, used to have a lot of snow. But now we don't get too much snow in wintertime, so that's how come it melts out fast.

» *Clouds used to be whiter?*

Yeah, it's true.

» *Sun is hotter, no good for fish?*

Yeah, I guess so.

» *What could we do about it?*

Have to live with it. That's the way it's supposed to go.

» *Back in the old days people had areas?*

Oh yeah, that's right. Like when they go trapping they got their own trapline, when they go fishing they got their own fishing place. But everybody shared anyway. I don't know about a caribou deal. When caribou come around they don't do that. When they go trapping for muskrat, that's when they got their own place, their own trap, muskrat. That's all I know.

» *Marten around here?*

We never had no marten up here?

» *Good or bad?*

Good. I think more animals, that's good y'know?

» *What could Arctic Village do?*

Nothing they could do.

» *The world?*

The world is changing.

Old people, they don't have many things to work with, they make their own with that tree, rocks, and all that, skin. They make their own rope, they use tree vines for a rope. Rope to tie stuff together. That's the toughest one, they say. Babiche? Babiche too, yeah. Use from that tree, use from that . . . use animal [*inaudible*].

Allen Tritt | 06/09/05 | Time: 1:10

» *Somebody said it's muddy and slushy during fall-time?*

Depends on weather. Now it's different, because there's a lot of vehicles, compacted, it's not like that. Used to be, what they talk about, early days, when we don't have no equipment.

That's when it happened, long time ago, it really does. Really! Really mushy and muddy, bad! 'Cause it's not compacted, that time no vehicle run over.

A lot of vehicles nowadays, really compacted.

» *Fall-time comes early?*

Yeah! It is. Right now, compared to when I was a kid, fall-time comes early. First week of September it starts freezing up, it's snow. I know that from early days.

Everything freezes up and after everything freezes up, it snows. It [the process] works really good that time even before October, and springtime too. That ice goes out early, like about the first week of June, every year, first week of June.

Nowadays what we call a "crazy weather," 'cause right now, it goes out about the third week of May, third week of May, that ice, that snow gone, water coming out, creek, stuff like that. Last week of May, even ice goes out. Even fall-time, it depends on what time it's going to get snow, get little snow, then freeze up, then get a lot of snow sometimes, then it freezes up and melts again from the snow. That's why we have a lot of water on top of ice, under the snow.

I remember the last 3 years now, we got a hard time setting fish nets over Old John lake, because by October it's still not enough snow. And the warm, it's not even freezing up, it's still thin ice, so we can't take a chance.

» *Why is it important to put the net in in October?*

It depends on the weather, if the weather is bad. That weather it not like it used to be. Like in my day in September it freezes up, then we got snow, then we got no problem setting fish nets under ice, about October.

» *Early freeze-up? Bad for caribou?*

[In the] early days we got no problem, that's the way it's supposed to be, but nowadays it's just crazy. Like right now, at the fall-time, we not have no snow, sometimes we [have] no snow the whole month of October! Nowadays.

Sometimes it snows for the first week of October. Sometimes it don't snow for a long time and we got hard times.

» *When it snows and it doesn't snow [for a] long time, why is that hard?*

You might know better than I did. Nobody knows. Time is changing and weather is changing someway somehow. How do we know? Like a long time ago, we can tell by the sun, by the clouds how the weather is going to be, but now it's hard to tell.

» *Springtime is quiet?*

That's true too when I was a kid. Like Trimble, Kias, and them, when they was kids, ptarmigan was so noisy. They can't even hear good some-times, so noisy, there's a lot of them. Make all kinds of noise, that's what they're talking about around here.

Around there too, same time grouse, Cha'ta'kwan, there's a lot of them down there, they make all kinds of noise. All those birds, loons make all kinds of noise, but let me tell you this too, that's the time when I was a kid there is some animals. There are a lot of animals, like you said.

But before that, when my mom was a kid, she said you couldn't even hear so many animals make noise. That time when I was a kid there was no animals, but when she [was a] kid she said more, but when I was a kid, yeah, there were a lot of animals. But before that she said more, my mom, she can't even hear nothing. But like you said, you walk up to the lake right now, paddle down, you won't hear nothing, you won't even hardly hear Tah'qwaii. Like loons, little ducks. Maaaaa!!! Loon is different. Two different loons, they make all types of noise.

» *You don't hear that no more?*

Sometimes, not all the time.

» *But a long time ago you heard them lots, huh?*

All over, even right here, [*points to a lake below his house*] over here, up that way, on the river, gee, we use to go upriver with boats, so many ducks, Ahan'luk, we even shoot them down with 22–2. Hardly any ducks in the river, black ducks.

» *People say less ducks nowadays.*

Yes, it is. Like right now, . . . geese line up, I don't know how many thousands of feet in the air. They fly up north, sometimes they make lines like this, [*making a V*]. They just keep going over and over and over, we hear them all the time. Jee! They make good noise too, Dachaa, Haii, Gwegeh, maybe 30 to 40 to 50 at a time. Going by, fly over, but not anymore since that William Sound, that oil spill? That makes it worse, also, when they building that pipeline, we never see caribou for 4 years, even how many miles out from here. Since then we never see caribou like we used to. Farthest they go is up here on the mountain, they went down little ways and they come back and go back.

» *Do you still see the Vs?*

Going north, I don't see them no more. Sometimes I see little groups go by. Even at night we spend the night at Red Camp, we hear them.

Yeah, a lot of changes like . . . when I was a kid, your grandpa and them, we used to go up to the glacier. Up there, one caribou supposed to be up there, every glacier, one caribou stay there. Sometimes we go up the mountain, we know where we're going to see caribou, somewhere not even that no more.

» *Kii vaataiin Lii, there was caribou up there before?*

One time we were up there in the mountain, we shot caribou up there, Kii troo. We took it down the mountain. We were coming back this way, there was lots of caribou, lots of caribou! Sometimes they walk this way or coming down here, that time they shoot them at open place, Shrijyaa Haalii. Shoot them up there.

» *How come you don't visit those camps anymore?*

You got that right. You blame yourself too. That is a good question. It happened. The times are changing. There is a TV there. There's a telephone there and there's a movie there, who wants to work? [At] that time we [had] no choice, we got to do it, that's the only way to eat. When we go out, we got to shoot good before we eat. What we aim at we got to shoot him, but now when you go out hunting you're going to go out for fun. You're going to have a candy bar in your pocket, cracker, you're going to have pop [soda] on one side, what you worry about it? When you go home you know what you're going to eat, there's a hot pocket, pizza there.

» *[Food and a nice home] waiting for you.*

You're right. So what [do] we worry about?

That's true too. When I was a kid, that time, it was really hard. We [were] always hungry, always hungry, always hungry. What we get, that's what we eat. That time, old people, my grandfather and my grandmother and my dad, even my mom said, "Yeendaa, in the future," there going to be a lot of food is going to be lot of white man too. There's going to be a lot of food, you guys are goin' even walk on the food. "Really?!" [Allen said].

» *Gwich'in prophecy about walking on food?*

Right now there's a lot of food. When I was a kid, if I find a piece of candy on the floor I got to eat it, but now if a cracker drops on the floor we put it in the dog pot.

We got to eat it (food on the floor). We got no choice, or otherwise, where we going to get some? We got to eat what we get. No matter what it is you got in your hand, you got to eat it, unless it's dog food.

» *Forest fire?*

We just go by what the Elders say, times are changing. There's a lot of food stamps, welfare, stuff like that, that's why it's like that. Right now there's a lot of people looking for oil, cutting the lumber, looking for gold, and that's where the money goes. That's where the government gets the money, so he can feed us with that welfare and food stamps. Electricity going.

» *Fire lines? In the old days?*

They do it by hand. They got better equipment, better axes, and they got helicopters, they got better food. At that time we got no food.

» *Bush growth low long ago?*

Like you said, it's different. A long time ago, this whole thing was nothing but ice, that's melted, become just like this, that's why there's just nothing. Just hardly. Even down Yukon Flats, same way, like you said, even from Venetie, somewhere like that they can even see steam boats follow up the Yukon [River], that's how low that timber is, but now everything is just going back.

They said a long time ago this country seems like Africa. Thousands of years ago. That's true, too. The people, sometimes, they find like elephant teeth around the glacier sometimes, sometimes they find the big bones too. That's what lot of people said. Sometimes, a slot of people find pieces of weird bone like big animals like. I hear that.

» *Elders said there's going to be warming in the future?*

I don't know, maybe after we're all gone.

Try to get this thing in the future. Fifty years from now if you're still living, look at the country, what's it look like? A lot of different, maybe this whole village caving in [erosion], you never know.

» *Permafrost? Houses and building collapse?*

Lookout Hill even caved [in]. A lot of lakes even cave into the river, stuff like that. Lake down there is like that too, [the lake below].

» *Bushes in mountains thicker?*

Yeah, it's thicker and longer that's why those Elders said the caribou try to stay back, because that willow and stuff like that is getting longer. They try to scare [them], so they get attacked by other animals like wolves and stuff like that, that's why they don't want to go through the long brush. That's why they stay up there and look.

» *'Cause they can't see wolves in the bushes, huh?*

No, they can't, they know that.

» *Creeks are shallower now?*

Yeah, it is, because like you said, when that early spring melts fast. Sometimes it gets cold, then it dried up, then it gets warmed up like that again, all of a sudden there's not much water.

Only time that river and stuff like that raise up is when the rain water, lots of rain. The water goes up. When I was a kid—15 or 16 years old, when I move here I guess—that spring [there was] lots of water in the river, lots of water! Callahan's house [on a bluff] to the end of the house, that's how far the water is, how high it is, holy cow! There was a lot of water, just water all over the place up here. The water [is] that high, I don't know why, I remember them. That time your grandpa [Trimble] and Kias said they got a little boat they went by the creek and I just went by like that. Just went all over with the boat, went everywhere.

» *If there's more water you get to more places?*

It is. Even Yukon is like that. A lot of Yukon Channel got dried up. I used to go down there, 2 years ago, I try to use the same channel I just went down, so they have to go all the way around now. Venetie we get, but some places down the Yukon where we make shortcuts, you can't run a boat through there anymore.

» *No blackberries?*

Hardly, hardly, not like [it] used to be, yeah it is, nothing.

» *June 5—green leaves? Not like that?*

True, that's right, that's what I mean, that June 5 that's when the ice goes out in my days.

The first week of June it like that, it's good that day, it's good for animals, very good.

» *Clouds used to be whiter?*

Got to be whiter, long time, like you said, that day it's not a jet [air liners]. Even my day there's no jets. 1958, that's when I went down to state, there was no jet plane. There must be an army jet plane, but no commercial flight. You got four-motor we fly down with, I remember that. But right now so many motors going on, generator, snow-go, outboard motor, airplane, truck go back and forth to pipeline road. Jets fly over all over. That makes it seem like this. I don't know what you call it. I wonder if scientists test it, what's the air [like] compared to my day?

» *Sun used to be less hot? It was this hot? The sunrays didn't hit you directly? No sweat?*

You're right that must be it to, but that day people get a lot of exercise, a lot of exercise just like animals, they walk everywhere. Nowadays you eat too much junk, too many junk food, even right now people young like you get into diabetes, cholesterol, high blood pressure, all that's coming out right now cause of all that food, too much food.

» *We grow old fast?*

If you want to get old fast you get old fast. If you don't want to, you won't, you got to do a lot of exercise, only way to keep your body up. Your body, you take care of it. Just like Johnny Frank said that old man, he said, "This is my body, I'm going to take care of it. I'm going to live 100 years," but he missed by one year, almost made it. He's right! "It's my body I'm going to take care of it." He said that's how everybody is.

Like you, sitting right there, what you think about it yourself, you got to take care of your body. If you don't care [for your] body, unless somebody take care of you it going to go ruin. I got two legs right here I barely walked 4 years ago. I keep walking, if I hit this one the wrong way it's going to hurt for a while. I don't pay attention to it, I just go out and walk. I walk down to the airport [one mile] and back. It's going to go ruin one way or another, but I try to take care of it the best I can. Doesn't mean I'm good at it.

» *If you take care of your body, you're taking care of the land too, huh?*

Yeah! You're right! That land is hard to take care of nowadays, too many laws to it. Nobody goes out, like you said. We can't even go up there and spend a night and look for caribou stuff like that anymore. Can't do that anymore now, cause there's a boat there, there's a four-wheeler there, there's a mashed potatoes there, macaroni and cheese, hot dog there.

» *In the 2004, winter caribou moved around fast?*

They had to move around 'cause they always look for food to eat. My grandma told [me] caribou are like people, when they go there they look [for] something to eat.

Sometimes they sent one caribou to an area to gather food and he comes back to them [the herd] and tells them where the food is, and they go over there. That's what my grandmother told me, Sarah "Ghoo" Tritt. [She] said they're used to it.

That's why the old people watch for it right now, me and you go up to Dachanlee. We see one caribou running this way by himself, can't shoot them because that's a messenger. Go around look for food, go back. If you shoot him, he's gone.

Even us, you know, we send somebody out there, if he don't come back can we go over there? [Laughs] That's how the people take care of the animal like that. But nowadays nobody listens, they just go up there and over towards the caribou, they're just there and shoot caribou. Caribou know there's shooting up there and know they shoot the messenger, what they going to do? They're undecided. Either they're goin' to go down or they're going to go around or they're going to go through it, hard for them.

» *How many caribou did they get this winter?*

I dunno.

» *Winter last year?*

This year we have a hard time getting caribou, because you're right, they're moving so fast. They were all over and they go someplace. They went that way, some of them down that way, sometimes we got a hard time finding them.

» *Has it been there for the last couple years? Getting harder to hunt caribou?*

Yeah, plus snow, like snow gets deep so fast, can't break through with a snow machine.

» *No trash long ago?*

That trash bag, nothing, we don't got that. Now people are just throwing everything everywhere, that's the thing you young people should talk amongst yourselves, how you're going to solve a problem like that.

» *Did Gwich'in just know when to kill animals because of animals' population increase?*

Nothing bothers them like that, like I told you, when we do something, we try to go get something to eat, that's what we're doing, getting ready to eat it. Stuff like that, but what're we going take that we need, that's all. We can't take more or less, because we got to take it back with us too when we move it, if we get too much, how we going to move it? We can't just leave it behind cause we just going to waste it, but that's how the Gwich'in people all over (did it).

They can't leave the food behind, they take what they need to move, to survive with it. Like they go fishing at Old John Lake and up here they dry some to keep it, until caribou come around that's how they do it. If caribou come around, they [take only] so much they can handle it, so caribou won't rot and stuff like that. They get so much so they could dry them and keep it fresh.

» *In summer of 2001–2002, little to no caribou?*

Yeah.

» *In summer of 2004, one caribou killed?*

Uh-huh. Sometimes there's caribou, sometimes there's no caribou. Last year, hardly any caribou up there, nothing! Fall-time, nobody got nothing.

» *Dried lakes?*

Yeah.

» *Ice? Ice goes out so fast they don't fish as long at First Bend?*

Nobody goes out anymore, because it's so easy today, too much food. They just go out for fun, that's all. When we was kids we have to go out and get fish to eat. We got to eat, that's why we all piled up there to get fish.

» *Blueberries?*

Depends on the weather, hardly nothing sometimes. Last year some here and there, hardly nothing sometimes.

» *Women said they are scattered?*

Uh-huh.

» *What can we do about it?*

Can't do nothing, its nature.

» *What can the world do?*

Like in the creek, less water, and more water dried up, don't take enough water. Sometimes, we don't get rain for a long time. Like that springtime, ready to melt then it gets melted, then it dried up, freeze-up.

It don't get warmed up for a long time, the wind dries it up, heating it, then it warms up again, it's not enough, not enough for water to go into that ground, like mucky, wet, but it dried up.

» *They said they see marten too? Forest fire scared it up this way?*

Yeah, there used to be . . . I don't know, there's marten, sometimes there's a lot of marten, coming down from way back, it's like that, sometimes they're down the Yukon Flat, sometime there's a lot of mink, fox, moose, stuff like that, sometimes there's a lot of beaver swimming all over the place, like 10–15 years ago when we was down Yukon Flats guard training, beavers were swimming all over the place, now we hardly see hardly one. In 1979, I go trapping down Christian Village, there's lots of marten down [there]. Four to five years, then there's not that many, price went down, so [I] don't bother to go trap no more.

» *Best way people of Arctic Village can handle this weather is to live their traditional life the best they can? Don't buy candy so they don't have to throw the wrapper away?*

I don't know, the time is changing. The weather is changing, that's the things nobody can do nothing about, the weather. Anything grows on the ground, the berries. Who knows? Like you said, we just guess. Lake dried up, not enough water, there's lot of snow, but it don't melt like it used to. It just melts halfway [and] it freezes up again, it gets cold again, then it gets dried up, then it gets warm again. It's not enough to melt. That's what I think myself.

What I tell you right now, all [the things] I said, it's not a true or it's not an interest for you. There must be two or one word from Elders.

Like us, we the last ones to go, we went through these things like I told you. Every time we go out hunting, we got to shoot. A lot of times I went hunting for my brother and sister for the next meal. Before the guys go out tonight, we got to eat, I got to go out and get at least two rabbits or more. One rabbit's not enough, because [there's] thirteen of us in the family, we got to have two rabbits. My mother got to chase me out, sometimes I got a headache, "Get out! Get the rabbit!" So, I always go out, I was hungry too.

» *Big change, huh?*

That's why I'm living here, healthy right now, that's why I am not worrying now. There's lot of food, nothing to worry about. [During] that time, that's a big worry, we don't know if we're going to starve or not sometimes. Right now, you sitting there, you got to go out, get something before your next meal, you got to shoot good too. If you miss it, [you're] going hungry overnight. But nowadays, like I said, *easy*, but you got to have money. You got to have money, food stamps. You got nothing in your pocket, you can't eat.

» *A long time ago it was bow and arrow, now it's money?*

We don't have bow and arrow. Like my grandfather's young days that's when they get bow and arrow, but it's not hard [in] that time. People [are] like animals, they know what they're doing. They really move around, better than we do, even when we was kids, we do better than anywhere else, right now we can go to Old John Lake and back one day. Tea pot, something to eat, sometimes we get moose and caribou, pack it back, store it really good so animals won't get to it. Next day we got to go get it.

Trimble Gilbert | 06/25/05 | Time: 1:20

» *Porcupine caribou herd turned around at the cabin point?*

Summertime coming back from Sheenjik from calving ground I think, Sheenjik River is 75 miles northeast, that's where the trail is coming this way. Sometimes they come out that Vyuh Dzraii' [Black Seagull Mountain], sometimes at Dehst'eh Va'ddhaa [20 miles north of Black Seagull]. Next one is Dehst'eh Va'ddhaa, the last one and the next one is Deh st'eh chan leh'eeh, and then Vyuh Dzraii'. Migration coming this way, different area, and Old John Mountain, that's where they come from that time they're crossing Old John Mountain to Veetreegwangwaii, at the other end is a trapline, sometimes they cross the other end.

» *Looking over map:*

When I was a kid, sometime Veetreegwangwaii is covered with a herd, 'cause there's so many caribou at a time, [they] just cover the whole mountain. In early July, middle July, they follow the ridge all the way down to Brown Grass Lake. Then they're crossing Vinee Dachan Dhi'ee [mountain south of Arctic Village], I don't know how far they went from Vinee Dachan Dhi'ee, maybe Wind River somewhere, and then [in] August, the caribou's skin is just black, first week of August the old hair comes out, black, short hair, that's the time they're coming back. They're shooting [them], I remember them shooting young, one yearling, for the parka, so they shoot that young one, young caribou. That's the only time that skin is good for a parka, [so] they make a winter parka. They're coming back even, the bulls are down that way in September, they start coming back. Sometimes they start coming back Dachanlee [mountain above Arctic Village], sometimes on the other side of the river Kii vaataiin Lii mountain [east], then they're up Junjik [River] crossing. Sometime [for] 2 weeks everyday there's a bunch of caribou, you can watch them from here.

Heading north we call Haii ts'a' [fall], velvet on just about ready for October 'cause they're fighting. Maybe 1970, that's the last time caribou

[were] crossing Junjik [River], since then, no more. Even the village here, caribou are crossing where they built the airport, Elen Vaatąįh. Even down by the old village Shrijyaa Haalii, people kill lots of caribou. In 1970 and before there was a lot of them like that, I don't know why caribou are not crossing the river like that anymore. Even Nets'ii Dhah caribou are crossing all the time, ever since, there's no more caribou on other side. Now sometimes they're coming east northside of the Old John Lake, they're crossing to Veetreegwangwaii, but it's not very many, compared to a long time ago, just a bunch of them crossing now, just about half maybe. There is only 75,000, sometime less.

Coming this way towards Venetie, but farthest they can go is Tłoo Tsoo. They don't cross the river down that way anymore either, so they turn back, coming back and heading north again, so we don't see too many Haii ts'a' [fall]. [In] September just very few times, not like a long time ago, old people like my father said, those young caribou, those young generations don't know the old trail they used to have—the old leader—they lost all that leader, the one that knows the country and those young ones, they don't know the country. Porcupine caribou herd, they call them baring caribou.

Brush, even 1960, in picture I saw, today pictures is really different, you could see that hill west [of here], there's a hill across the river—1960, there's no tree on it. But now you can see the tree is growing everywhere [on it]. I think baring caribou, they don't like the brush, so they don't use the old trail, so there's another way. That's why they don't go across anymore.

» *Choo tsik' klok is gone?*

You know where Raih Junjik? There's a hill a quarter of a mile behind that hill. Choo tsik' klok was a big lake a long time ago, it's a rich lake, I remember. Lots of muskrat, lots of whitefish, maybe 15-pound whitefish, not too big, it's really wide and just fat. Full of fish on it. So that people hunt ducks all the time there, good place for ducks, we hunted ducks all the time when I was kid up there. And Choo tsik' klok, the creek come out to that Nun'elyii small creek. When that ice breaks up [in] springtime, the hole comes out, and when they come out, the creek is running on the wide grassy place, shallow. Everywhere on the grassy place, you just go over and pick it up, people kill lots. Drain out. Choo tsik' klok is nothing but grass now. Choo tsik' klok is Shee'choo [whitefish]. Good fishing place, that's why that one old man built a cabin right here [pointing on map]. He lived here and he's fishing, right here, putting fishnet in, that time he hunted black ducks.

» *Pointing out things on the map about the lakes draining out, Gideon referenced.*

We lost Noah Vavan, Grass Lake, Haaglii'n.

Noah Va taii' old caribou fence. Lake trout used to be in Blackfish Lake. [*Inaudible*].

» *Caribou don't stay in one place all winter?*

Well, um . . . the Porcupine caribou herd, [there's] so many of them, 150, 170 sometimes, that's a big herd, so there's not like a Central herd or 40-mile herd. They're different because their migration is a couple hundred thousand, so many of them. They go to different winter areas. That lichen is growing slow, they know it.

After they spend winter here, they move to another place, maybe Fort McPherson, Canada. They just take care of their own food, they can't eat everything one time. They think about future. Sheenjik area, Colleen, Old Crow, probably now Dempster Highway, McPherson Mountain, they spend winter [in] different areas every other year. They spend winter, and next year they might not come back here, because of that lichen. It grows slow I think, they know it too, so they move to a different area.

» *Spring is quiet now?*

It's getting less and less, maybe the last time, 1950, that year is the last one, so many birds, ptarmigan, we stay in the tent, May to June 6, we have a hard time sleeping 'cause it's so much noise, lots of birds, ptarmigan, everywhere.

1953, that's the last time I see ptarmigan in this flat area, there up in the mountain. The reason is they're nesting, males sitting on top of the tree watching the female, lots of ptarmigan, lots of ptarmigan sitting on top of trees, we don't see that anymore. Not very many people use a shotgun, they used to, but they don't shoot very many of them. Lots of ducks, everywhere.

» *Are there lots of ducks there anymore? No more geese in Vs over Arctic?*

Maybe they're going another way. Lots of them stop here. A long time ago, you could see them, forming a "V." Not many yet. Some of those birds we don't see that. Some of the birds make different sounds? Some of them I don't hear anymore. Some snipes, little brownhead snipes, all over when I [was growing] up. I don't see that, and some birds, I don't see them anymore. Even this year, I don't see that black bird either, I don't see them, gee! That's sad, maybe dying down that way with oil spills, lot of them gone. Something you can't replace. Oil businesses, I know they're killing a lot of birds.

» *You can't hear loons anymore?*

I see a lot of them, but they don't make noise. Dah'stii, that big one, I don't see them this year. I see T'salvik this year. Another one looked just like T'salvik, but its head is smaller. Lives on the river, we call it Kah'eetreh. I don't see that make lot of noise all the time either, I don't see it anymore.

» *When did this start happening?*

A few years back.

I don't see many birds either. I mean certain birds, they don't come back.

» *Seagulls late?*

Yeah, seagulls usually sit down on the river, the other side of the river, lots of them. Arctic turn I never see them. Bank swallow. Lots of them a long time ago, flocked down by the village down there, thousands of them. Not anymore. Brownhead swallows, they make a house along the house, I don't see them.

» *They don't make house anymore?*

No, nothing, this year has really changed, I didn't see none of them. The other day I looked for that bank swallow, I don't see them.

» *When I was little, I used to see lot of bank swallows.*

Lot of stuff are disappearing now, but they don't talk about it.

» *There's no blackberries anymore too?*

Blackberries, grizzly bears really need it too, up in the hill there's a lot of them, they [grizzly bears] eat it all day, then hardly any, Deh'netchoo.

» *Raymond said there are no more salmon berries on the mountain too.*

Blueberries disappear too, Nałyuu klut is cranberries. Last year [there's] nothing. Kii vaataiin lii [mountain] on the side just red, we fill up a five-gallon can in no time, nothing like that no more.

» *Clouds are darker?*

Weather is changing, that's why, talk about old songs, they call zhee zaa loo talk about the ozone, a big hole.

» *Creeks?*

Even that Bear Creek, Bobby said he drove all the way up last summer to that Bear Creek over there, no water he said, that's the first time. A long time ago, there's always [water] running all the way down to the river, dry all the way up! A lot places are like that, even this East Fork River is getting lower and lower too.

» *Banks eroding upriver?*

Permafrost is melting, some areas we lost because that permafrost thawed out.

» *They say that's why the lakes dry out?*

Uh-huh, that's why it's dried up.

» *Remember that there's a lot of snow in the higher mountain?*

Kii vaataiin Lii, a lot of snow, warm spot just like refrigerator, never melts. Sometimes you can't see the mountain, because caribou lay down on it one whole day. Hot weather, same as a glacier. [*What mountain?*] Almost every mountain, thaa 'eh kyit, that's where that snow is there all summer, never melts, now it's all gone. Caribou need it too, hot, mosquitoes, glacier up here Raymond house [Look out Hill], Kii vaataiin Lii [mountain] bottom [of it]. All summer, you can see the glacier now it's all gone, all melted, that's where caribou lay down on it all summer. When there's lots of mosquitoes, they lay down on it all day. Animals need it, now it's all gone.

» *Permafrost bad for houses?*

We always have a problem with it. You know, behind that church, if you walk towards the river, there's a big dipper there, another one by Rih' Junjik too.

» *That never happened a long time ago?*

No, never.

» *Can't catch fish [at] certain times anymore?*

Netsii' dhah, we fish up there, clear water, you can see the fish jump, even Junjik you can't see that anymore.

I go muskrat hunting with my mom and dad sometimes. I stand on the bank, I can see a bunch of them, grayling. Like Raymond said, we don't catch many. Every bend we catch some for lunch, supper, now it's really hard to catch, just a few here and there.

» *Caribou mobility increased due to less vegetation?*

Vegetation, it don't grow very much anymore. No berries.

Right now, they live on vegetation, huh? Leaves, uh-huh they eat lot of leaves and grass right now, they got a lot of food, but wintertime they're having a hard time right now. They move around, they don't spend winter together, 150,000 they just spread all over. They know they don't have enough food for a bunch of caribou, so they just spread all over. Crow Flats, Fort McPherson, Dumpster Highway, that's the only way they can survive. There [were] some caribou last winter, but not too many of them.

» *We can't move around too much, because there's too many bushes?*

One guy came from the northeast, Koness, he asked me, why is there such thick brush?

Hard for that caribou, Porcupine caribou herd, 40-mile herd, Glen High-way this spring, we saw quite a few 'cause they get used to it that brush. Porcupine caribou herd is not like that, Baring caribou, hard for them, that's why they never go to Venetie.

» *Back in the old days, did they make fire lines?*

No, there's fire here and there, but they don't fight fire.

Just smoke signals for communication. When we see smoke, we know someone is coming.

Venetie, Fort Yukon, up there FYU trail, they're going to burn one tree. So, they're just going to let people know that it's coming, once they see that smoke, and then they make an answer here too. Really important they make that smoke a long time ago. They never had a problem with forest fires, because [of] permafrost, you know? Not much brush.

» *Forest fire, when it spreads all over, what animals move up this way?*

Marten, moose.

» *You think they'll go back?*

Maybe [in a] few more years, even this summer, I flew over that. The grass is growing back already. That burn place, that food, better food too, I think. They going to go back.

» *No rain?*

Even now I'm worried about blueberries.

» *We had a fire right up here?*

I'm worried about it, I call Fairbanks, but they don't want to do anything about it.

» *Back to the old days?*

If something happened to all the animals we're using then, we're going to have a hard time. How [are] we going to survive? They said hard times are always coming, the whole world is changing. It might happen. Same time that fire and water is destroying everything, too much human activity, that might affect that wildlife too, polluted water. If they do then, we're going to have a hard time, starvation.

» *Invasive species?*

Fort Yukon, they're losing lots of trees, lots of dry wood, maybe that same thing is going on already. I'm sure that different bugs are going to arrive, kill all the trees, not only that willow, vegetation.

» *Gideon said he's never seen green leaves on June 5 before?*

That's why some of those birds never arrive on time, same with black ducks, they thought there's never going to be black ducks, but they came in same time, early spring.

» *Porcupine River melts before the caribou make it, so calves drown?*

I think people over there help them climbing the bank, that's when we lost a lot of calves.

» *Caribou herd? Hunters' yearly harvest? 2004 worse? One taken?*

Yeah, we didn't see caribou August, September. There's too much smoke, so they didn't come this way. Lucky me and Gregory got four or five up there.

» *2003?*

Not really good, hard to get caribou now. Like, a long time ago, a big herd was everywhere, there's probably lots, but it's hard to get into it. You kill caribou somewhere, you can't get into it, you lose the whole thing?

» *Fall come, melt, came again?*

N/A

» *Dried lake?*

Dried lake, someplace where the water [is] deep, there's still puddles there. Still muskrat there, ducks, the rest is just willow, it's good for moose, too.

» *They say there's going to be more moose around there, more moose?*

Yeah, nature does that.

» *Ice conditions?*

Nobody fishes up there, ice is melting from the bottom so it's going fast. A long time ago, at Old John Lake the ice [was] maybe several feet thick, not anymore. Three feet, that's all. Ice don't get too thick anymore. After Freeze-up, then it takes a long time to freeze, I keep warning the people to not take chances with ice anymore.

» *News of deaths?*

They don't expect that thing I always warn them about ice. Ice is not the same anymore, so we got to educate young people.

» *Alaska heating up two to three times more than rest of the world, really bad for the rest of the world?*

Elders' story is that, you know that oil when they hit the oil, it's just thick, that black. That oil they said [is] like a refrigerator, keeping the earth cool, the reason it's there. Everything is connected, water, oil, subsurface they call it. When they get rid of all that oil they replace it with water, but it won't work, because that oil is cold. [It's] one of the reasons the whole world is changing, they probably know it, but they don't want to say it.

They pump the oil over there 20–25 years ago, everything is changing slowly. That's why they have earthquakes here and there. They pump it out and replace it with water, but it won't work, so that earth is warmer, erosion. Everything is changing, lots of animal die. The whole world is changing, and people are changing.

My time and before my time, people really took care of themselves, good spirit. They're really good spirit people. If they say one bad word, they'll never forget it.

They'll always correct themselves. If they steal something, they tell everybody. Nowadays, "I don't care" is the word. A long time ago, [it wasn't] like that, whatever they do they'll ask for forgiveness.

Animals change, weather changes, time is going fast too, faster and faster, so much going on. You don't have time.

Every day you see something going on with TV and everything. A long time ago, [it was] really slow, time is going slow. Everything is going too fast. People's minds go along with it too.

A long time ago Elders had area, they did that to control population [*specifically muskrat?*] [*Pointing it out on map*]

» *Animal population control?*

Since there's no dogs, people don't fish that much anymore. They kill more, lots then there's more animals. Every year we kill a lot of muskrat, but there's more and more. Since we quit, they're all gone, not very many. Not very many, here and there I see Muskrat, but not like a long time ago. When you kill more, the animal knows it, so there's more. More we harvest, the more next year.

» *We were busy?*

Busy people, busy all the time for living, even right now. Maybe my father goes 4 to 5 miles to fish with a dog pack, down Haalii Van he goes down every day to check his fish net with a dog pack, brings fish, people do that all the time.

I told someone the other day, what am I going to do? I never go hungry, so I never go out, but when we go out, it's more healthy.

In 1960 [there were] lots of old people living here. Muskrat [was the] only income we got, now it's this time there's nothing. If I go downriver to cut wood I pack it to the bank, maybe I can bring back five loads of wood and then I pile it down the bank. The one who got pension, they go down and they want to buy it, so they give me three and a half a loads for dry wood, so I don't look for free stuff.

We have to work for everything, that's a good life. We had a big store that time, we didn't ask for credit. Now it's different, I drove a boat past *Netsii Ddhaa*, Jothom [Jonathan], Walter Newmen, Donald Tritt, we hunt wolves. We walked halfway up to Red Sheep Creek we only got two wolves. That's a long ways, lots of mosquitoes, this is how hard we work for money, but when we don't feel it, we like to do it. When everybody works hard for a living, it's better, old people, they put fish nets around the [river]bend, they check it every day, paddle with a canoe. They don't use that motor, they check it out and bring back fish. When you work hard for something, you feel better about it.

» *Work with Fish and Wildlife more?*

They got scientists and everything, so they don't listen to us. Before they come, traditional law, they [Gwich'in] got their own law, they got their own area, they don't kill everything, they save a lot of them for next year, trapping, wintertime too. Just like Gregory, he traps down Cat Trail, he caught a lot of marten, but he sees lots, but he said, "Oh I will kill some more next year."

» *Wolves eat only half?*

Wolves kill caribou, leave bones here and there, puppies are born and then they bring that bone for a little puppy, so they can chew on it. They raise the little one like that.

We got only one breed [of] dog when I grow up, big one, working dog. They're all good working dogs, and strong. After that, I don't know where the house dog come from, they bring house dogs into this village and they ruin all the good, strong dogs. They're all small. We have big dogs a long time ago, working dogs. We lost all those good dogs.

» *Outside dogs?*

They're good for racing, but not for working.

» *Grizzly bear? Behavior?*

When I [was] growing up, they were really wild. When they shoot caribou, sometimes grizzly bears get into that meat. They're smart, they stay away from people. They don't go near that camp, once they smell you, they take off. In 1970 people fed them in some places, they got into camps, they couldn't get rid of them. We have a problem with them down this way too, they get into cabins, our tent. They'd never done that in the past.

They get into meat cache, but not tent. They're not afraid of people, some of them, that's one hanging around camp, people camping. Grizzly bear is different, it comes in the village a couple times now, they shot one up there. That Tri'h [roots], lot of them growing aside the road it's easy to dig them out. They start way up there and come all the way down here, Galen got one, and before that, I got one. They're acting just like dogs.

» *Trail up that way? You and Kias know it?*

Start from Trii'Junjik, if I can see it, I can follow it.

» *How come they made it?*

If you don't have a trail up that way you're going to get lost, you're going to spend more time going around big lakes, maybe take you one week to get up there. If you know that trail it will take you maybe one day. A group of people went up, started from here. My Grandpa Dehts'e', medicine man, he's the one that went up with hundreds of people.

They don't know the trail, but they're making the trail. So many lakes up that way, so he just use the medicine, go to sleep, and he knows where to go, he tells the people where to go and he makes the trail all the way up. My mom said a long time ago it [was a] couple feet deep, the roots you step over, they use it all the time, that trail from Tritt Creek all the way up to Tsiivii Tit, maybe farther up to Thundercloud Mountain. Down this way Ottertail [Creek] all the way down, down here to Haalii Van, fish camp. Vashraii Van, another one going to Dachanlee [Mountain].

Vashraii Van to here, we use willow cutter one day, we cut the willow we going to be good for fish. Bobby's cabin, that creek, that's what they did a long time ago, they take care of it. All that trail, summer trail, creek, re-do it again, mark all that trail.

» *Birds that make a nest on that house? There used to be lots on the school, but I don't see that anymore?*

Brownhead swallow, I don't see too. Brownhead, bank swallow, down there by the river, thousands of them. My father knocked them down with a stick [in midair], so many of them.

» *No sounds of loons?*

There's still a few of them.

» *No geese?*

That's what they say, but there's lot of geese this spring.

Tsal Cho, blackbird. There's none.

Del' I used to hear them all the time. Yeah, the oil did something to them.

No Aahanluk [mallard], just five this spring.

Bobby Tritt | 07/24/05 | Time: 33:38

» *Salmon timeline from 1980–1990*

» *10-year period from 1980–1990.*

Well, from those years from 1980 to 1990 to 2005.

Well, it seems like now there's more fish now than there was then. The king salmon, there's more king salmon now, you know. I don't know what Fish and Game is doing, but it seems like the numbers are going up too.

They [Fish and Wildlife] set up sonar down there. Over 200,000 went by, so that's good.

Now they're [Fish and Wildlife] keeping track of fish, maybe even moose.

As far as fish is concerned, I think we're doing good.

» *1990–2000, how was the harvest intake?*

The Native community, a lot of them don't do harvest reports, but it would be good if they did. That way they'll keep track of how much they're catching between Beaver and Fort Yukon.

» *They'll know when something weird happens?*

Yeah, you know how Native people are, they don't like to do what the white people said, but if we explain it right to them, it's just a report, it's not a big thing there. It gives us the basic idea of how to raise more fish down the road. Lots of people don't fill those things out, especially Native people here in Alaska. In this area, that's how I see that.

Basically, it gives them a good idea of population, how much we're eating.

» *It would make more sense if Native people did harvest reports?*

It would be better if a Native person is doing it. A lot of times, Native people, seems like they're willing to help us, they don't want to. Me and you, we'll go check the mail, but some other person from the local level, we'll all check mail and he'll get one of those harvest reports from CATG [Council of Athabascan Tribal Governments], and they'll throw it in the trash, [laughs]. A lot of them do that.

If you go to Chitna, you're only allowed one king [salmon]. Up here the harvest report is important to Fish and Game. Us, we pretty much rely on subsistence too. The villages, a lot of Native people rely more on subsistence than the store. It'll be better if we continue more . . . we depend on subsistence [more] than the store, because of the way the world is going today. War, we got a war going over there and, being in Alaska, we're kind of a big target here because of the pipeline, you never know what's going to happen.

» *Salmon: when did it start changing?*

Sometimes, I see people coming up from Fort Yukon or in Fairbanks, I ask them how's the fishing running? And they always say it's good, so I'm assuming it's good. As far as I'm concerned the fish, the numbers are up there. The state, feds, hopefully they'll all work together with us.

» *Moose: more or less?*

One of our Elders passes away and we always throw a good potlatch, doesn't have to be open season, we can just get one now. Us, we depend on moose, we've always depended on moose, it's important we keep that tradition going. As far as population, here in the Yukon Flats, it's lower because of the wolves, brown bears, maybe Fish and Game, Fish and Wildlife, they should control the brown bear population.

Hunting season, August and September, during those times there's lots of sports hunters that come up here [from] different states, they're only there for a trophy. They're having the same problem, it'd be really nice if those people, even if those people don't eat moose meat, bring it to the nearest community, to someone who eats moose meat, that way it don't go to waste. 'Cause a lot of times state land, state jurisdiction, the hunters kill the moose, they just take the head, they throw away the rest or leave it. There should be some kind of law to say, "Hey! You shouldn't do this." It's wildlife. Once you kill the moose it's not going to be there again, it's got to have a young one.

If we don't take care of the young ones or try to keep the bear population down or wolf population down then, the moose can come up. Restrict some areas for sports hunters. They could only go hunting certain areas. Like, um . . . I'm not telling them not to hunt . . . on the other hand, Alaska Railroad, they kill a lot of moose, they kill anywhere from 600 to 700 moose a year just with the train. We should do something about that, a lot of moose go to waste.

» *Highways?*

Highways, a lot of moose get killed there.

Maybe out in the wild like us out here, bring bears and wolf pups down. For moose and caribou, we need to look at the whole picture, but it's hard to look at. If we all work together, lets talk about it, instead of sending a letter here and there. There's a few people in Venetie that are willing to work for Fish and Wildlife. It's better if it's someone from here, maybe you.

We need more Native people in those kinds of positions [with Fish and Wildlife], maybe 5 miles upriver from fish camp. Federal [government], they give the state $5,000 to $6,000 a year to count fish. Native people could do that, put them on job trainings.

Somebody will benefit from it down the road somewhere. If we get some interested people from the village, local level. It'd be good. That way if somebody from outside wanted to come over all the time in person; be here and deal with the issue here. Maybe they'll have a lot of trust in that person because that person will be from the local area.

» *Water levels?*

Well, it seems like now we're probably sitting at average. You see how cold it is outside now, the wind. It's what, July 24 right now, it's supposed to be a little above normal or hotter. It wasn't like this in the '70s and '80s, but now it seems like this year we got an early spring, but it's cold. And maybe we'll have a shorter summer or early fall.

The weather, there's something going on. All of a sudden, its super hot, and the next day, it'll be average, below the normal temperature.

Seems like when you get older, days fly by faster. One year is like nothing. I was first chief of Venetie Council 3 years ago, it seems like last year.

I'm just happy it's nice and sunshine and we're all alive.

» *Tells of when he was in Arctic Village as a kid in 1970s, really cold in wintertime.*

Hopefully, we'll try to be here for even past our time.

The weather now, is like, seems like, it's getting shorter, the days go by fast, the weather is really cold for July. A couple of weeks ago, my sister says fish are even freezing at night. They couldn't even dry their fish, [it was] too cold at night. Funny weather we got nowadays.

» *Dried lakes?*

Lots of dry lakes here in Venetie, Big Lake dry a little, guys around here is telling me the water is getting low.

I told them, "Well, you guys got an escalator [tractor] down here, you can dry that up there." There's a creek above Big Lake, they need to open up that old creek. So next spring when water goes up, water will go to the lake. If they do that, years ago, way before our time, they used to have a fish trap up there, they used to have a lot of water up there. It's not like that up there anymore. We need to look at stuff like that. Get it up and going, that way we'll have whitefish here in Venetie. There's no whitefish up there, not now, not on the creek, but way towards the mouth of the creek, but not up here.

There's probably one, two, three, lakes from here to Big Lake, they're all dried up. Maybe if we open it [the creek] back up, everything will come back to life. I'm sure they can get a little money to open up creeks. I'm sure they can get a little money to do that.

» *Cave-ins?*

You see that mountain? Maybe just at the bottom of it, there's something like that going. We're landing here, we're circling, I see below that mountain a big ground just fell off the cliff. I don't know why, but I never seen that earlier, big land that slid off the hill. Permafrost is bigger and thicker in Arctic Village.

» *Bush growth: bushes and trees weren't as high. They didn't grow as fast and thick?*

When I was a kid trees like those willows, they don't grow as fast, as fast as today.

» *Growth rate sped up?*

Yeah.

» *Spring birds: robins, swallows?*

I don't see that many swallows anymore, robins, there's a few probably. I don't see that much no more.

» *Ducks?*

Seems like the numbers are low on ducks, I ask the people, "What's the duck hunting situation this spring?" They say, "Well, there's not enough." Seems like the duck population is down, I don't know how or why. Maybe wherever they migrate to, they eat more ducks than us.

» *A long ago around this time, would you hear birds?*

A long time ago, there [were] more birds. There [were] more birds singing. Now I hardly don't even hear any birds singing. Birds don't even sing anymore.

I don't even hear birds sing anymore, even in the springtime, they hardly ever sing anymore.

» *Robins? More robins a long time ago?*

Yeah, there were more robins a long time ago.

» *Swallows that made mud houses a long time ago?*

More a long time ago, less today, maybe about half-less today, comparing then to now, probably half.

» *Ground squirrels?*

A long time ago there used to be lots, but that oil company blasting the grounds with explosives, I think that's killing them off, they just get caved in. Seems like the population on ground squirrels are low, seems like the only answer is the oil company blasting the ground. One strong dynamite is one strong bomb to use. [*Note: Bobby is referring to Roush Oil Company doing seismic tests for oil on Venetie Reservation in the 1970s, when they had a partnership with the tribe.*]

Ground squirrels, they live in the ground. [Every time] the ground moves, that's a disaster. They all die because they get trapped in there. Seems like the population is down.

» *Big forest fire 2004? Were you here?*

No.

Trapping, it's going to affect the trapping. All the little animals, like the rabbits will move somewhere else, and all the little animals will follow them. They'll eventually be back, but not for a couple of years. Still need to keep track of the population, because a lot of people depend on those little animals for subsistence like our Elders.

When Jim Christian was alive [in the early 1990s], he said we used to kill lots, but not much anymore.

» *Salmon harvest timeline.*

» *When did you start seeing changes in fluctuations in salmon populations?*

Local salmon population species, one would be chitnooks, also known as kings. The numbers have greatly increased. In the last . . . my goodness . . . probably in exactly those years caught 97 in 6 days, to give you an idea. I stopped. They may not have been as fat as in Fort Yukon, but they were good tasting!

» *97 in 6 days.*

I was catching those ones that look like [they're] from the ocean, that's how good they were.

The dog salmon, the chums seem to increase. I don't know about the silver, but those two have increased greatly.

» *When did you start seeing this spike in salmon and dogs?*

In the last 5 years.

» *Moose? Noticeable changes with moose?*

Moose are always hard to get for one. I don't see no variation in time for that fact. Other than one spring I harvested a moose, and I grabbed ahold of it to skin it, the hair came off, and I pulled it a little bit more. I noticed there were circular rings throughout the skin, and it was seasonably warm, in fact, much warmer than it has ever been. And I was wondering about that too, cause of the big talk of the ozone. I wondering if it directly affected the skin, which is the largest living membrane they got, just like us. I'm wondering, yes moose are being affected, but I don't know how much yet.

Like that old saying, "When its 40 below and a sparrow falls off the branch and falls to the ground, does it feel sorry for itself?" No. They weren't given that conscious-thought-process like we have. Animals do and die. I don't know the numbers; I don't know the hardships they endure other than the predations is a big part of the gameplay. Moose are still moose. They're sought after for the skin. I raised my kids on it year in and year out, even if gas prices go up to $5.50 a gallon. It's not going to stop, so I can't really answer that question. I have not noticed anything great or anything less.

» *Dried lakes?*

This year is totally different, water tables seem to have [risen] quite a bit, in the areas I've gone to so far. It may be due to the fires that we had, and no collections of melt off and rainfall to be absorbed in the ground, that's definitely attributed to that. But the areas like Ginnis va von, Enuk va von, and them lakes down the way, there's been a recession of the water level. How much? It's dropping, there's no question about it. I haven't been down there to take note of any dramatic changes, but I'm sure the changes have increased again.

» *What was that, Enuk and Ginnis?*

Good moose country down there. [*Tim is marking spots on the map.*] Enuk and Henry va von, good moose country.

» *Now you're saying they receded?*

Yeah, I walk the lakes. Everything runs downhill, right? When that's the case you can safely assume that the water table has increased.

» *Permafrost and cave-ins?*

I can't see any, that would almost have to be a subtle change there. I don't see anything standing up.

» *Increase in bush growth?*

Only because we never had any fires around here, so the growth is going to be tremendous as it is.

» *Birds? Numbers?*

We favor the sea ducks, old squaw, and white-winged scoter. The surf scoter, Dee Tree aah, and ahon luck, their numbers have dropped. Big time.

» *How do you know?*

Twenty-two years [ago], when I first come up here they were flying in flocks, waves, and in this day and age, they're not. I mean, you'll see small numbers of flocks here and there, but no great numbers anymore. Drii'n daw, their numbers seem to have increased a little bit, but mallards, their numbers seem to be stable. All the other puddle ducks seem, just all the sea ducks seem to be the diminished number. There used to be a lot of sea ducks.

» *When did you notice the changes?*

Probably in the last 4 to 5 years. My harvest numbers have dropped like you can't believe. Normally I get anywhere between 40 and 70 jaw—quite a bit of duck. I pass it out to those who don't get [any], the Elders and what have you. Then I smoke the rest and keep some during the summer. In fall-time I go get some again and catch some before they're about ready to head out. Nice and fat and plump. Not wise either, but those numbers have even dropped too, something's amiss.

» *Robins?*

I don't see any sparrows; I see quite a bit of robins.

» *Decrease in sparrows?*

Yeah.

» *What about the ones that make mud houses along the homes?*

Just little bit.

» *A long ago, there were a lot?*

Yeah, a lot more. They were flying all over the old village and everywhere else.

» *Big geese Vs?*

The geese populations seem to be pretty good, speckled geese numbers are . . . Watch wave after wave after wave, how come I'm not there when they're doing this? 'Cause the hunt is so hard, only because the winds have changed in the springtime to make it worse. Winds have definitely changed. Here in our area, the winds have changed *dramatically*, oh yeah.

Even the talk of wind energy is becoming more apparent year after year, their thoughts of alternative energy sources, we can't afford fossil fuel anymore.

I've seen different color birds. When I did see them, there were just a few.

I shot a brant goose one time that wasn't supposed to be here. They normally fly by 80,000 freakin' feet in the air. The brant geese are normally not in this region, this is not their fly zone at all. I shot that probably 5 or 6 years back.

I shot a wood duck this is not its habitat either. Saw another one this spring, whether they're flying with different species or what, I have no idea. But the scoter ducks are here.

We have two species, that's the white-wing and the surf. White-wing we'll call the jaw surf, we call the Dee Tree aah.

» *Blueberries?*

Small in size, not too many around, that's maybe because of the region, but that's what I noticed, maybe when you get past Key'drii cho (Big Hearted Mountain), I heard around there the berries are vast and huge.

» *Fire of 2004 affect hunting or health? Trapping?*

I traveled it [the burned area] this winter. I seen very few moose signs here and there. Around the village here there's pretty much a resident moose, if you will. They got out of the way, they either got onto the river and the other side. And they got out of the way they either went on the other side or after the fire burned out, winter came about, they moved back in. Like I said before, moose are pretty versatile. When I got up to Bob Lake there was hardly any moose at all. Eddie's traplines, the turnoff before it, just before you get to it, you come down the hill. There was always moose in it, this winter there was hardly nothing. I didn't hardly see a squirrel track this winter. It was like traveling through a remote, destitute, desolate . . . oh! I traveled it one time, I didn't want to travel it again!

It was horrible, I was just amazed by what I seen.

I was hunting caribou up on the other side of Brown Grass, trying to catch that cat-trail Jimmy John came back this way on, I try to connect to his trail and caribou were up in there. They wandered this way here, but of course the feed was gone, so they went back over again. I think Venetie is going to experience some hardship in that regard, to what extent how many hunters go out, 'cause that what the success ratio is based on, how many hunters go out.

» *Do people go by season?*

We don't take part of the state's regulations. I had state troopers come in here and question me about that, and I said, "You guys can't judge us this way, it's not just, it's something you're expecting someone in Fairbanks to do. But not us, it's something we've been doing for thousands of years, it's something you can't regulate. The need base far outweighs your guys' rules. It's understandable you guys got to do this cause you guys just do it for the horns." But I said, "We use everything here." We hunt when we have the need, or when it feels right.

» *When is the normal natural moose season?*

August is generally a good time. We know if we get them before August. It's well before rut. They're definitely in their prime, and you and I know meat is a valuable source of subsistence, and the fat plays a big part of it. And if you start hunting them in September, which is fine because they start moving around and you start seeing a lot more and you could start calling them and be more successful if you didn't get anything in August. Even July is good, but the freakin' bugs on those moose when you're skinning them is horrible. August is a good [time] for hunting moose.

» *Early summer?*

As far back as I can remember the temperature seems to be as aggressive as it always was, and I keep telling that to these guys here, maybe there've been a few temperature increases, some hikes. I welcome [it], personally.

» *Why do you welcome it?*

I like it.

The water in the Chandalar, as everyone suspects, is . . . too hot. I think there [are] a couple years back it was really low, really low; I choose not to even drive most of July. I wouldn't even go set a king salmon net, it beat up my lower unit, I wait [to] catch it at the end of July, or when the water table increases, summer may be early, pretty warm.

» *Do you have very high weather variability?*

We still have an Indian summer, that's in September. Then in August it starts chilling out, and it gets up to 80 degrees.

» *Anything you want to add?*

Snow fall amount is less than quite a bit. [*When did you notice?*] Ten years [ago]. [*How does that affect you?*] I'm able to profit in the wintertime cause I'm able to get my animals easier. We're not getting stuck all the time, but because of that, spring comes early, as soon as we start getting some more.

We don't have 70 below. Me and [my] old brother Ben and Horace Cadzow, a couple different times we were setting marten lines and it was not uncommon at all to have 70 below out there. We don't see it anymore. Only because the skin prices are not in demand anymore and of course the gas. [*The food too.*] Yeah.

» *Inflation of prices? Going to change subsistence values?*

It's not going to change subsistence values at all; cause subsistence values are always going to be maintained; irregardless of what the world does and the problem thereof. We have a good fallback the city-dwellers don't; they're going to be hit—we're not going to be hit, not that dramatic. We'll notice many effects, the luxuries we been able to obtain in the last 40 years will be cut back dramatically, but our way of life—unless these climate changes really increase to where animal species start dying off. If the world doesn't do anything different, a dramatic change will [come] really quick, not just the Gwich'in, but everyone in the world is going to feel it, it's awesome to think of the damage that's going to take place here [before] too long. And you know I'm hearing old-timers saying for years that the hard times are coming up again, so these questions are pertinent, to be aware so you [aren't] caught off guard and to raise your kids up to the standard. Not just in the subsistence value, but ethically, because what ethics speaks about—I'm able to help my neighbor out. These can never be hindered by climate change. I think we're going to survive, to a point, far greater than most. We have to. [*We're going to survive far greater than most?*] Absolutely.

» *Alaska is going to be hit first? Same thing with economics, if our electricity will be shut off and this will spread all over the world?*

Absolutely.

For Native people to survive they have to be aware, they can still walk their trails, they can still live their lifestyle, which is a real rich blessing, 'cause it is.

» *Yeah, cause Gwich'ins are very adaptable*

We're still very versatile. I think there's many of us that still know the old ways what our grandparents, and the type of wood to gather for smoked cash and how to cut meat and how to get firewood and still how to raise our children. And those values, man, they can't be forgotten, no matter what takes place.

» *The old people used to say the springs were noisy?*

Yeah, it's tough in the springtime. [*A long ago you used to hear birds singing?*] All the time, it's apparent. It takes a lot of patience and skill to even come close to the numbers for harvesting again that which we use in the springtime, everywhere. You can choose any lake and we all back and forth trying to get some numbers and we can't get them.

» *More mobility and more money?*

There's a cost sneaking up on us that we're not aware of.

I see the wolf population increasing. [*How does it affect?*] It's going to make tremendous change in subsistence, any which way you look at it. I don't care what animal you're looking at for taking, whether it be rabbit or whether it be moose, they're good hunters. And if the snow levels are not high enough, nature takes its course in the animal kingdom. If it gets harder to survive, they die off from weakness or sickness. If the winters are mild their numbers are going to be increase. Fish and Game came in here probably 7 or 8 years ago, said we had 3.5 per square mile, combination black bear and grizzly bear—lots of predation. I suspect that's increased, there's no one doing anything.

The caribou population this way is practically nil, in how many years? Six years maybe and a couple of years before then, they say they come in cycles, well, this has to be the biggest cycle I've ever seen.

They used to go up right below Big Rock. [*You guys get caribou here?*] Yeah, they used to wander around all over the place here, off and on in the years past, and we don't see that taking place. Definitely after the fire, there's not going to be anything. We used [to] hear the herd was up there around Big Rock, [so] we'd go on up there. We haven't seen too much happening anymore.

Robert Frank Sr. | 06/26/05 | Time: 43:59

On the Chandalar River, that river down here, I've been traveling on it ever since I was 13 years old. On the river, the channel always changed, and the place where I used to drive my boat, there's a gravel bar, I used to drive my boat, I even stood up in the boat and there's an island, I used to drive my boat right there. I think the river is sinking.

The water is getting shallower and shallower, it's just weird, man! Because I been asking quite a few people in different areas and they said they seen something like that too. They said it's sinking. We used to have that river down that way, there's only a few islands, but today, a few years ago I went down there and it just looks different. I could draw the whole channel where it used to be. The place where I used to drive my boat is a big island and the willow is growing on it, lots of stuff. Same time right now too, all those islands covering all those open areas too. Now they had this channel right now it's just like it's a little slough all the way . . . down.

My grandpa James Robert, he used to have a launch, that's a boat he got a big barge on it. He drifted all the way up this way. Way before that 1906, they used to have a steamboat come up here. You could still see the wood pile down by the river that was for the steamboat. You know the East Fork up here, up here about 30 miles up, there's an East Fork, that's where the steamboat turned around. He went up into the river . . . up to Arctic and he backed up into that one that's coming down from Caro. Then he turned around like that way back in 1906. See how high that water is that time? Look at today, whereas today you got to have a jet unit [a boat motor unit mostly above water level], you cannot even drive towards Venetie with prop [lower unit in the water], maybe if you're good driver.

» *No lower unit in the future?*

Yep! They got to use that inboard jet or something. How about later on in the future everything is getting dry, what will happen? The only time we might have a river is when [it's] raining up that way. We never know what will happen. There are lots of places just like erosion. Erosion, we're losing big land on our side, 'cause up here, 20-mile, they call it David Henry Cabin, used to be [a] big bank sticking out way out in the middle of the river. Right now, that time that house was way back there, maybe about 600 hundred feet, that's where all those houses used to be, right now that erosion took that whole thing away. Look at how 600 feet.

Down here at the old village, the reason we moved that school is 'cause that erosion almost took the school—BIA school. Seventy feet, it just washed away one spring. That was around 1980s, '79 or '78. Our old village used to be waaaay out there too. Right now, you see that bank down here? From the river to the bank is like from here to Maggie Roberts's house [roughly 400 yards]. Look at how much erosion [it] took? I got an old picture; I don't know if I still have it.

That's another thing I was looking at too, it's just like when you said way back in the 1980s too. The river and the whole bank is like, in the angle, that's where the erosion took place.

Just like Hump on the middle, that side of the high water and you got to jump on this side to be on the highwater. Pretty soon it's just getting worse and worse and worse. Our Chandalar River is sinking, because the place where I used to drive the boat, there's a big island there. The main channel used to be right on top of it.

When will happen in next 20 to 30 years? Everybody is blindfolded to what is ahead, but lots of old people, I visit lots of old people, Henry John,

Sophie John, Ned Robert, I still remember what they say for the future. They seen it. They see it in a vision, just like Martin Luther King. Everything's been changing—I had a dream, he said. Quite a few Indians in this area, that's the kind of dream they had, that's one that [they] bring down to their grandkids.

The grandkids will relay it [to] the little ones, that's the reason they're saying it, old people. Just like what Henry John say, we were working for him, I was 7 years [old] that time. He said near future, if our enemies coming over our boundary, they won't even make it over our boundary line, they'll all [get] shot down. Look at it, how long ago, I was 7 years [old]. He was talking about laser. There's lots of Native [people], they see something in a vision.

That Venetie village council, they used to have a meeting when I was growing up. They even said, "Keep our land clean, make sure you bring back all the things you used, don't leave it out there," they said. So, we bring it back. Cans or anything, we'll just bring it back, because they've seen, these people in Venetie, they see a moose down in Beaver, they hear about it, down there in Beaver, somebody shot a moose and there is a can on his foot. The can and toenail grew, it's like sheep horn. If we keep our ecosystem clean it will never happen, if we bring back trash, because he [the moose] don't know about cans or anything. That's why all that Native [people] say, "Keep your camp clean."

Where we shoot ducks, all the time, look at the place up there, nice and clean, that's the way they taught us, those old people. If we don't listen it'll be like trash up there, big dump. How many places they've been doing that up there? Another thing too in the past, not only us, we're making our environment dirty, look at those guys that're way ahead of us, way before us around here. Or maybe while we were here, geologists, surveyors, topographic mapping people, they go there and there and do stuff. Right above the karrow there's a big lake, [on the] other side of [the] lake there's about 1,000 or more 5-gallon cans, they just dump it into the big lake, it's still there. I keep on telling TCC, I don't like it. Right on top of [the] hill there's a can on [the] other side, USGS, it says on the can. I told that [to] Davy James too, CATG, he says we're going to bring some people to show where it is, right now I've been waiting 3 years now. How much damage that can do to animals on the food chain. Maybe that's how we're getting all that cancer and all that disease, we don't even know.

I work on the environmental down here at tribal. I did research on food chain, they had a conference in South Africa, I wrote a resolution, they passed it. I said on the resolution, "Us Native [people], we don't have a USDA to inspect our food, what we catch, what about those wildlife animals we're taking? We should start doing that. The meat [has] never been tested, that's a big question for me right there. That's the reason I wrote that resolution. What I'm trying to say is that we got to protect our ecosystem. Clean air and water, because there's lots of caribou, we got to keep the land clean, if we want to keep the caribou safe and [in] good health, we got to do that."

We got to help the animals to make it happen, that's what I'm trying to say. Just like us, they said we went across the icebergs a long time ago [Beringia], we just found a good place around here. A few families stop here, and that's the way it is all the way up to the ocean. Just like [the] Navajo.

» *Forest fire (2004) last summer?*

There's lots of ways, but us, we didn't do anything about it. We got to have a forestry, a forestry on our land, so we know how much our land will [be] worth, because white men will do that.

» *That's what the Doyon Land Exchange did, they set the prices for us.*

Yeah, uh-huh. They just roughly guessing it, they should go out and investigate what kind of rock we got, what kind of timber we got, if it's white or black spruce, how much it is worth.

» *Dried lakes?*

Yeah, the lakes too, all those lakes around here used to be full when I was 6 or 7 years old. They used to be all plum full. Six or seven years old, that will be like, [I'm] 61 one right now, look at how long ago, 55 years ago.

» *How does it affect animals or people?*

That is why the animals quit migrating around here, they moved to different areas, and the hunting is getting far, far, far, far, farther, farther. Just like ducks, we used to have all kinds of ducks around here, they got to go down 50 miles to get ducks. Gee, it's just been happening [since the] '80s, everything happened [in the] '80s. Just like all these lakes used to be plum full, just all grass, not even a drop of water. And some of them, you don't see the lake no more. There's one big lake over there, one of my . . . John Christian, he said he went that way, he said, "Where's the lake there?" I said, "It's there." Those willows are taller than you, too. We used to shoot muskrat and duck around here, right now no more lake, just willows.

» *Not many swallows or robins anymore?*

This spring I was sitting out here [on the porch] towards the windows, I was looking at those chickadees. They all act funny; they're all hanging down with their beak. Hanging down funny, I don't know, maybe they're doing a little contest, too many of them out here. Pretty soon I see a red bird with a blue like that [blue stripe down its back], that female it's kinda funny too, kinda reddish color. [*You never saw that before?*] I never saw that kind before, I thought somebody's pet got loose, [it was] blue on top. I never seen [a] bird around here like that. Just like you say about robins, sometimes they even get here right before the snow melts, today they don't even do that. Sometimes they come here just before the snow is melting, but the snow is covering the land. Maybe they're eating flies and also all our birds, just like ducks, we're getting less and less and less every year.

» *Mudhouse swallows? No more?*

No, just on the bank, the big cliff down there, they got a lot of holes there. Even [they are] getting scarce, I think the population is getting down. Maybe they died someplace, just like down there in [the states] they said, "A bunch of birds are dying," in the news, New Mexico, someplace. Those dil', look like dil', they said they think, they dig out claim, maybe that's how they got sick, they said a bunch of them are dead.

» *Summer came early?*

Early every year. What I think too, is really, it's early spring, too fast, spring come around too fast, and I think the sun is drying up everything before that whatever grow, grow fast too, because that sun is too hot around here. This summer I think 80 or 90 degrees around here. [*No blueberries?*] No, just big thunder, no rain though, nothing but hail. That time it [was] raining like hell right here, save all that trees, they're just about dying, look at that tree over there, it's all brownish color. Like those little spruce trees towards [the] airport and Arctic. We got to do something about that machine, you see how it looks on both sides of the airport, it will look like that up there on the mountain, from that exhaust, it will happen. Pretty soon we should just stop using those things to go hunting, let's go back to where we started a long time ago. Not an easy way no more, that's the only way we could save our own ecosystem. For animals will migrate around that area, once [it's destroyed] they won't come back.

Just like a long time ago [there] used to be lots of caribou down here. What happened? Big question? Maybe too much disturbance?

» *PCH's migratory routes shortened by pipeline? Sensitive herd?*

Yeah. Just like us. If the people impeach us [talk about us] all the time and living here from outside of our boundary, outside of our boundary, if they impeach us, we'll do the same thing. Just like caribou. Wherever they go, they always go to the same place all the time, same country, they always travel, but every so many years they change the route, just like ducks. They used to come in this way, those black ducks, now they come this way. See if you can just notice something. There's lots of stuff, just like when you trap, you see that one animal went this way, just like lynx, maybe there's about 20 lynx, but you see one track. Maybe 20 lynx went past there but don't even show. If you do like that on his foot, it's going to [be] hard, lots of them using the same track. When lots of trappers they see one lynx pass they pay attention, that's how I got three traplines, every 3 years I go to trap this one, next year this one, next year this one, next year this one they're all 3 years apart. Three years, that's the reason I made my animals grow in that one area, I leave it for 3 years, when I [do] rotation like this, next year this one, next year this one, and this year they already the first one will be 3 years ago. I come back here and trap that year and clean it out. When it's less tracks, I put all my traps away, I don't try to kill everything, I try to manage it on my own. Lots of trappers, they just go there and clean it until nothing, that's the one we got to watch what we're doing, too. Just like you and I, last year Ernest gave me a quarter of it, just like this one family, I count how many moose they shot, seven, how come they took seven and I'm living on one-quarter of a moose all winter. If they take care of their food, they can go by and those six will still be walking around, right. Waste, just like in Fairbanks somebody dumps, they had this caribou open on pipeline road, somebody shot five caribou and they left it on the Cushman Street, they just dumped it without skinning it. They should do something about it. [*Fish and Wildlife?*] Shit, they were there. Fish and Game should do some research, but [it's] not enough. They should write down everything just like what you're doing right now, so that way they're going to get help from the village because they've been there all their life. They know about the animals, they [know] about the animal population . . . going down. The village [is] always watching those things. Them, they just get hired, it's just a job, not to take this, that's about it. They can't fool around like that. They got to go out there and push it—make sure.

They should have some kind of station someplace. If they want to open the pipeline, the only place they've got to go through is Yukon Bridge, Yukon Bridge they should pay for it right there and see who got what. Before they're leaving the area, that's the only way. Some of them are leaving with airplanes, they should be over there at Frontier and or Wright, make sure they take the hunters to wherever they want, but don't overdo it. Let's cut down on their hunters. The more hunters they get, the more money they make. We should tell them to get less, all those guys. "Don't get that many hunters in there, you only got three hunters this year. That's it!" Ask them how many hunters you got to have so you don't have to be bankrupt to be a guide. We got to balance it.

» *If they're making money, they won't do it.*

Just like [on a] fishing boat. When I went to Hawaii, I had a meeting with the Hawaiian tribal council, they treated me really good, I was there for 1 week with them. What the tribal do, they show me the whole thing, but lots of fishermen over for tuna, but they need a partner because they're getting into a bankrupt. One person owns, and the fish prices are going down, and the population is going down too. What're they going to do? That's the only qualified thing they got to do. [*Very interesting.*] Look at the hatcher, they even got a whole bunch of hatcheries are in the state of Alaska, but they still go more . . . fishman to go out there. They buy those boats, 50 to 200 grand. They can't keep up. The reason I went over there is because that tribal council was thinking about doing business with our tribe that time. So, they can, we might join a venture that time so they're not going to file for bankruptcy. If they handle half and half, it'll be good for their business. Sometimes they get lots, sometimes it's a good day and sometimes it's a bad day. Sometimes the bad day comes a long ways, bad day every day. If you're a trapper, if you get broke, could you keep on going? No! Me, I always watch how much I spend on trapping, my gas, how many parts I pay [for], everything. How much money I put in the trapping; if I don't get it back, no use for me to do that. Today fur prices are getting low, everybody is getting no job, pretty soon what kind of resources [are] they going to have to improve their family?

» *Salmon?*

A long time ago they [were] coming up this way, it's not good. Yukon, when they're catching in Yukon it was really rich and it's good, but when it came up the Chandalar it wasn't that good. Dead. First time the king salmon came up here, some of them are really good look at it, it's like Fort Yukon fish, a long time ago it wasn't like that [*gestures to hung salmon strips*].

» *What was it like a long time ago?*

It was white. Now it's red and rich. Yeah.

That dog salmon go all the way up, all the way up to, sometimes, around Gold Camp, there's lots of them in the river. [*Do people still go to Gold Camp?*] People don't go there; they just pass by. I want to live there, animals are good there.

Caribou don't come all the way down anymore, maybe too much brush. The last time [they] came down [was] 1995. Springtime, there was caribou here. [They] could come to the marten lake. A long time ago [they went] all the way down.

» *Lot of caribou a long time ago?*

In 1959 or something I stayed with my dad in Gold Camp. There's lots of caribou. Don't come all the way down this time, they turn around at Brown Grass Lake, that's the farthest [they] come down anymore.

» *Main subsistence here is salmon?*

Hm-mm. Yeah salmon, right now salmon is really good. Moose too, but not too much around here, only sometimes. There used to be lots of moose by the river, when they go up by boat, they kill moose right there and come down the next day. Too many wolves and bears killing calves. [*How did they take care of that problem in the old days?*] Yeah, they kill wolves, and bears too, they're even eating them.

Today everybody lives like rich people, EA, wood, food stamps, and GA. Go up to 70 below. Even kerosene froze, sometimes there's two weeks straight of 69 to 65 below for a long time. They even bring dogs inside to warm them up. Sometimes they got no dog food too, but they use probably anything. They even make bonic for them. I saw all this; I went through all of it; that's why I say it. No food, kids are crying [because of hunger pains]. Today it's not like that. We're going back to that place right now. [*That's what some people are saying.*] Even those old people long ago [in pre-contact], they know what's going to happen today. They told all the people. No chief, but the person that is a good hunter, good worker, everything, he is the boss. Just him they follow, that's how they were. If he said one word, everybody would listen to him, no objections.

No gardens, but on the land, we got berries and [Gwich'in name for some kind of weed], they fry them and eat them and feed it to the dog. Also, they eat roots, but only in springtime. Ground squirrels and rabbits too, they even eat marten.

» *In Arctic Village they had traditional fishing spots they used to go to, do they have any here?*

They don't go there 'cause it's dry. That's where they go to fish for white-fish and pike. That big lake, there's lots of fish in there a long time ago, but not no more. Lots of weeds growing under there, I don't know how long it's going to last. All the creek is just dry. Some of lake is dry too. Really bad, it's going to be bad.

Old people said, "Always tell their people don't go down to Yukon to live down there." They know something, probably that Yukon River is going to dry up. Going to be no water. The only thing [that] is going to last long is Big Lake. There's fish in it too. The only animals [that are] going to last long are moose and beaver. Right now, long ago when it was cold it was really cold and bad, now year round it isn't cold that much. Maybe one day, next day it's warm. Old people said, "In the future that weather downstate and the weather over here changes" [*gesturing that it will switch*]. On the land, big animals, if [the] land is warm, the animals will migrate.

A long time ago, [we had] two winters that connected together, instead of summer. Maybe it will be that way again. Maybe summer or winter, either one.

Hang moose feet on tree, even the bone. Dig the hole in the ground and cover it. When you're in trouble, you will have to use it again. That's where we're going back to now.

Old people said, "War is going on, and all the nations will kill each other until there's one nation. Then all the people in the states will come up this way. In this time, we will have nothing, no planes. Those who are alive will live off the land again. No store, nothing." That is why it is very important to teach the children the old ways. You have to learn everything. If you were out on the woods, you wouldn't know what to do.

Whatever your grandpa is doing, watch him. I teach the kids, look how good a job they did [*gesturing to the meat*].

Right now, we don't see caribou, ground squirrels, and no birds and no ducks. Dil' is even scarce. When we went up to Big Lake a long time ago, ducks were so noisy, dil' was noisy, but now, no more. Rabbits are even scarce now. What's wrong? Even the sparrows that make mud houses on the homes are gone, and the birds on the telephone lines are gone too, there used to be lots of them.

A long time ago, when there was no food, they didn't come back.

Lots of wolves, more than caribou and moose. A long time ago when there used to be lots of moose, it was good, now no more.

Wolves kill them lots.

» *Salmon is still good?*

Dog salmon still come this way; we really use that. Sometimes that was all we ate in the old days.

We used dogs a lot too, because there were no vehicles.

Eddie Frank | 07/27/04 | Time: 22:37

» *Dead trees you've witnessed?*

I noticed when I got up the road lots of the larger trees seem to be falling, because there's no place for them to grab on the ground. Or possibly the permafrost thawed or something so that trees don't hold on[to] the ground, so they uproot themselves. I know that a couple of years ago I wanted to cut wood for my dad, it was a lot of big trees I cut up because they were down on the ground, didn't even have to knock them down.

» *Where is this at?*

Up that road to Tyii' troo' eeh. You see those trees in certain areas, those big trees are down. I think another thing that I see, if you go up the river on that bluff up here, you'll see like mud slides, probably happening because permafrost underneath thaws it out a little bit, and that creates moisture under that, and that side of the hill you could see where the topsoil just slid down. That has something to do with global warming. Lots of lakes dried up because of global warming, permafrost drying and lot of lakes draining out, I know that's been occurring. One of the things that

I noticed—probably somebody else noticed too—that little snipe, there's one particular snipe that used to pass through here every spring, I'm not sure what they call it in English, but we call it Nee jaw il'. The last two or three springs I've been out hunting ducks, [and] I've never seen that snipe, usually they're there. That's a strange thing for me, it is possible that the global warming is affecting them.

I always think about the caribou too, the Boreal Forest is moving northward. The caribou don't come this far south, it's been 10 to 12 years since we've seen caribou, what we call our "woodyard." They don't come down this far anymore, that's because there's too much growth.

» *Somebody told me that 1995 was the last year?*

That sounds right. We had caribou up here, timber up here on the side of the mountain, I mean we go out in the woods; to cut wood; and we run into caribou all winter long. After that, caribou never come down this way. [*You think they're shifting north?*] Well, I think there's too much growth getting in the way, they're used to open country. That could be a possibility. Because of the warming, temperature rises going north, things grow better, there's more growth going farther north. Again, people probably told you too, our springs are coming earlier, our fall is later. The temperature is—we rarely see more than 45 below in the winter anymore. I can remember [when] I first came to Venetie in 1980, 65 to 70 below was December and January, now December and January [are] 40 below, big change in the average temperature. Snow's been slow coming, especially for people who do trapping, sometimes it's even hard to get out there because there's either not enough snow or the creek is not frozen so you can't get out early. I remember a few years back when I used to trap, I tried to go to my trapline, there's a particular creek up there by Martin Lake that I can't cross because it's open water yet. That's toward the end of November going into December, so temperatures aren't as cold as they used to be. A long time too, snow, this last winter is the first time we've seen so much snow in our many years? Snow is early even, something is changing in the temperature.

The phalarope? [bird] Nee da jil? That's the one, I don't see anymore. [*My grandpa hasn't seen a special kind of bird anymore, maybe that's the same one?*] Maybe it is.

We even see strange birds sometimes.

» *Like what kind?*

Eider ducks, sometimes eider ducks pass through.

There's one that looks kinda funny too, his feet are like chicken feet, he's got a sharp beak. I don't know what you call them? I never seen him.

» *How is that bad for local habitat?*

It seems like our bird population—like the waterfowl—their numbers have decreased quite a bit, I think there's other influences on it. It's affected. Like the water in Big Lake was low for a long time. This year because of the fire, we got a lot of water again because there's nothing to hold it up in the mountains anymore.

» *How has that fire affected things?*

Game is a little bit scarce for a while there, we had a hard time getting access to going up because the trail was so plugged up.

» *How plugged up?*

Well, until we got a lot of snow; we were able to get through; when there's that much snow you can't get up there. This year they cleaned it out though. The other thing is—this global warming thing—this snow content, quantity of the snow, normally it's early when caribou migrate right. Sometimes they pass through up here, there's not enough snow, so they don't have anything to hold them back so they just pass right through. Last fall they said there were lots of caribou up there. The lack of snow makes it easy for them to move. That hurt the caribou migration in the sense that they don't stick around.

» *River receded 600 feet?*

My father said steamboats used to come up.

The moose are moving northward because the growth is moving north. I heard they're seeing lots of moose in Arctic Village. I heard they've even seen moose on the other side of the Brooks range because there's growth there they can survive on.

» *Couple of interviews they did say there was lots of moose around.*

That's what I heard too. This forest is moving northward. Inching northward.

» *So, what do you suggest we do to adapt to the change?*

Gwich'in adapt real easy. I'm looking from a household; if they do without certain things, they can do without it. They're a strong people; they adjust real easy.

» *[Showing him a makeshift map of global warming]*

Fire affected animals too, Wintertrail Fire [east]—last fall these guys got quite a few moose on the river because of that. They even shot two on the airport down here.

And then Fish and Game said moose population is doing good.

You can't believe how much meat they [Venetie] consume.

» *How will it affect Venetie when the moose shift north?*

Just go north and get them [laughs]. CATG is talking about re-introducing buffalo. If [the] moose population is coming down, they just replace it with buffalo.

» *Salmon, moose, caribou? Main subsistence?*

Global warming [has] affected the salmon movement too. We're getting more salmon now too, king salmon, more king salmon up this way. I can remember when I first came here, king salmon was never heard of, only a few of them come up. By the time they get here, their teeth were, they were too poor. Just the dog salmon, which is chum salmon, they have a spawning area 6 miles upriver, the early ones, late July, early August, that's probably the only ones that were edible, after that they get too poor and they're usually for dog food. That's the way it used to be. We rarely catch salmon that we could eat, but now its changed. I hear this summer some people got up to 40 salmon.

» *What's the usual intake?*

Four or five if you're lucky. Afterwards, they're probably too poor.

» *You guys used to catch salmon for 2 weeks, but now it has expanded into 2 months? That's what Fort Yukon people are saying.*

The king salmon, I know that. When my dad had a fish wheel down there, we put a fish wheel in at the end of July and [when] we were into August there was another run that come up and we were able to get enough king salmon for our freezers. That's another thing that's been changing. You know I was talking to a guy one time I was out on a fire too, he was down from downriver, Holy Cross, grayling area. Those big males? They usually don't catch them because they usually pass by under the ice; they don't get the big kings. When I think about it there might be some truth to that. That dog salmon, they're coming earlier.

» *Did it used to be this hot a long time ago?*

I can't remember, in the '80s it was always hot here. It's just that the warmth comes earlier now, spring. Usually, we have our Spring Carnival in the second week of April, by that time there's water puddles around town. That never used to be, too. That one year they were driving down in water and that was the second week in April, so our springs are coming earlier. Our falls, no snow. We're hauling wood with wagons in December; four-wheelers and wagons in December. Last summer we didn't get any rain, nothing at all. No rain. Hardly any rain this summer.

FORT YUKON CLIMATE CHANGE TRANSCRIPTS

William Flitt | 07/19/05 | Time: 29:15

» *River level? Can't get to Birch Creek, Chalkyitsik?*

Well, nowadays, it's not like it used to be a long time ago. Everything is just, huh . . . even weather is changing. All that river is changed, like long time ago, salmon running is 10 days, now it's running 2 months. Everything is different nowadays. River is low. And it's changed lots. Even water is low. And then, huh . . . hunting, hunting . . . even some few people don't hunt on account of the river, no water. Yeah, it's too, not like it used to be.

» *Ten days? Now its 2 months?*

Long time ago, it run about 2 weeks, no more. It run all summer, it's funny for me. It's, like, 2 weeks it's good salmon, and after 2 weeks it changed, y'know? It turns white, the meat, now it's nothing wrong with 2 to 3 weeks, it's funny for me. On account of, I don't know what's going on.

» *Pretty strange.*

You know, hunting too, hunting moose. Nowadays, a long time ago, lots of moose in the river, nowadays you can't hardly see moose on the river, you see tracks, but you never see it, it's out on the mainland.

» *A long time ago you could always depend on seeing moose by the river, huh?*

Yeah. It's always, you see a track and you hunt for it, it's like that, but nowadays you see tracks, you never see it, it goes on the mainland, way out. It's just, lots of things are different. Like geese, huh, some boys . . . they [go] hunting, and when you kill geese you have to put it in a five-gallon and put it in hot water and pluck it, y'know.

Nowadays they don't even do that, they just pluck it the way it is. It's just easy they say, that's what I mean, it's kinda a little different for me. When I grew up you couldn't even pluck it it was so fat, y'know? Geese is so fat you can't pluck it, you tear all that skin off. And then, before you tear all that skin off you got to put it in the hot water and then . . . like . . . heat it up, like, boil it up like, and then you pluck it, easy. Nowadays they said they pluck just like little ducks it's a lot different, I don't know what it's cause, but it's, huh . . . happen. Y'know, even them birds, you know, nighttime they always sing, huh? Nighttime. You never see birds singing no more. You know them geese coming in first time for geese coming in you can hear them makin' noise, they don't do that, just flying. Lots of different, I don't know what that cause, but it just happens.

Something I don't know is what it's cause. You know, right now they can't even drink water, you can't even go in the river and drink water, that's what we grow up with, y'know, now they don't even let us drink that water, see? I don't know what that cause is, pretty soon they won't even, there's lots of difference, lots of difference. You could see it.

It's getting hotter, you should see this summer, remember you was here. It's getting so hot you can't even walk around. It's like that. A long time ago my grandma told me that it's going to turn around, the weather going to turn around, but I don't know if that's true. That's what the old people say, but that's just their opinion. The world's going to change and it's going to be hot all year round, that's what they said, but don't know what will happen.

We're not going to even see it.

» *We're starting to see it though?*

Yeah.

Fishing is pretty good [this] year. Some people said there's still lots of, huh . . . different, maybe [on] account of water, I dunno. Maybe come early, or come too . . . I know the fish came in early, everything is early! Break up is early. You know what? Not even 1 week snow is gone, [couple of feet], 1 week later it's just full of ice. And then 1 week later it's just running water. It's just, ice just went like that. I dunno. They said ice is not thick enough too. You know, nowadays it's not even cold. Maybe 1 week that's only 58 below. A long time ago, my time, it was 60 to 70 below, you know? Year around, but now, last 10 to 20 years you see it we're just walking around with jackets, that's all. Lots of difference, lots of difference. I dunno. We got to look at it, the way it is. Only thing I could think is you just got to survive in it, y'know?

I cut fish and I dry fish, I never hunt for moose for long, but the way them boys tell me what's going on, sometimes now, huh, water is really low. Last how many years. Someplaces they don't even go down [to the hunting] area, they can't even go down there. Like, huh . . . Venetie, that's pretty low water now, and Chalkyitsik, it was not like that before. Now it's kinda high water, but later on it's going to be really low, I bet you.

» *How is that bad?*

They help each other, they help each other to send fish to each other. But there's Birch Creek, there's no king salmon there, Chalkyitsik, Venetie, there's no salmon, but only thing that they catch is silver and all that, to place here, but Birch Creek is nothing. Silver is going to run pretty soon. After king salmon. There's a lot of difference for me, so my comment, the best I got is "this is it," y'know?

» *No solution, just adapt to it? I mean, it would help if people cut pollution? Years 2000–2005? Salmon?*

Well, it's same. Some years [it] is kinda poor. This is all right, it's good, I guess.

» *What else do they catch here?*

King and silver, that's all.

King salmon go first, and silver second, and third is dog salmon. That's the last, but some people, they use dog salmon for dogs, and all that and silver is good to eat, just like king salmon. Same as king salmon but good eating. You know part of native you got to survive throughout winter with fish and meat. You know what I mean?

We got to hussle about fish, meat, ducks, all that. Like, we . . . some old people, they really like, they grew up with meat and fish and caribou. When I eat them I put some caribou on and fry it and make hot cake with it in the morning, jeez weez it's good.

» *No caribou down here, huh?*

My grandmother said they used to crossing Circle, right below Circle a long time ago. Above Circle, and then with boats, they get it. And then from Venetie they get it with a dog team from here, a long time ago. Well, people travel with dog teams, transportation is dog teams a long time ago. Nowadays they don't even go out for caribou, like, that far. Them younger generation, nowadays, the hardest part is [that] all them older people are all gone, you know what I mean. Part of Athabascan Indian, some new generation, they grow up with them chips and pop and micro-wave stuff, that's all they grow up with. One year, a bunch of my boys, I tell [them] we got to fry fat meat and cook some fat meat, "No, no we're going to go [to the] store and get some microwave stuff." They went and took some little stuff and heated it up, boy that one is a good stuff. "This one is a good stuff!" They tell me. See? They won't eat that meat, well, they grow up like that, that's why. [This] world is really different from a long time ago. Kids are like, they go [to] school, they have education. They're part of white people nowadays, some of them, almost all of them are half-breed.

» *Same problem in all the villages?*

Nowadays people are involved with alcohol and drugs, that's the two they have a problem in every village. Some people destroy themselves with that, but you got to teach your young generation about two thing, so they'll have nice good life and someday in generation, their generation. I want them to have [a good] education and skills, and they can carry their own problems [for] their family and their kids. Like me and you, we know what to do, we can survive, but they're the ones that one day we're not going to see it, we're not going to be there, they're going to carry their own generation, carry their own, they got to survive. I want them to [be] well-educated so they can teach their own kids the same problem like what we said. It's hard but it's got to be carried on like that.

They against each other so they don't solve the problem.

When you're talking real good they don't like it. I talk to kids about driving, about staying out late, one woman said that's not your kids, don't worry about them kids.

Nowadays they don't even talk to their kids. Look like them kids are grown by themselves.

» *Different with people and the land, huh?*

Yeah. That's right. Same time too, nowadays them young people they hardly ever hunt too, you know what I mean? They hunt, but they hunt maybe 1 day with a fast boat, 90 horsepower, they just zoom around like that. And then they [say], "I don't see moose."

They want to see that moose standing right on the river, they don't want to go on the mainland and hunt for it. All my father, my grandfather, they go out and hunt for it. And then they go a long ways and pack it in with a boat, nowadays they just want it standing right on bank, so you can just put that boat right by it and cut it up and put it in the boat. That's what they want, but it's not like that.

It's funny nowadays.

» *Get together with like-minded people?*

Only way you could solve problems like this is have a nice, good meeting and they'll talk about it. That's the only way! Make a nice, good Indian powwow and make a meeting like that chief and council and all that, get all them guys together and all that. They'll fix it up.

» *Earliest spring in Arctic too?*

My father told me it's going to change lots later on. Before he passed away, he told me that. Everything you see with your own eyes [is] going to change, even animals [are] going to change, lots! Yeah, people begin to not even go to hunt no more. I could see it now. More important thing they want is going to liquor store and put music on full blast, you know what I mean?

» *Gwich'in doing good under Corporations?*

I dunno. It's hard to say.

Land claims, that's the one that screws everything up.

Well, you got to have real good, if you're going to go highest court, [you've] got to have a good lawyer and all that.

....

Richard Carroll Sr. | 07/19/05 | Time: 8:46

....

» *River level been low?*

This year, real low.

» *More moose?*

I think it's about average.

» *Plants? Trees?*

No, I don't. Seems like every[thing] growing pretty good this year.

» *Last 5 years?*

Kinda drying up, all the creeks, drying up, even the river.

» *It was hard to get to Chalk?*

Yeah.

» *Birch Creek too?*

Yeah, it will eventually raise this fall?

» *Anything else different from 20 years ago?*

Compared to this year?

» *Spring came early?*

Yeah.

» *Snow melted in 1 week?*

Not much snow to start with. Very little.

» *Fall freeze-up?*

Froze up pretty low this year. Seems like it's getting that way every year, less and less. It freezes up quick when its low water.

» *Summer getting harder?*

Seems like it.

» *More fires?*

Yeah.

» *Habitat changes? Moose?*

There's always something, when they move out there's another animal that takes over.

» *Small game?*

Rabbits? Seems like there's more.
Wasn't much snow.

» *Salmon harvest in 2000–2005?*

It's been low but it's coming back.

» *Your own questions?*

Staying up pretty good, cause there ain't too many trappers now. I think that's why the animals are coming back.

They don't trap them all either, they always leave enough for next year.

Eva Carroll (*Elder*) | 07/19/05 | Time: 8:23

» *Blueberries?*

Blueberries grown in hilly country in Yukon Flats, there's not too [many] berries growing, since I know, when I moved here in 1947. We used to pick little berries, but there wasn't much.

They grow around Fairbanks. Around maybe on the highway or . . . Circle.

Cranberries and high and low bush.

» *No berries so you go farther out?*

High-bush, they grow way out by the river, Sucker River. Up the Yukon River. Up here in Circle. I haven't seen blueberries since I moved here.

I came from Canada, lot of blueberries up there.

I haven't seen salmon berries around here.

» *Fish meat? Getting soft?*

When they go farther up the Porcupine or Salmon River? They get soft, when they get to Old Crow it's pretty soft by then. Not as rich as down here.

» *Moose OK?*

Moose meat is alright.

» *Different when look out the window, hotter?*

Rain helps lots. Last year there was no rain all summer. Big fire. But this year there's [been] quite a few rains, that's why the willows are growing big. Yeah, rain always help.

Keep everything fresh.

» *Anything else different?*

No, not this year. Last year it was pretty dry, smoky, fire. Different this year, no smoke, that fire up here Sheenjik, it quieted down.

Different from hilly country.

» *5–10 years ago? Anything different?*

Uh-huh.

Rain is a big help.

Doris Ward | 07/20/05 | Time: 16:30

We used to go out in the woods, nice beautiful timber, everything is nice right now. Did you notice all these dead trees all around here? It's just awful! That got to be from some global change or something, we think of the water here, but I haven't been out in the woods, how is it? I don't think it's not that bad, I think it has a lot to do with pollution. There's steady dust here, all those willows over there are coated with dust, the leaves must have air to survive. You know all that traffic, all that traffic especially at night. Fumes from that exhaust and everything gets on those leaves and stuff, especially the spruce boughs, it gets in there. A lot of that has something to do with pollution.

» *Hunting areas and animal habitat area; you have to keep it all clean?*

Over there, lots of Neetsii. I pick a bunch of them, I took all of them stems off and washed them good, then I cooked it. [*Describing a couple-inch ratio*] around the pot is just like oil. So, you see all that, what I see on that berry must be affecting those trees.

They have to have air to breathe.

Nowadays when they catch salmon, they said they got a lot of sores on them. When you think of it the other way too, you know what they call those wears? If the water is not clean, they have sores. I think a lot of that is caused by traveling and pumping things. Because if that water was that bad it causes sores on the salmon, why don't we get it? Whitefish, you don't see those sores on them. This big [*gesturing*] big eggs inside. They get in fish wheel. In August, close to freeze-up time, we get big ones, one side of that eggs fill up that frying pan, gee it tastes good.

» *Shellfish harvest good?*

I think so.

» *Tell me this little theory again that this might turn back into Africa?*

Well, eventually it's going to be. It's got to change, it can't stay the same.

» *Your grandson found an elephant tusk?*

Bison.

You know, we have summer and winter. Millions of years ago, it was hot country, all these prehistoric animals used to be here, is that where they get all the oil from, from all the animals that died off? [*Someone mentioned that.*] So, you see, I think slowly the world is coming back to that. It rotates every day. It's slowly. We'll never see it but it's coming back to that time. And this modern living nowadays, all these gas . . . engines, I mean trucks and all that that, use gas and oil, that's what's spoiling the timber and trees and stuff. Things spread around.

When we first got this house, a long time ago, this is one of the first houses they build back in the '70s. And . . . we had these little black bugs sometimes crawling around in the wall, you know, we always find it on my windowsill, that I'd never seen before. What I think is when they ship this stuff in from wherever, bugs, even mice, they like to get in insolation, it's warm. One time I visit Sally Lawrance, and she told me lots of them little black bugs are on the wall. So how do we know all them little bugs came and eventually get in them spruce trees, its spruce bugs, spruce beetles. I saw it myself when this house was new, in my bedroom I got windowsill, see I got this white stuff, and I got my pillow over there, these little black bugs. When I was growing up, I remember spiders and a bunch of other things but not that little spruce beetle. I never seen it. Now we see lots. So, I always figured, what they call this, when they come and . . . so much, a number this big by this big. That thing is shipped up and you don't know how long it sits somewhere. I figure those beetles get in the insulation.

» *Moose OK?*

I think so. They say no moose in Yukon Flats, I mean not as much as there should be, but you know what, these people around town, they go out and hunt them all winter long. And they sell that meat. That's why no moose.

» *Referring to the old days.*

We didn't have no furniture. We were poor. We lived off the land. I always remember, my dad would kill maybe two or three moose during the winter, y'know, when we need it, he didn't go out to kill it just to kill it. Now everything [that] moves, they kill it, that's why everything is just . . . disappearing. I know Christmastime, between Christmas and New Year's, they have potlatch here for 1 week. Native villages give them gas and shells to go hunting instead of appointing a couple people and all that meat should be brought back to the Native village and cut up for the potlatch. They go out and sometimes they give only one hammer, some little thing, and they keep the rest because they want to sell it. This is past Christmas, between Christmas and New Year's, for the potlatch they kill four moose, we had one day meat only. [*That's really bad.*] Really bad. [*Who do they sell it to?*] There's lots of peddlers around. Bootleggers, drug dealers, and just like right now I got nobody [to] hunt for me. If somebody came here right now, "Oh I killed a moose, you want to sell ham?" He's going to sell it. That's how we get little meat sometimes, that's what they do. And then they go to all these meetings, they worried about no moose. When they find out and hear about it, they should do something about it. But they don't. There's going to be a day, you see, they're trying to transport bison to this area.

» *What the heck are they trying to transport bison here for?*

'Cause there's going to be a day when there won't be enough moose.

If it's doing good in this country there [will] be a day when you can buy a permit to go out and hunt buffalo. Buffalo burger, talk about good meat!

Stanley Jonas | 07/20/05 | Time: 19:38

» *Old people?*

The old people tell a story, they tell a story they're predicting, about this year, they said long time, they, people, will . . . we going to [have] hard times again. They said that in lower-48, where things grow it's going to be cold, lots of fire, strong wind, it's a hurricane they're talking about. It's now started, it's really covering the whole state of Alaska. Not only that but down [in the] lower-48. So, you see it. I can see right now about what they're talking.

Right now, you go up [to the] store, buy a loaf of bread, it'd be about $4. Price is still going up, gas price, so it's really you come down to think of it, you really know what they're talking about, those days we don't know forest fire, there's no forest fire, all kinds of game; ducks. Even summer birds, you don't see a lot of them no more, I don't think I see [any] black-birds for a long time now, robins last year [were] hardly around, now this year there's a few around.

» *Store prices are so high you can't buy anything?*

No, you can't buy nothing, $40–50, you buy one meal, that's all.

Yeah you, that one old woman told me that they're not going to even be one dog around, just iron dog: snow-go. Big iron dog, big sled ahead of it.

Lots of people don't see this, they hear it, but they don't think about it. Me, I think about it all, this the old people talk about it, it comes back to me.

» *What to do to get ready?*

While you're still able to do it, get ready for it, they say. Nobody is getting ready for it, even my father-in-law, he talks to me when we go trapping.

» *When you can't afford [things] in the store, you pay more attention to hunting?*

It's pretty hard, too. Look at those trees over there, see how brown they are? They're just drying up from that water, it don't rain much here, everything is just turning brown here. Up 20-mile, that's where I grew up, if you go around these islands with a snow-go or dogs you can see no willows. They're all drying up, whatever that didn't burn, they say that burns and new growth, don't need new growth, look at all those little islands, that mud bar is all green with willows. They just run out of water, they run the water out of the lakes, you see trees and willows, they shade the permafrost underneath. About 6 feet down now that everything is burned up and everything is thawed out. That's where all the water went, those lakes are just meadow now. I see it, lots, all the lakes that way up 20-mile. Everything is just . . . that's where moose fat comes from, the lakes' underwater plants. There's no more [of] that, so moose are not even as fat as they used to be.

» *Hard to live off land because land is different, huh?*

Yeah. Uh-huh. Last year we got only one fish, today somebody gave me six fish. Yeah, I don't know, people are, looks like people are getting more hungry now than those days. Those days you could buy one whole bag of potatoes, one size paper bag, now it's not even half that much it's $7–8, too darn much.

You go up with $40–50, you can't buy what you wanted.

It's like that all over.

Long time ago nice green, green all over, now it's just black. Sorry-looking world we're living in. I been all over, almost and I see it from the air. Jeez, where it's burned it looks pretty . . .

Trapping for fur too, hardly anything to catch, and what we catch hardly brings any money anyway.

» *Not like long time ago? Live good off of one fur a long time ago?*

Silver fox $1,000.

» *Land changes because people change?*

Well, they change as we change, we change too. We're not . . . back in the '30, people helped each other, no income, nothing, people eat, kids hungry, they call the council chief, they sent two or three out with a canoe, there's no inboard, that's all. Sure enough, they bring back moose, that's how the animals are, even close by you don't have to hunt very much to find them. So those guys that go out, they just take as much as they give out to everybody. That's how people help each other. Gee, my father working for $2 a day, I feel like I'm rich myself. They start cutting brush pay $2 a day. They cut wood for steamboat, that's the only way they make money.

Summer, lots of them go to fish camp, one wheel there's five families, they're all getting enough fish. Up here at four-mile. My father is one. So, it's I think those days are better days than today. Today everything costs high, something to make your mind no good.

» *Weather is no longer predictable?*

Those days you get an old man or old woman they look out and they say what kind of day they're going to have the next day. Today you can't even predict that. Look at that, in July I turn my stove on. Crazy world. One time in January it was raining outside.

We never have long cold weather, I think this is the longest cold weather we've had in about a couple weeks. Used to be 1 month, [all of] January, we even see 70 below, now it just barely goes over 50. Get caught in the snow with the car and they freeze.

Too bad.

» *Gwich'in 50 years from now?*

Wondering how it's going to be myself. Gee, the other day they showed the little kids starving outside, terrible, you can count their ribs, I always pray for those kids, that those leaders will help them out.

1946 I trapped 20-mile above Chalk with three dogs. Now three dogs can't even pull the sled, that's right, they have to have about 10 to 13 dogs.

» *Someone said nowadays those dogs are worthless?*

That's right, nobody got working dogs, just those racing dogs, scrawny things.

Those two dogs out here, they cost me over $40 a month. Cheapest bag [of dog food] is $37, right there.

Fire really ruining the country, they say new growth will grow real quick. They don't need to look at this one here, you could see Freddie's house not too long ago, now you can't even see through that now.

» *Makes it hard to get around?*

Yeah, uh-huh.

One time we went hunting my son and I went hunting up Black River, all the way hunting up Salmon Village. We see lots of moose but they all cows, gee one place he really wants to shoot a cow, but I told him no way, you drive my boat. We got back and he went back to Chalk, beautiful day, 3 o'clock in the daytime.

People hunting, bad luck, all those cow moose, the single one, but I told him I don't want to kill cow moose.

You have to lay over for a couple weeks to go out, last couple years me and Fred (Thomas) maybe 1 or 2 days and that's it, and the rest of the time it's all warm.

» *Salmon harvest?*

This last couple of years the water in the summertime is pretty low, it's way lower than it should be, I guess.

» *Not much rainfall?*

That's half of it, last fall we couldn't go up Black River hunting, we just went up below Chalk, that's all. We generally go way up where Fred is, up grayling. Last couple years we never went there, no water. Last winter we had a lot of snow but I think, the fall, the ground was so dry, in the ground, instead of runoff.

» *What do you hunt at Black River?*

In the fall-time we generally hunt moose. Two to three years now there's no water, I don't want to tear up my motor going up there.

» *When did the weather start being like this?*

In the fall-time; it's always low; but in September you generally get rain and it raises the water so you can go up; but the last couple years it wasn't enough rain . . . to raise it; people go up, but I don't like hitting the bottom with my motor all the time.

» *People will probably need jet units from now on?*

There was a guy that had one of these airboats up there 10–15 years ago, you can hear it 10 miles coming. I don't know how you hunt with that.

Gas here is $3.90 a gallon now too.

» *Food expensive.*

Paper sack like that you fill up, it'll be about $50. Two dollars for water.

» *Don't last long too, huh?*

Yeah.

» *Have to shop in Fairbanks?*

Water is $6 a gallon and gas $4 a gallon.

» *Today is cold, that's not normal huh?*

Generally, in fall-time you get cold weather. This month is generally hot. This here is 3 days that's all, hot weather.

» *A week, snow was all gone in 1 week?*

Grace: Second of May, ice went out. And the swallows were here early.

Harry: I think the swallows are getting ready to leave already. It's not even August yet.

When the ice starts breaking up, generally in the middle of May, this year it's 2 weeks early.

Grace: Everything is 2 weeks early.

» *When you have early spring, you have early fall, right?*

This is the first year its really that early, but it seems to me that it's getting earlier and earlier all the time; break up.

» *Birds?*

There's the same birds but they're like robins, and like, they were flying a couple of weeks ago; but they should be flying about now—young ones. A week ago, first of month, some of them are ready to fly, that's pretty early for that; generally, about end of the month [is] generally when they're about ready to fly.

» *Animals are getting out of their normal cycles?*

That's the way it seems to me. They're getting earlier; they come in earlier and are nesting earlier; maybe [by the] end of the month we might not have no more birds.

Grace: It's really different, it's just really different.

Even the gardening, I'm a gardener, the flowers are this high [*gesturing*] they're just stunted; it's from the heat and the cold. We had a hot spell and it got cold; they're not like they are normally; cabbage are not doing so good and zucchini.

Harry: I think we only had 3 or 4 days real hot weather this summer, other times it's like this, rain, cloudy, no rain but it's cloudy.

Grace: It's cold, usually July is up in the 70s, 80s, 90s; it's not like that. We could see our breath, I think it's 45 degrees. I went out this morning I swear I saw my breath, it's like fall-time.

Harry: Three to four days she made a fire, too cold in the house.

Grace: I had to build a fire—cold, down to below 58 degrees.

Harry: I went down [to the] Elders today, I had to wear a jacket in the house.

Grace: I know people are getting sick too. Like colds. [*Cause they're not prepared for it?*] No.

Harry: I guess you're not really prepared for it when you go up in that weather. [*You don't expect it.*] Yeah. [*Go up there and its 70 degrees and another day it'll—*]

Grace: drop down to 45.

Grace: It's really different, it's totally different. People seem to be very highly agitated, I don't know if that's from the weather change, very high-strung, antsy. I noticed that in people. Very touchy, quarrelsome.

If [there's a lot of] moisture, I'm irritable, like Sunday it was very humid, I was really agitated, I had to come home and lay away and read and stay away from people. Just keep completely low, and then I could feel the change by midnight it was going to change next day. Yeah, it's different.

» *Growth? Can't trust weather?*

Potato patches? They're just scattered, not fully grown?

» *What do people garden for?*

Their own use.

» *If you can't trust the weather to grow things, and store prices are too high, than food is going to start being difficult to get?*

Grace: Mm-hmm.

Harry: Yeah.

» *You can't even go to hunting grounds too, like the Black River?*

Harry: Yeah.

Grace: We're kinda concerned about what we're going to get this winter, if we don't get our winter meat. I sure don't want to eat beef.

» *We're having some problems with the PCH too, unpredictable.*

Harry: Yeah.

Grace: I'm sure hoping to get meat.

» *Moose season good?*

We generally try not to, I wouldn't kill moose in the summer, but our next month I think 20 it opens, and Joseph's here, I like to dry a little meat too.

» *Gas prices are going up too, huh?*

I don't understand that gas, when you buy and you're going to sell it, buy now and you're bringing it here and you're selling it. And you got enough gas for all winter, and the price in Fairbanks goes up, why is the price here going to go up? You already bought the gas.

If you bought the gas at $2 a gallon, you should sell that gas at that price until it runs out.

When the boat came in, they raised the price to $3.80, and about a week ago they raised it to $3.90. by fall it's going to be $4 a gallon.

Who wants to eat beef?

It takes a little over 100 gallons to go up to where we hunt, so that's $400 for gas, plus your oil, plus your grub, plus your wear and tear on your motor.

Grace: Yeah, that meat is expensive, thank God we don't got eight or ten kids.

Harry: Yeah, but when you got eight or ten kids you go up there and get that questcard.

Grace: Oh, that's the thing that's ruining them people.

Harry: That's really ruinin'.

Grace: Ruinin' them younger generation.

Harry: Don't have to work, you can't get nobody to help you work. If you want somebody to work outdoors you can't pay them enough. If they don't have to work.

When I was building my garage, I got one guy to help me, I said let's get your brother, he can help us too, he said. I went up there and he said, "Hey I got good clothes on, I eat good, so why should I work?"

Grace: It's terrible.

» *I just got done interviewing someone and they said volunteering is gone*

Harry: That's right. Nobody is willing to help anymore.

Grace: No.

Harry: Just a few people.

Grace: They could care less. Sharing if you get meat, they won't share with you. Nothing. It's not like it was in the '50s, when they first got moose, the town got meat, it's not like that no more. It's just dog eat dog. It really is.

» *What about the youth camp teaching kids to live off the land?*

It's good, I guess.

Grace: They really want people to go down.

» *That guy really said that to you? "I got nice clothes?"*

His mother was alive at that time, he just stayed with his mother, and he don't have to work.

» *Questcard? People buy pizza and stuff like that?*

Grace: All kinds of stuff, steaks, porkchops, they could eat good.

Harry: A lot of time we make soup, and our grandkids will come here, and we tell them to eat soup and they won't touch [it], that's no good, they want pizza.

Grace: Bad, really bad. They're just changing so bad, all that cholesterol, all that fat.

» *Land is changing 'cause the people are changing?*

Could be. When I was small, there was lots of us, everybody had a job when you assigned to this job you do not ask questions, you just do it.

» *Climate forces them to pay attention to traditional ways?*

Last winter or [the] year before, me and my brother Fred, we go out and we trap. We got about 5 days. When we first set it out, we try to shade about every 6 days. So, we keep just going over, we never lay over for cold weather. When its 20 below we say, "It's too cold," and we don't go out. All that time it got 20 below today and the next day it's warm, it don't stay cold. Johnny said 40 below one day, a long time ago you got 56 below for 2 weeks at a time?

» *Do you pick berries? Five years?*

Harry: They seem to be all right. Fairbanks, a week ago, blueberries [were] already ripe, we always figured end of the month. The guy told me the other day they're just getting good now.

» *Women [pick them]; they're ripening really fast in Arctic Village, here?*

Harry: Like I said, over a week ago blueberries are already ripening we figure end of month is when they—

Grace: July, end of July.

Harry: Just like I said, the first of the month, young geese are ready to fly, we figure about end of month we generally go hunting geese. It'll be flying by them.

» *Weird psychologically? Going hunting for geese in July?*

Harry: The first week in August, like I said, we went up fooling around the other day, first week of August. We, already, the heads are turning like the old ones black and everything already.

» *Forest fire? Does that play into climate change?*

Grace: I think it ruins the plants, the smoke. They say ashes are good for gardening, but they're not as big, they're stunted, they're poorly, they're not as big as normal, their growth is. It's really different this year. Very poor.

» *Fall early?*

I'm just wondering maybe in August it's going to freeze up.

» *You get ready to go out to get ducks? Find out they're already gone?*

It's really bad, it's scary. Especially the water situations, can't get anywhere.

» *50 years from now?*

[Gasps from both of them.]

» *Best thing to do right now to prepare for this insane weather?*

We didn't have much rain this summer, just a week ago, rained a little bit here, that's all, all spring we didn't have rain here.

» *A laong time ago? Rain?*

I remember one time me and Donald came up with boat, we [were] coming up on the main road, the water didn't have time to run off the road, it's just water standing there and pouring off like that [*gesturing*] the road it's raining so hard. You don't see rain like that anymore.

» *Fort Yukon flooded?*

This spring it flooded downtown here and my garage, the water didn't get so high. I thought last winter with all this snow we had we'd have a flood.

When Porcupine floods too it comes across the country, through town, then a lot of the people that don't get flood when Yukon floods, like my brother Johnny, gets flooded when the Porcupine comes through. Cause little low there from the backside, water comes through there. This road used to be a river, before they build that dike before Porcupine come through that way comes run through down there.

Twice it come up, went up above my garage there and went down and pretty soon went back up again.

» *Porcupine, you said, does it still flood across the country? Does it still do that?*

Well, it never did that for 10 years now. We hadn't had a flood for quite a while now. I really can't tell you when the last time we had a flood [was].

Grace: '82 I think.

» *What could we do about it?*

No answer.

Harry: That one year the water was high and we had a friend here, and she walked out and she stepped on that porch and that step is moving with her, and that guy come and picked her up with a boat.

» *That swallow thing again? About them being on telephone lines already? That means they've given birth already and they're about ready to take off?*

Yeah. They, generally about end of the month, they go on lines, these telephone lines. And then they're like that for 3 or 4 days and then they take off. Well, they're already on the lines and its 28 already, they been like that for 3 or 4 days now. I figure one of these days they're going to be gone.

» *Hunting seasons going to shift to an earlier time?*

Yeah, probably.

» *[Showing me the garage]*

It was on that table there. [*Pointing to workbench 3½ to 4 feet off the ground.*]

Water down there too [now]. [*Pointing to line on garage 1 foot off the ground.*]

» *Salmon coming earlier?*

Yeah, early, too early, middle of July, yeah. And still running.

» *When do they usually come?*

Around the 20th of this month, supposed to. This year it's a little early, so it's still running.

Me, I don't [go] fishing, but for kids, in camp, couple days, I caught fish, so they watch me how I'm doing [it]. Oh, just for 2 or 3 days, and then I came back.

» *Trees didn't grow as fast as they grow today? Land clear?*

Everything changed nowadays. I went up [to] Arctic, first time, the trees, some of them, some of them is dry, but that long [gesturing a couple feet high]. Now everything is growing. Jeez, the willows are thick, growing big.

» *Bad or good?*

Nobody knows. Around here it was like that too.

» *Trees used to be smaller a long time ago?*

Yeah, that's right, now look at that! It's all growing up.

» *How did it get like that?*

How would we know, nobody knows.

» *How about the grass? Was it like that a long time ago?*

Yeah, it's growing.

» *Moose? Tell me about moose.*

That little calf, little calves is born once a year. Cow, it's pretty hard to say.

» *Anything different with them?*

Just one or two calves, not three or four. But I hear over [in] Fairbanks [there's] one cow and four little calves. I never hear about that. First time, maybe some trouble.

» *A long time ago did the moose ever give birth to four calves?*

No, this is the first time. Over [in] Fairbanks, just talk, I dunno.

» *Where do you go to hunt for moose?*

Big country around here. Trapline, a lot of them. Trails, Birch Creek trail, Venetie trails, Black River, here and there, lots of lakes.

» *More or less of them?*

More, gee, lots of animals.

» *Summer really earlier?*

Funny. Everything changed. Even kids, they all, they don't eat fish or meat, that's bad. They eat chips and pop, that's it, that's all they live on. The kids, it's a half-breed, even full-blooded kids, they talk English, not all Native. Different life.

» *Land is different too, huh? River is going down?*

Not enough water sometimes. All the lakes . . . just dry up.
All kinds of birds, there's nothing, just a few.

» *No robins?*

Just robins and ravens, and some little birds, that's it. Lots of different white color.

» *[I attempted to show him bird book.]*

No dil'.
Solitary sandpiper.
A long time ago, nowadays its lot of different. [In] 1938, the first school of Venetie, John Fredson school, '38 or '37? There was no school before.

» *Telling me his life story.*

Now there's lots of planes around, when a person is sick you know they're right there, the hospital [is] down there, but no plane. Now when they're, sick [the plane] just took him over.

» *Land is changing?*

Yeah.

This is not Gwicha Gwich'in, that's what them old timers said. When I was a kid, I always listen to [the Elders]. There's only two people in this Fort Yukon, one is an old woman, [she's the] only Gwicha Gwich'in. That daughter died, too. Rest is from downriver, Chalk, Tanana, Beaver, they moved up here a long time ago. [To] Venetie.

Two days ago, cold, it's September weather, this is July month, never had that kind of wind like that, maybe early fall. [Very] different, even the kids are like that, they don't care about out in the woods. Different mind[set]. They've been [to] high school, graduated, [and] they don't do nothing.

A 2013 Gwich'in Elder and Youth Climate Solution Statement to the World from Arctic Village

GWICH'IN ELDERS AND YOUTH ON CLIMATE SOLUTIONS AND ADAPTATIONS

By Matt Gilbert

DATE: 6/28/13

Climate Change is no longer a question in the world, but a devastating reality. The Gwich'in Elders and youth of Arctic Village gave their ideas on climate solutions and adaptations in the days following President Barack Obama's major push against climate change.

According to the Associated Press article "Obama Opens Drive Against Climate Change," Obama launched a major second-term drive on Tuesday, June 5, 2013 to combat climate change and "secure a safer planet, bypassing congress." The president said that the world has done far too little to stop it.

Obama planned to implement new controls on new and existing power plants that emit carbon dioxide—heat-trapping gases blamed for global warming—boost renewable energy production on federal lands, increase efficiency standards, and prepare communities to deal with higher temperatures. Obama called for the United States to be a global leader in the search for solutions, according to the article.

https://doi.org/10.5876/9781646423361.c002

Last year, the Gwich'in Elders and youth spoke out about the impacts of global warming on their village in the remote north. They were heard around the world through Cultural Survival, Inc. (CSI), and now they speak out again, but this time on solutions and adaptations.

Allen Tritt is a Gwich'in Elder living in Arctic Village who keeps to himself despite his wisdom on worldwide issues such as global warming. He opened up on the issue. "Make a road up that way [a mountain above the village], bring the rocks [flat rocks] and put it along the creek, all the way up [the creek], along the river too, get a good dump truck," Allen suggests.

The flat rocks along the banks would act as a wall to prevent the eroding creek- and riverbanks from eating into the village and its roads.

Allen says we need cold weather to maintain the permafrost, because the permafrost is melting everywhere and it's drying up the lakes and creeks. "Our Elders already talked about it [long ago]," he said. "The permafrost melt, at the graveyard, there's a big ditch in there, caving in."

After mentioning readers from Fiji who read his words in CSI and claimed the same events were happening there, Allen gives a grim statement, "We're the last ones like this, no more history."

Regarding how cities can change to combat climate change, Allen has little to no ideas. At the mention of overpopulation, Allen says, "There's nothing we can do about it." He then mentions the rock wall again but with the idea of government funds running dry, he says, "We can do it ourselves if we do it right."

Sarah James is a Gwich'in Elder and a spokeswoman and chair for the Gwich'in Steering Committee. She travels the world speaking against oil and gas development in the Arctic National Wildlife Refuge and global warming. "Global warming is getting worse. It's going faster and faster. We can help President Obama and start in our own house, everybody does their recycle, reduce, and refuse. I refuse to play bingo to waste my time, paper, and marker."

She advises everyone to know how much energy everything takes to make. For example, why do parents have to buy a new backpack for their children every school year? She says, "We got to find a way to use what we already have and reuse things, people are too materialistic."

"We're getting all this from the earth too." She says the earth has to have clean water, clean air, clean land, and clean life in order to operate. "It's scary, enough, we have to try to do something about it, starting at home, teach it to our children."

There's not enough good air, and it's affecting the weather. The weather can't decide how to act, so whatever it can produce is getting faster and faster, "and it's getting scary. We *have* to do something." Sarah says one way people can fight climate change is with the use of their time. Instead of playing cards, bingo, or going to a party, one can do other earth-saving things like planting a tree, repairing one's house, or bringing one's own bag to the grocery store.

Trimble Gilbert is the traditional chief of Arctic Village and says it's been the hottest June he has ever seen. He says that it may be too late to do anything about climate change and overpopulation. "There's more and more pollutions in this earth, because of the human activity and oil. Seems like there's more and more sick people and no one is happy anymore because of the climate change."

Trimble says we have to stop using things that are not good for the air and teach young people around the world. "We got to renew the earth. The president is worried about it, so we have to have a big meeting and have foreign countries get together with Native people. That might help Mother Earth for the next century."

Again, the Gwich'in youth had their own views on climate solutions and adaptations. Clifford and Kate were in high school when they were first interviewed but have since graduated.

Clifford David is an 18-year-old Gwich'in boy who recently graduated from high school. Like Trimble and Allen, he had a similarly grave outlook. "Honestly, I don't think there is a huge amount we can do. There is the obvious: Try to cut down on pollution, use some renewable energy to power vehicles, dispose of trash properly, but we've gone so far on pollution, there isn't really a turnback point. It's only going to get worse and worse."

Concerning his fellow youth and advice for them, he says young people of the world need to keep their pollution minimal and try to enjoy their lives, because the next generation will inherit a worse world.

Kate Hollandsworth is 19 years old and also graduated from high school, and she is now a utility clerk. Kate says the government should pass a law that requires schools to track what kids and parents do to take care of global warming. "Parents can teach their kids about taking care of the place they live in and around, so the world won't be so polluted!" She says kids need to learn the responsibility of having clean air to breathe and clean water to drink.

Ask what young people of the world can do, she says, "Get more involved!"

Her further solution for the youth of the world is to learn what will happen if there is no solution and everyone continues doing what they're doing. "Start caring about the world so it can be better for their kids." She goes on to comment on school reform, "Teachers should get kids/students into environmental activities so they could learn to get a better world for a better future."

CONCLUSION

The Gwich'in Elders' and youth's main message was directed at the destructive lifestyles of people around the world. They believe the key to the global crisis lies in the way we live and what we learn. It starts at home.

They had no comments on worldwide engineering projects or worldwide quick fixes, because they do not exist. Even if a quick fix were to be developed, it would not fix the root of the problem: What caused climate change is the unhealthy and destructive lifestyle humans have adopted, and now has to cease for the sake of the world and the children.

If a quick fix were developed and climate change reversed, it still would not matter, because our destructive lifestyle would cause it again. It's our destructive lifestyle and the way our society is run that has to change in order to resolve climate chaos for all time.

PROJECT DIRECTOR INTRODUCTION
TO 2020 CLIMATE INTERVIEWS

In 2005, I did a series of interviews that got rave reviews at the time, and I was invited to conferences all over the world. However, I was not interested in pursuing a career in climate change science at the time and had other opportunities. I did not have support in Alaska either, so I tabled the materials I obtained. I figured someone else would do the work later on.

Fifteen years later, in fall 2019, no one had yet done the type of work I did in a way of quality and rawness of traditional ecological knowledge. I was shocked my work was still new and unique, so I pitched it to the US Fish and Wildlife Service. Funded by USFWS, my climate materials was reawakened from my personal archives and published into a report, and again it achieved popularity.

I was asked by the National Wildlife Federation and the University of Alaska Press to conduct updated interviews in summer 2020, 15 years after my first round of interviews.

In spring 2019, I finished one last research project that took a whole year, a mapping project. I was officially retiring and writing a letter to the tribe to announce it, when the call requesting these updated interviews arrived.

https://doi.org/10.5876/9781646423361.c003

Frankly, I was not interested at all given the lack of support the first time. I had an opportunity out of state, so I wanted to leave. Besides this, I was retiring from research work among Gwich'in. I did not know at age 25 what I now know at 40—that this work would not let me go and did not provide enough pay for a living. It's been very hard.

It's a very hard living on "soft money" (grant money), so I wanted a change in lifestyle, but I felt God calling me to do the work. I was very reluctant to stay and do the updated climate interviews, especially considering the outdated materials were not my fault; but the fault of the environmental groups particularly in Anchorage who were not only unsupportive, but rude and contentious, it was not my fault it aged 15 years.

Nevertheless, the UA Press demanded updates for publication. So, even though I was very reluctant, I knew the scope and difficulty of the work. I realized I was the only one who could do them. I gave a shaky agreement that I would try at least writing summaries based on the audio recordings.

I also found that the Elders interviewed did not have much more to add and not much more to share, because the 2005 was so voluminous. They covered so much.

I am a lot older in 2020 with two more degrees, and a lot wiser from living in the Gwich'in villages off and on through the years since graduating in 2005. I have experienced climate chaos and had a lot of observations myself. I gleaned a lot of Elder wisdom from the 2005 work, and made observations based on them. I had learned so much about the land from the Gwich'in Elders and hunters.

GWICH'IN CLIMATE INTERVIEWS IN 2020

Many topics were covered in 2005 that do not need to be revisited. Every Gwich'in knows the culture has changed more and more with the modern world and cultural and language lost is a stark reality. Every Gwich'in knows the destructive climate effects along with the rest of the world. Anyone reading this knows the climate has changed rapidly and become more unpredictable and destructive. These topics will not be broached too much.

The focus for the updates is the unique observations and ecological knowledge of the Gwich'in.

Millions have mobilized to do something about the changing climate and massive demonstrations and political pressure has been put on governments around the world to address climate change in the last 15 years, but not enough progress has been made. Climate change's destruction is no longer a debate across the world and in Gwich'in country as well; we see it destroying societies around the world on the news all the time.

The unique contribution the Gwich'in can add to the worldwide conversation and movement on climate change is their intimate ecological knowledge. They know the land better than most people, possibly worldwide, and can see changes in the land years before the best environmental scientist can see them through computer models. They have this to offer, as does every Indigenous tribe like them around the world.

They also have philosophical and spiritual advice for the world. Especially in regard to everyone's attitude toward the land.

This is why I chose to do the 2020 updated interviews. My time is a lot more precious to me now and I have long since moved on from this project, lobbying and advocacy, but I'm the only one who can do it and the world deserves the knowledge of the Gwich'in on climate change.

PROJECT DIRECTOR'S OWN OBSERVATIONS

As mentioned, I spent the last 15 years coming back to the Gwich'in villages off and on and saw changes myself. My name is Matt Gilbert and I'm Gwich'in. I'm 40 years old, and I grew up in Arctic Village and spent a lot of my professional life there doing research on climate change and cartography.

I'll go from big to small: The biggest change is the weather; it changes very quickly now. It can be raining and heavy cloud cover, and then a mere hour later, it will clear up and be sunny with blue skies. It's very odd. It makes the weather very unpredictable and causes anxiety and sickness among Gwich'in.

One Saturday a Gwich'in man named Julius Roberts in Venetie, and I were at the Washeteria, doing laundry. We walked there in T-shirts because it was sunny and hot in July with hardly a cloud in the sky. But we got stuck there because 20 minutes later, because it started pouring rain outside. This is how quickly the weather changes.

Thunderstorms

The thunderstorms are now a lot stronger and more violent. The thunder has become so loud that it shakes houses and, in summer 2020, it even shut our electricity down in Arctic Village. I saw thunder and rainstorms my whole life in Arctic Village, especially when I was a kid, and never did I see a rainstorm so bad that it knocked out our electricity and shook houses and scared people and dogs. It is very strange and a bit scary.

In 2011, the thunderstorms got so terrible that dogs scrambled for cover and children hid under tables.

This is my personal account of the thunderstorm that knocked out the electricity in the summer of 2020:

> Even during the writing of this very climate report, the weather had huge chaotic impacts on Arctic Village. On June 30, 2020, we had a tremendous thunder rumble that shook the houses, which is becoming a common phenomenon. It shook everything so much this time that the electricity went out all over the village. I'd never seen that in my life. I grew up in Arctic Village and have lived there off and on my whole adult life until now, at 40 years old, I have never seen such an event.

More will be told about this in the summary section on topics.

When the violent and ground-shaking thunder first started in the summer of 2011, I interviewed Gwich'in children in Arctic Village. Caitlin Hollandsworth, a high schooler at the time, said, "My cousin Allison called me scared and asked me what to do. I told her, 'Just get down!'" She giggled. There were other accounts of children hiding under tables. Raymond Tritt said of the 2020 thunders, "It's a big thunder, even my house was shaking. I thought it was going to break a window!"

Lightning Strikes

There are more and more lightning strikes (Bieniek et al., 2020). I was walking home from checking email at the school when I saw lightning approaching, I was scared. I wanted to get indoors immediately. I had never had this type of fear from lightning my entire life in Arctic Village. They never used to be a problem.

A few years ago in 2016, a Native man named Wilbur was walking to town when lightning was striking not far from him on the road. I have never seen this in my whole life growing up in Arctic Village.

Cold Springs

Spring 2020 was the coldest spring I ever experienced in Arctic Village; the cold spell lasted well into the summer months. We did not have a real spring as we traditionally know spring.

The winters are very warm up until Christmas, then it gets cold in the spring.

Increased Rains

The rains are more frequent and heavier, which explains the rapid overgrowth and increased forestation. Gideon James mentioned this briefly in the 2005 report.

Overgrowth

The next-most obvious problem is overgrowth (Grabinski and McFarland, 2020, p. 12); a person only has to take a look at Arctic Village's photos in the 1980s and today to see the overgrowth. The village council pays the teens to cut the willows every summer and they have cleared whole areas of the village, only to have the willows shoot back up again the next summer. The tribal councils now make it a point to clear cut willows in the village because they are being shrouded in vegetation.

As I said to Charlie Swaney, a bunch of us kids used to visit his stepdaughter Marjorie when she was a child and watch John Hughes movies in the early 1990s, while he was playing cards at night. I used to be able to see Arctic Village very clearly from his porch, but not anymore, the vegetation is too high and thick.

Charlie confirms, "Yup, you can't see nothing. When I built this house, these trees were only a foot tall, and now it's taller than the house!"

Bank Erosion

Canoeing upriver in 2011 and on, I noticed the riverbanks had eroded and the river had widened. The river being wider has also made it shallower. The banks are eroding farther and farther back. A hunting area I frequented a lot as a kid, Han Geeraatąįį, upriver from Arctic Village, is seeing its bank disappearing by almost 100 feet.

According to the Environmental Protection Agency's website, climate change has increased heavy rainfall and therefore has caused more erosion (EPA, 2021).

Animals

In terms of animals, the caribou are still plentiful and migrate their normal route. Moose have mixed reports, but surveys and studies on moose in Arctic Village are hard to do because moose are a relatively new animal in the area, being that they only migrated into the area a century ago. Ecologically speaking, a century is a very short time. However, moose seem to be normal.

CONCLUSION

When I was a kid, my friends and I would hunt muskrats with our 4-10s and fish grayling with our fishing poles. We would walk up to the first riverbend, called First Bend, where we hunted muskrats, ducks, and fished grayling from the river. We used to sneak up to the lake behind First Bend to shoot muskrats sitting on the ice, but they are no longer there. The whole area seems like a lonely reflection of what it used to be. Muskrats have grown scarce.

Beaver houses are large mounds of yellow grass. They were in many places I hunted, and I have not seen a single one lately.

The mountains and lands are devoid of animals. During my childhood, when my grandfather Trimble Gilbert took me to the mountain for a caribou hunt, it was an entirely different world. There were Elder camps all over the mountain, the skies were clearer, as Gideon says, animal sounds were everywhere, birds sang on almost every tree, the caribou migrated in giant herds and were all fat.

In Spring 2020, I went up to Duchanlee Mountain with my late father's snow machine to hunt ptarmigan, and it was a completely different world. It seemed like a desolate wasteland, now empty of animals and lonely, compared to long ago. I stated my account to Audrey Tritt, a well-known hunter woman, and she replied, "Nothing, yeah."

Many things are different on the land, and it's scarce of animals and people. Not many Gwich'in hunted like long ago when whole families would be at camp and kids running everywhere. The trees also seem different now compared to long ago in the early 1980s, where they seemed lush. Now they seem parch and "sick." There not as many birds as well.

In conclusion, I believe in the words of my great-grandmother Maggie Gilbert, who said so long ago, "When the animals die off, humans go next."

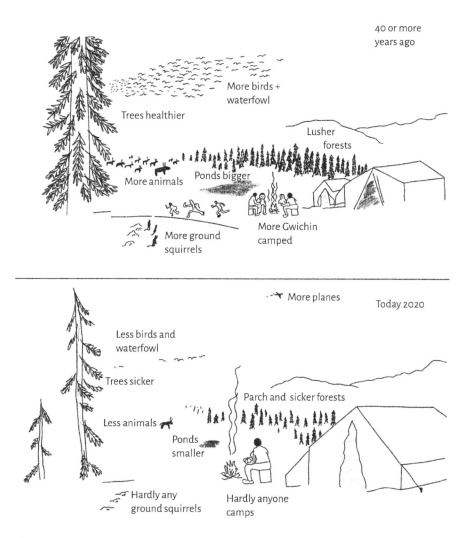

Figure 21. Gwich'in Life on the land 40 years ago compared to 2020 (illustration by Matt Gilbert, redrawn by Lulu Kachele)

Mosquitoes

Mosquitoes seem to have increased in numbers and aggressiveness for Gwich'in in Arctic Village. For myself, they have changed a lot since I was a kid. They have gotten so bad that you have to run to your house to avoid them. They used to bite you casually, as they buzzed around you. However, now in 2020 they "attack" in swarms, like bees attacking you after knocking their honeycomb down.

I was also seeing mosquitoes in my house as late as October 10, which is very peculiar.

Lakes

Every Gwich'in and non-Native Alaskan knows the lakes have been drying out, so I did not ask about it in the 2020 interviews. If a Gwich'in person wanted to bring it up in his or her own context, I allowed that. It is an Alaskan fact that lakes have been drying out and becoming dust bowls and gravel pits. This does not need scientific confirmations; all one has to do is fly over Alaska to see them. This has been continuing steadily for 15 years.

There is a lake on the eastern embankment of our airport, I had a lot of fond memories of that lake, especially with duck hunting and school trips. It is now drained out so much that it is no longer a lake but rather a sand pit.

COMMON CLIMATE IMPACTS

Based on the 2005 report, there are climate impacts that are taken for granted by Gwich'in people. For example, the more frequent rains, dry lakes, lower waters, quiet forests, and scarcer game are changes all Gwich'in communities are adapting to.

The overgrowth is an everyday reality, and Arctic Village has started a massive brush-cutting program to implement every summer. The Gwich'in agreed that there are fewer birds, but some birds have returned. The forests are still quiet from the scarcity of animals, and it is lonelier. I can attest to this fact myself because of the numerous trips I took up to the mountain in the last 15 years. It has been barren. It's not like long ago.

The poor berry quality is a fact to the Gwich'in women and that berries scarcer, and the berry patches are less dense and smaller. Kathy Tritt, a Gwich'in woman who moved to Fairbanks but grew up in Arctic Village and Venetie, said of Deena Tritt's testimony, "Yes, the berries are less in one place now. They're not stacked up, you know, like berries on top of berries, where you can pick all day in one spot. It's not like that anymore, so she's right."

Deena also added that the berries are not ripe anymore and they pop easily, which makes them inedible. Deena says in the 2020 updates that this is still true.

SHORTCOMINGS OF THE 2005 INTERVIEWS AND IMPROVEMENTS

In 2005, some of the Gwich'in jumped around with their testimonies, some saying there was less snow and some saying there was more snow. It is important to read and understand the Gwich'in climate testimonies in context and "read between the lines," so to speak, because there have been extreme variabilities in the seasonal climates (Grabinski and McFarland, 2020).

For example, when Trimble Gilbert says, "Animal populations are going down," and a lot of animal species returned to Arctic Village in 2020, I figured he meant it in general. It is wonderful that a lot of animals have returned, but they are not as plentiful as they used to be. Their behaviors have changed as well. "The animals are not happy no more, the birds don't sing no more," Trimble says.

I was very young in 2005 and spent nearly 10 years away from my people after that. I had to get to know them again and I did. This time, I knew my people better after spending 15 years helping them, so I knew who to interview—who had the best materials.

In 2005, the Gwich'in Elders, hunters, and gatherers made predictions that, for the most part, came true. These are the predictions that came true:

1. The lakes have dried up tremendously.
2. Human diseases have worsened (Coronavirus).
3. Weather volatility has increased.

15-YEAR STABILIZATIONS

The Porcupine caribou herd was behaving strangely during the early 2000s, and population fluctuations were occurring, and it had the Gwich'in worried, but the herd has stabilized. The hunting has been more than good for the Gwich'in in the last decade. However, some Gwich'in say it is getting harder and harder to find "fat caribou."

Moose population has more or less been the same.

As far as birds, the yellowtail has returned to Gwich'in lands in spring 2020 and its fire alarm–like sound was much welcomed. The small number of bank swallows returned and made holes in the gravel pit at the Arctic

Village airport. Muskrats were seen swimming the sloughs again as well. However, beavers were still hardly seen.

CHALLENGES OF CONDUCTING A 2020 UPDATE

University of Alaska Fairbanks (UAF) scholars wanted updates to the 2005 Gwich'in Climate Impact Report. The original report was a unique snapshot of the Gwich'in, but an update was sorely desired, so a quick one was done in summer 2020. Although I had grave concerns about the time and unpaid work involved, I did it nevertheless.

The Coronavirus of 2020, known as Covid-19, utterly disrupted the world and all its business, including mine. It made my formal research in Gwich'in communities impossible. The virus basically shut down the world and, along with it, Gwich'in villages; the communities had travel restrictions and quarantine requirements for anyone outside. Venetie and Fort Yukon shut their doors to nonresidents, so the two interviews for Venetie and Fort Yukon had to be done remotely on the phone.

Coincidently, Gideon James predicted the Coronavirus in 2005, when he stated, "This climate change is going to create conditions for new diseases, and they're going to be worse." Unfortunately, Mr. James's prediction was realized by the world in 2020 with the outbreak of the Coronavirus, an unprecedented pandemic that has killed over 1,000,000 people worldwide and caused enormous disruption in everyday life.

My life has also changed since 2005. I am a lot more conscious and sensitive about my time and did not want to do a lot of research work for free. Nonetheless, I realized if I did not do this update, no one would.

CLIMATE IMPACT FOR THE LAST 15 YEARS

The 2020 Gwich'in Climate Impact Report itself is chaotic, because, as mentioned, it was not possible to visit Venetie and Fort Yukon due to funding shortages and travel restrictions from the Covid-19 pandemic. However, I conducted interviews in Arctic Village and got some interesting findings.

In regard to changing land, wildlife, and weather over the last 15 years, some things have stabilized, some things have actually improved, and some have gotten worse. It was not a straightforward update. Some change rates have stayed the same, such as the drying of lakes. They have stabilized in their rate of drying but the spring of 2020 had record-setting cold temperatures for Arctic Village, so there was hardly any meltwater for the lakes and rivers; therefore, the water was substantially low.

The spring was cold and did not warm up for more than a day, so the snow was dry, and evaporated. Therefore, it did not melt and create water to run into the valley to fill the lakes and rivers.

The climate has become very chaotic and hard to keep up with. As Audrey Tritt stated so well, "Something weird happens every day." Climate reports such as this one become outdated quickly too because, as Audrey stated, the weather changes and does new things all the time. Climate change has sped up and is hard to report on because changes are happening at a more rapid rate than 2005.

The particulars of the changes can be explored by studying the transcripts between 2005 and 2020, but I will only touch on the categories of change in this report. The two main changes between the reports are the enormous overgrowth and increased weather chaos. In Arctic Village, the most pronounced incident was the giant lightning strike of 2019, which was explored and discussed extensively among the Gwich'in.

The 2020 update interviews from the Elders are briefer, but there are some more lengthy interviews from the hunters and gatherers. A lot was covered by the Elders in the 2005 reports, so there was not much to add. There were some new and fascinating traditional knowledge gleaned from the 2020 updates. I had become skilled and knowledgeable in traditional ecological knowledge over the years working in Native cartography and climate knowledge, so I was better able to glean the information.

Below, the topics of change are organized into their respective themes, like in the 2005 report. The interview transcripts that follow are a little rougher than the 2005 interviews, because they were conducted more informally.

And as mentioned, I was unable to conduct many of the Venetie and Fort Yukon interviews because Covid-19 shut down access to the villages by visitors. Also, many of the Elders in Fort Yukon passed on. But I hope that the readers will enjoy the updates, nonetheless.

A unique observation of trees was given by Audrey Tritt; she believes birch trees are starting to appear in the area, although no one else talked about invasive plants and trees.

PRESIDENT TRUMP OPENS ARCTIC NATIONAL WILDLIFE REFUGE TO OIL DEVELOPMENT

The rise of President Donald Trump caused changes to the Arctic Refuge. In 2016, the Republication congressmen were able to add a provision into the Defense Bill that allowed the Arctic National Wildlife Refuge to be opened to oil and gas exploration. They had been trying to open it for decades, and the Gwich'in people, along with their environmental allies around the world, had successfully stopped them; however, the Gwich'in people's nearly 40-year battle was lost that day.

The refuge has yet to be developed, but a lengthy Arctic Coastal Plains Environmental Impact Statement (EIS) has begun, and the Gwich'in have been testifying in the hearings for this EIS. Chapter 1, Section 1.10.1 of the statement reads:

> Scientific evidence confirms the earth is undergoing a change in climate. Climate analyses suggest that warming in the twentieth century was greater than warming during any other century in the past 1,000 years, and the 1990s were likely the warmest decade in 1,000 years (Mann et al. 1999, Folland et al. 2001). The arctic climate has warmed rapidly during the past 50 years, with annual average temperatures increasing nearly twice as fast as the rest of the world (Arctic Climate Impact Assessment 2005). Warming in Alaska rose sharply beginning in 1977, concurrent with large scale arctic atmosphere and ocean regime shifts (Parson et al. 2000). The greatest warming has occurred during winter and spring.

The Arctic Refuge EIS itself dramatically describes the globally dire situation of climate change.

SUMMARY OF ARCTIC VILLAGE CLIMATE IMPACT REPORT

There were many complex areas of observation in Arctic Village of the changing climate, and I have organized them into their respective themes the best I could. I include a section on the giant lightning strike of 2019, because it illustrates the sheer drama and shock it caused Gwich'in in Arctic Village. Therefore, is deserved a section of its own.

I also combined all the fascinating weather knowledge of the Gwich'in people, which I term "Gwich'in meteorology." The last section discusses the dangers of lightning storms; the Gwich'in feel threatened and anxious about storms now when they never used to be.

GWICH'IN METEOROLOGY

The Gwich'in possess brilliant knowledge of the weather. This has been built over thousands of years of observation. I obtained some Gwich'in meteorology information from this report, but I can't help but to think of so much more the Gwich'in people have lost. As you will read in the following sections, the Gwich'in knew a lot about the weather. They observed that the cloud formation and air currents are different on each side of the skydome opposed to long ago when there was one pattern. They also knew that the weather was supposed to vary regionally, but it does not anymore.

Dust Storms

The small dust storms that used to be so common to Arctic Village are hardly seen anymore. Gwich'in called them Ahtr'ii Vee. They are giant tornados but invisible and weak, so no one sees or notices them, but only the tips of the funnel are seen from the dust they pick up. They are seen as dust storms on the road. This Ahtr'ii Vee blows away bad weather and makes good weather, "but not no more, because these clouds we're getting are different." The clouds seem to be denser, so do not blow away now.

Audrey Tritt explains it as her Elders told her, "But we don't see them anymore." Darrell Tritt from Venetie confirmed Audrey's account.

Small Clouds

Allen Tritt of Arctic Village says that when small, puffy clouds are seen, it means the weather is going to be nice for a long time. However, he says with climate change, this predictive weather pattern no longer works. "Now when I see small puffy clouds, it doesn't mean it's going to be nice weather."

Cotton Balls

Long ago, the Gwich'in used the floating cotton from cottonwood trees to predict fish runs. In July, the cotton would float through the air, and

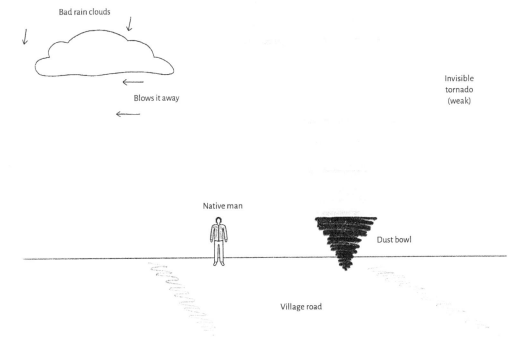

Figure 22. Illustration by Matt Gilbert based on Gwich'in Elder knowledge (July 2020), redrawn by Lulu Kachele

the Gwich'in know Big Fish was running. In Fort Yukon and Venetie, they would know the king salmon were running, and in Arctic Village, it meant the whitefish were running, or the pike. This goes back to a Gwich'in legend. Kathy Tritt explains, "Long ago, raven told the Gwich'in people, 'I'll be back when cotton balls are in the air. I will bring Big Fish.' This is how the Elders knew when the big fish were coming in all the Gwich'in villages."

Mosquitoes

Traditional Chief Trimble Gilbert says he heard a Gwich'in Elder in Canada once say, "The mosquitoes are going to be gone tomorrow" and they were gone. He predicted it by the feel of the air, Trimble says. "When mosquitoes go, birds leave right away, too. The birds eat mosquitoes." When asked about pre-contact repellent, he says mosquitos never use to be a problem long ago.

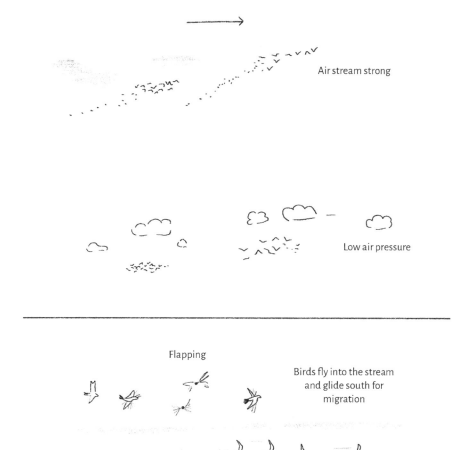

Figure 23. Illustration by Matt Gilbert based on Robert Sam's statement (July 2020), redrawn by Lulu Kachele

The River in the Sky and Aerodynamics of Birds

The Gwich'in have knowledge of birds and airstreams high in the skies as well. Robert Sam is a lifelong Gwich'in hunter who lives in Arctic Village. He has had thoughts on bird migration south during fall migration. He says there is a strong airstream high up in the skies and the birds wait for it to get strong, so they can jump in it and glide south. "They don't flap their wings when they migrate, because they would get tired in no time," he explains. Robert continues,

The small birds, *Glak tsoo* we call them. In the fall during their southern migration, when the air pressure is lower toward the ground, they know

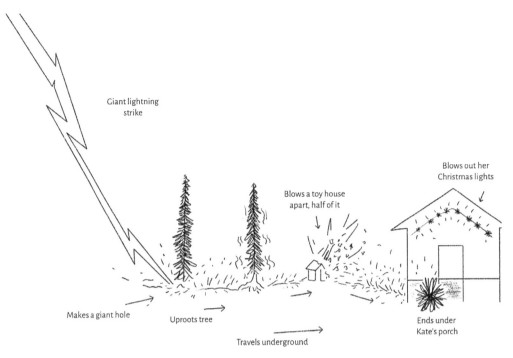

Giant lightning
strike

Blows out her
Christmas lights

Blows a toy house
apart, half of it

Makes a giant hole

Uproots tree

Travels underground

Ends under
Kate's porch

Figure 24. Illustration by Matt Gilbert showing the summer 2019 giant lightning strike near Kate Hollandworth's house, redrawn by Lulu Kachele

the airstream high in the sky is strong, so they fly up and get into it. They then ride the stream south. They don't flap their wings, just glide on the stream.

After hearing of Robert's explanation, I brought it up to the Traditional Chief Trimble Gilbert. He agreed and added, "Yeah, the swan flies south, little birds hang on him, swallows." Trimble also says there are aerodynamic reasons geese fly in V-shapes, too. "The lead one flaps hard and makes it easier for the goose behind him to fly, and they rotate and take turns being in front." The lead goose makes the airstream smooth for the geese behind him to simply glide (see figure 24).

THE GIANT LIGHTNING STRIKE OF 2019

The most talked about climate impact incident was the giant lightning strike of summer 2019. It was during one of the unusually bad thunderstorms Arctic Village has been enduring lately. A giant lightning strike hit the ground outside Kate Hollandsworth's house, creating a crater. The lightning traveled

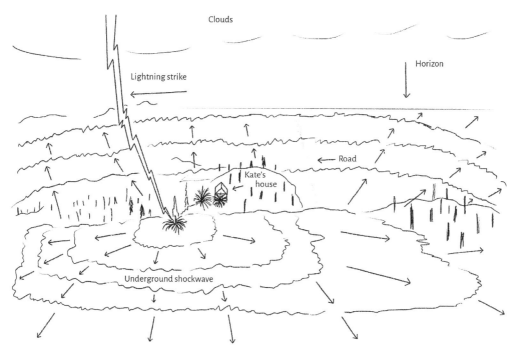

Figure 25. The giant lightning strike of 2019, sending an electrical shockwave out (illustration by Matt Gilbert, redrawn by Lulu Kachele)

underground, uprooting a tree, blowing half of her son's toy house to pieces, and finally ending up under her porch and blowing out her Christmas lights (Kate Hollandsworth smartphone video interview, October 9, 2020).

The giant lightning strike also took out landline phones, and it took a month for the telephone company to restore services.

It was surmised by Kate's aunt Deena Tritt and Kathy Tritt, that the giant strike sent an electrical shockwave underground across the land, killing plants. Deena says after the giant strike, blueberries and cranberries were found dead all over the land. "That was a big shock to us," Deena says. "The next day, no blueberries. The leaves looked old [too], all of it, not just one place, all of it."

She says it impacted the animals too. "And then, we realized there's no more birds singing. It was quiet last year. Even now [summer 2020] it's quiet. No woodpeckers [making noise with their beaks] on the trees."

It's concluded by these Gwich'in women that the birds may have been shocked by the lightning and thunder that summer, which explains the lack of singing.

Kathy Tritt, a Gwich'in woman from Arctic Village who lives in Fairbanks, after hearing Deena's statement about the giant lightning, added, "Yeah, it probably killed the ground squirrels too." Deena, having heard her statement confirms it, "There's nothing up on the mountain."

Audrey Tritt added his own statements about the giant 2019 lightning strike, "I wasn't here to see. That lightning struck a transformer right outside Caitlin's house."

Mike Lee, a Gwich'in hunter of Arctic Village recalls the strike, "Yeah, it blew apart that toy house, right by it, even went into the ground—under the ground—and blew out of the ground." He says he examined the crater it left and described it, "Like somebody dug up the ground with a shovel or something."

Audrey Tritt of Arctic Village and Darrell Tritt of Venetie said that in their entire lives they had never seen lightning behave like that in Arctic Village or Venetie. "We never used to deal with lightning hitting stuff," Audrey said. Darrell Tritt of Venetie added, "They don't come close to the village [Venetie], way out there. It comes close to village now. Hit right across the river. Boom!"

The Gwich'in interviewed believe the worsening thunderstorms and lightning strikes are from rampant technology usage in the villages, satellite TVs, smartphones, and more landline usage from rising populations.

LIGHTNING STRIKES ARE MORE FREQUENT AND DANGEROUS

The Gwich'in say lightning has always been natural and something they saw from a distance. It never struck near the village or inside it like it does so frequently now (Bieniek et al., 2020). It was a visible phenomenon they saw in the distance and nothing more, but now, with climate change, it's literally outside their door and a danger.

Charlie Swaney of Arctic Village says a lightning strike nearly hit his stepdaughter Casey John when she stood on his porch outside his home. "Casey almost got hit by lightning last night!" Charlie said with wide eyes, "It's way more intense than in the past. When the thunder starts roaring, your house shakes."

Swaney says that in 1997 lightning struck the ground by him, but he was shocked a little by it. It was likely a tiny shockwave under the ground, like the giant one Deena described of the 2019 Strike. Charlie says, "It traveled underground, and it shocked me. That's something I never forgot, because of that happening, that's why I really don't like lightning."

Traditional Chief Trimble Gilbert adds, "20 miles north, that's where thunder hit. It hit that rock, that red rock ocher, so all that water is red." This was an event in 2020. It created a landslide that poured the red ocher into the river and turned the river red.

After hearing Deena's explanation of the phenomenon, Audrey claims that another giant strike took out the electricity some years earlier. "Before that, down by that old generator area, the lightning hit too and it [caused a] power outage in all that area. Then the transformer caught on fire."

It is clear from the multiple dramatic accounts of lightning damage and danger, that it has become quite a natural threat to Gwich'in of Arctic Village. I don't personally remember walking home quickly to avoid a coming lightning storm for fear of being struck. Mike Lee said, "You never heard of it damaging somebody's house." Charlie Swaney of Arctic Village says rains are heavier now, too. "It doesn't just rain, it pours."

The lightning is now a threat to Gwich'in people. They believe it's only going to be the first of many to come if climate change progresses.

WEATHER

The weather has been the biggest change between the 2005 and 2020 reports; it has gotten a lot more chaotic and violent (Grabinski, 2020). The weather changes very quickly, which will be and McFarland later in this report. Audrey Tritt of Arctic Village says even the skies above her house are not balanced. She says there are puffy clouds on one side of the sky and flat, misty clouds on the other side, and "that's not normal, it's supposed to be same all around."

Allen Tritt of Arctic Village said, "You listen to the weather report closely and you watch the weather, it's going to be a big difference," demonstrating how the official weather reports can't keep up with the rapid weather. Allen also says that long ago, each village had different weather, but "the weather is the same all over now." On the village level, the weather supposed to be the same, but regionally, it is supposed to vary.

Gideon James mentioned in the 2005 report that the "skies are dirtier" from all the planes in the sky. He says when he was a little boy in the 1940's, the skies were cleaner and the clouds healthier, puffy. He says that nowadays the skies are dirtier, and the clouds are unhealthy, misty, and not puffy anymore. Arctic Village Traditional Chief Trimble Gilbert confirms Gideon's statement on the dirtier skies, "Yeah, Gideon is right. I can barely see the stars anymore."

Deena Tritt confirmed the Elder's statements about the skies, "That's right, we could see all the satellites [a long time ago]. Now we can see only one."

Clouds Dense Like Coastal Clouds and Dirtier Clouds

Trimble Gilbert says, "The clouds look different. They look like Inupiaq clouds, I lived in Kaktovik once long ago, and these are their clouds, not ours." Gilbert says when it gets cloudy, it never goes away. "[In] Kaktovik, clouds cover us a long time and go all the way down to the ground. That's what we have here." Gideon James adds, "The clouds are black because they are soaking up the emissions from the North Slope Fields." It's these heavy, dirty clouds that the Ahtr'ii Vee [tornados] are not able to blow away.

Trimble agrees with Gideon's statement about the North Slope Oil Field emissions polluting the clouds. "That gas was burning over north slope. It makes the clouds funny on the bottom [along with making it blacker]."

It's also these heavy, dark clouds that make the summers darker than they should be. During the interview with Audrey in late July, she said, "It's not supposed to be this dark right now, it's only July." Her house was very dark. She said it's the dark clouds that don't allow the sun to come through most of the summer and did not allow the berries to grow as well.

Winter 2020

The same rate of change has been seen since the 2005 report, with warm winters and hot, dry summers, shifting spring and fall, and causing warmer falls. However, winter 2020 was cold, the Gwich'in stated.

Mike Lee: We had a pretty cold winter this year.
Matt Gilbert: It spiked up?
Mike Lee: Yeah, it was a rough winter.

Franklin Tritt of Arctic Village confirms, "We [hadn't] seen 50 or 55 below for long time, and [in] 2019 and 2020, it went up to it. Too cold, got really cold, it was kinda weird for me."

Snow

The winters have for the most part been normal, but the falls and springs have been shifty (Grabinski and McFarland, 2020). The snowfall in winter is less, Raymond Tritt of Arctic Village said in the 2005 report, and he reported the same thing in the 2020 update. I discovered from the 2020 report that the properties of snow have been long understood by Gwich'in Elders.

Allen Tritt of Arctic Village explains the record-low water levels of spring 2020, from the "dry snow," as his daughter Audrey Tritt termed it. Allen explains:

> The creeks in Arctic Village were low this year. The snow in the mountains is what feeds water to the creeks. We had a very cold spring, so the snow did not get to melt, because there was only 1 or 2 warm days. When summer arrived, it melted everything immediately. Since the snow didn't melt, it was dry, so when it melted, there was no water. (Allen Tritt, interview June 29, 2020)

Mike Lee confirms Allen's statement, "We had a weird thaw this year. a 'dry thaw,' you could say." The dry snow evaporated and spring was "skipped," as summer arrived. The dry snow did not provide water to lakes, creeks, and rivers. The winter jumped to summer and skipped spring.

This may explain why the whitefish were found frail and skinny, and smaller, because they didn't get their normal feed from lakes and creeks due to unusually low waters. Mike says the ice on the lakes was dry too.

However, sometimes there is too much snow. Mike stated that one year there was so much snow that it broke the snow machine frame twice and he had to repair it.

Summers are Cold and Rainy

The summers are cold and rainy in Arctic Village. During the summer of 2020, in which I wrote this report, the sun was hardly ever seen. Deena Tritt said, "It's cold. We didn't even see summer, we just been in fall [all summer]."

RAPIDLY CHANGING WEATHER

The weather change has become a lot faster since 2005. A few years ago, in Venetie, I walked to the Washeteria wearing a T-shirt because it was hot and sunny out. I went there and put in my laundry and waited, and 15 minutes later, I wanted to start home, but it began pouring rain outside. I did not know how I was going to get home. A Native man named Julius was there too, and in the same situation. He came in wearing a T-shirt and was stuck there too.

Audrey Tritt of Arctic Village explains a similar incident this summer when she visited Sarah James on the hill.

> I went there dressed for it being warm, doing little odds and ends, but it was too cold. We even had to build a fire 'cause it was cold in her house.
>
> I had to spend the night there because it was raining really hard and lightning. I wasn't going to walk home with shorts in the rain.

After the rains stopped for a brief period, I saw her sleeping in her summer shorts at Sarah James's when I sought her out for this climate interview. These dramatic stories clearly show how quickly the weather has been shifting, even while trying to write this report.

Matt Gilbert: It's like two winters, huh?
Deena Tritt: Yeah.

LAND

The land itself is said to be unhappy of the changes, according to Kathy Tritt of Venetie and Arctic Village. "The snow used to sparkle, and [it doesn't] anymore. The flowers used to smell, and they don't anymore. It's just dead out there." This was illustrated in a drawing I did earlier in this report of the differences between Gwich'in camping in the last 40 years (figure 21).

The main concerns about the land are forest fires, melting permafrost, and overgrowth. The Gwich'in go into detail on each one.

Permafrost

Gideon James explained it best in the 2005 report when he said, "A long ago, I used to walk on the ground with my grandpa upriver, and it was good ground to walk on, but now, there's holes everywhere, it's because of the permafrost."

Charlie Swaney of Arctic Village said, "The winter two years ago, the ground cracked a lot, and I know it had to do with permafrost thawing out, and then farther down, it's still frozen, the cold air hits it and it cracks. It

Figure 26. This telephone dish used to be visible long ago, but now it's not, July 2020. (Photo by Matt Gilbert)

would even shake our house. Yeah, it's sometimes [in the] middle of the night, we wake up, it's almost like a gun going off in our house." This refers to the ground cracking from melting permafrost.

Overgrowth

The most visible change, other than the more violent weather, since the 2005 Gwich'in Climate Report, is the overgrowth (Grabinski and McFarland, 2020, p. 12). The overgrowth has been dramatic. The Gwich'in agreed with me when I said, "Our villages are turning into jungles."

The Arctic Village Council began a massive brush-cutting campaign in summer 2020 to stem this rapid growth all over the village. Right outside of the house I was staying to write the 2020 update, it was clear in the spring, but when summer arrived, the entire yard was filled with willows. The change was astounding, and I had to cut the willows for weeks.

Charlie Swaney says, "When this willow gets thicker and thicker, are we gonna see the caribou anymore?" Traditional Chief Trimble Gilbert looks for the caribou every fall through his telescope and said, "I can't even look for the caribou anymore, too much brush."

Deena Tritt of Arctic Village said it doesn't take much for the enormous growth, too.

Matt Gilbert: It's starting to look like jungle.

Deena Tritt: It's scary, 'cause in the village, one rain and everything grows, all these different flowers that're coming out. We don't see those purple ones, but they're around.

Forest Fires

Forest fires have become more frequent and regular to Interior Alaska (Grabinski and McFarland, 2020, p. 3). The Gwich'in Elders say forest fires were never a problem, but due to runaway forestation and brush overgrowth, it's a problem. Their lands used to be bare tundra as far as the eye could see, so there was nothing to really burn.

Gideon James of Arctic Village said, "Forest fires cause a lot of ash to fall onto the rivers and when they do, they take oxygen out of the rivers. It kills the fish."

MOUNTAINS

There are small effects seen on mountains from climate change. Robert Frank in the 2005 report, says half of a nearby mountain was collapsing from rapid erosion. A mountain in front of Arctic Village, Kįį vaataiin Lii (meaning "pointed mountain scattered all around it"), the rear end of it seems to be warping and tumbling.

I noticed more and more crevices on the mountains, which usually contain streams. Audrey confirms that the mountains are cracking more. She says it's caused by the warming climate that is heating up the rocks and the permafrost, "sinking land" everywhere. Darrell Tritt of Venetie says it's occurring in Venetie as well. The cracks down the mountain are called *Gwehnaatin*.

RIVERS

The rivers have been changing a lot from climate changes in more ways than one: water level, shifting channels, disappearing channels, and abnormal ice behavior. The different areas of change are explored before, but the river themselves have become wider due to rapid bank erosion. Charlie Swaney says, "The wider the river, the shallower the water."

Trimble Gilbert says they used to go up the East Fork with no problems long ago, but now they can only go to certain places because of the shallow water.

Shifting Channels

Climate change has altered the rivers. The channels have shifted, split, dried out, spread, and lowered and gotten higher in other areas. The river has gotten wider due to bank erosion, and this has lowered the water level and some channels have narrowed. This was confirmed by Gwich'in in Venetie and Arctic Village.

Changing Water Levels

In spring 2020, the river was unusually low. Audrey Tritt of Arctic Village sets fish nets at the creek below Arctic Village, Vashraįi Kǫǫ to catch grayling and white fish. But she said the water was way too low this spring. Allen Tritt gives an explanation: "Early in spring it's supposed to be real high; it's really low."

"Fall Ice Jam"

Ice jams and the loud sounds they make are common to Interior Alaska and are as normal as spruce trees, but with climate change, they are now happening in the fall. Audrey says that Arctic Village had its first fall ice jam in 2019. "Fall-time, the ice jammed, that's not normal either, because when the ice freezes, it stays, and it freezes. Only time it jams up is springtime, 'cause I fish down there, I see it around that corner, it's just like a big ice jam and that's not normal!" It was the first time she saw an ice jam in fall, because they are strictly a springtime event.

LAKES

The lakes have been drying up for decades in Arctic Village, but they seemed to have stabilized since 2005, but in the spring of 2020, low snowmelt has caused even lower waters in the rivers and lakes. The permafrost thawing under the lakes and melting away the ice foundation causes the lake water to drain into the ground. This was illustrated and explained by the Gwich'in Elders in the 2005 report. Darrell Tritt from Venetie believes this is still the case in Venetie too.

Audrey Tritt of Arctic Village believes it is the overgrowth of trees and vegetation that is sucking the water from the lakes too. Mike Lee says that the lakes have been drying out at the same rate as they were in 2005. He says, "There's a couple places upriver that blew out [broke out into the river], and it even changed the [river] channel. It blew out the lake behind First Bend [the first river bend north of Arctic Village]."

ANIMALS

There are many animals that are scarce in the Arctic Village lands now. Many Gwich'in testify that the mountains and the camps are "empty and lonely" compared to long ago. The forests are quiet. Darrell Tritt of Venetie says it's the same in Venetie. "Our forests are quiet now too." Deena Tritt of Arctic Village says that it's because of the loud thunder and big lightening Arctic Village is now having every summer.

The unusually bad weather and scary storms "shocks" birds into silence. As far as the absence of animals, Audrey says she has no explanation. "First time in my life, all these years, I stay out in the woods all day. I never see animals come up to me."

The animals themselves are changing. Audrey says that some animal numbers have increased and become a nuisance, like tree squirrels. "They never used to be like that," she says. They are increasing in number and digging holes in the homes. I have had to trap a few tree squirrels myself that were wreaking havoc on my house's insulation and logs.

Some Gwich'in claim that some animals have grown in size and others have shrunk. Audrey Tritt of Arctic Village says she saw mice nearly 9 inches long on Duchanlee Mountain above Arctic Village. "They look like almost as big as rats." On the other hand, some animals have become smaller. Audrey says whitefish shrank dramatically in size this spring, "Its long and really skinnier . . . it almost looks like grayling." That spring the waters were low.

Allen Tritt of Arctic Village says it was very noisy with all sorts of animal sounds in almost every direction long ago. A person would hear a loon crying on a lake over here, woodpecker knocking on a tree there, and a swallow singing away in a tree here, but now it's quiet everywhere.

"The animals are different, they're not happy no more. You never heard that [bird] singing, not too much anymore." Traditional Chief Trimble Gilbert adds. The Elders also say they don't hear wolves howling too much anymore.

Porcupine Caribou Herd

The Porcupine caribou herd was described in detail in the 2005 report, including the migration, the downsized migration route from human activity and climate change, and many other things. The Gwich'in believed the herd was resilient against climate change and, fortunately, did not see many destructive changes. In the 2020 update, they still did not see many destructive changes to the herd.

The herd has been seen around the village a lot lately, especially in the spring. Traditional Chief Trimble Gilbert explains, "Too many wolves [are] back, so they [caribou] get close to the village, feeding on the lakes and shoveled snow, more lichen around here too." Trimble is concerned about the rapid overgrowth affecting the herd. "That tree is growing fast around here . . . it's kind of a barrier to caribou."

However, there are a few accounts that claim the herd has gotten skinnier. The late Timothy Sam said the caribou weight loss was because there is less snow, less food, and the herd moved more to look for food and perhaps run from predators. Franklin Tritt of Arctic Village says, "Bull caribou [were] fat, went from 3 inches thick on the back to 1 inch thick now."

Charlie Swaney from Arctic Village, who hunts the caribou every year, says the traditional single route into Arctic Village has disassembled. "It's not just one direction like before. They're showing up from the south, showing up from the north, and from the east."

Moose

There have been more moose seen by Gwich'in and they have been skinnier. Charlie Swaney says, "[In] the last 3 years I'd never seen so many moose here, [more] than ever before." A known moose hunter of Arctic Village, Mike Lee says he's seen more moose too.

THE ANIMALS THAT RETURNED IN 2020

Many animals that have become scarce, and which many Elders thought were extinct, did return to Arctic Village in summer 2020. There may have been more, but these were seen:

Snipe/Yellowtail (Dil')
Porcupine
Bank swallows
Muskrats

Animals Go Where it's Clean

In the Roundtable Climate Talk with Audrey Tritt from Arctic Village and Darrell Tritt from Venetie, they said the animals are returning, because "they go to where it's clean." The Gwich'in have stewarded the land so well that they returned, because likely they're finding more and more lands inhabitable everywhere else in the world. Audrey adds, "They go to where it's clean water too." Animals want to live with Native people, because they take care of the land.

ANIMALS THAT ARE SCARCE

I drove to the Duchanlee Mountain this spring to hunt ptarmigan, and I looked around the timberline and saw nothing. I told Raymond Tritt of Arctic Village that I did not see any animals, and he confirmed it. "Yeah, you don't see them anymore. Just probably, I could see tracks around glaciers, yeah about that. Not that many." I asked him if you even find them anymore. Raymond replied, "Yeah but you might have to go real far though."
These are animals the Elders of the report saw less and less.

Ptarmigan
Snipe/Yellowtail
Porcupine
Lynx

FISH

Fish have been impacted by climate change. The Gwich'in gave various accounts of abnormalities in fish and hardships of fishing they never had before. A Gwich'in said, "I used to catch fish all the time long ago, but these days, I fish all day and I'm lucky if I get two." The scarcity of fish has been a grave concern among Gwich'in. Audrey Tritt of Arctic Village said of spring 2020, "No grayling where we usually fish, there was nothing. We only barely caught one or two grayling and then the ice ruined [went out]."

Raymond Tritt of Arctic Village confirms, "Long ago, in the morning, you could catch 30 graylings in one place, but it's not like that anymore."

Another strange trend is that predominantly whitefish were caught this spring. Usually, it's a mix of pike, grayling, and lush, but it was just whitefish this spring. "Month and a half, I had a fish net in, I been catching 40 whitefish a day." Audrey says she also caught an unusually large lush. "That lush, I swear it was as big as a salmon, it couldn't even go in my net."

DUCKS

Duck hunting has always been a huge part of Gwich'in culture. The topic of waterfowl was heavily broached in the first section, but there have been updates. Keith James says he hardly sees any ducks in Fort Yukon: "In the fall-time, you see a *lot* of geese, not no more. We never see swans around here [too]. Even black ducks, we hardly see black ducks in springtime."

Although Arctic Village lies mostly in the mountains, the spring duck hunts are a huge event. Mike Lee is one of many Gwich'in duck hunters in Arctic Village. "Yeah, I noticed this year, I didn't see much wigeon, there's usually quite an abundance of them, but this year I see only a few pairs."

Allen Tritt does regular drives down to the airport lakes with his ATV and looks for ducks. "I drive down to airport, look at ducks, and [there are] no ducks, there's not even little ones. Two years ago, there were two families [of] young ducks swimming around the lake, but now, not even nothing."

Allen also says that long ago he would hear the loud splashing sound of ducks landing on lakes, but rarely hears it now. The geese do not fly in giant V shapes anymore either, because "[there are] not enough flying around," he says.

Darrell Tritt mentioned that in Venetie, the skies use to be covered with flocks of ducks but he says now they are lucky to see a few flying by here and there. The ACIA report states: "Changes in water regimes are likely to dramatically alter the quantity and quality of aquatic and riparian habitat. . . . Aquatic mammals and waterfowl are highly dependent on the availability and quality of aquatic habitats for successful breeding and, in the case of waterfowl, nesting. Northern species will possibly have diminished reproductive success as suitable habitat either shifts northward or declines in availability and access" (AMAP, 2005, p. 418).

BIRDS

Birds were covered a lot in the 2005 section, but in the 2020 update, the Gwich'in had a lot to say about birds again. They were gravely concerned about all sorts of things they saw with regard to birds: the low numbers to the complete absence of some birds, the migration patterns, new invasive birds, and possible depleted food sources.

Deena Tritt of Arctic Village believes some birds are starving, because they're not finding food on the land. "They knock on our window like they're hungry, so I get oatmeal and dump it all around," she says.

She says there are a lot of birds she doesn't see anymore, but she did not specify which ones. Franklin Tritt of Arctic Village says he hardly sees swallows anymore. "There used to be a lot of them, now [they're] not around anymore. The Gwich'in all agree that there are no flocks of birds anymore either, only single birds or pairs flying over." Trimble Gilbert adds that "the brown-headed swallows are not around [bank swallows are back], brown-headed ones, I don't see them." I made a list below based on the observations.

Keith James says they see little to no swallows in Fort Yukon anymore. "Going down Yukon River, you can't even see the sky . . . so many of them. They sat on the power lines; two whole wires, nothing but swallows. You don't see that no more."

Seagulls

In 2005, the Gwich'in see no seagulls sitting on the sandbars on the shores across from Arctic Village, and Darrell Tritt said they don't see them sitting on sandbars in Venetie anymore either. They are seen flying occasionally, but do not sit on sandbars anymore.

Ptarmigan

As stated previously, there has been a scarcity of ptarmigan. I could not find any when I went hunting for them one spring. Trimble Gilbert says,

"There's nothing [in the] last 2 years. I remember when I was a kid there was thousands of them taking off. It's just like an airplane and sounds like an airplane, so many of them." But he says they are no more.

Dried-out Lakes

The Gwich'in interviewed in the 2005 Climate Impact Report gave a lot of attention to dried-out lakes. They were very concerned about it, and they have even drawn diagrams to illustrate the many effects on wildlife that occurs when a lake dries out. Flying from Arctic Village to Fort Yukon, one can see the sheer number of lakes that have dried out.

NEW AND INVASIVE BIRDS

There have been new birds seen by Gwich'in. I have seen a strange yellow bird behind the Arctic Village church. I saw the bird before in Arctic Village and tried to take a photo, but it was hidden in the high branches and soon flew away. Deena Tritt saw another new bird that looked like a "purple robin," whereas our robins are normally red. "It was purple, blue, gray, but I think they're a robin," she said.

She had a pet bird that kept a nest under the eaves of her porch.

I got a bird nest up there, that bird never came back yet. Maybe they never flew. He never made it up here [to the arctic], 'cause of the bad weather down there [that] they're flying from. See his bird nest up there on my porch? Every year he comes back, and he goes in there. He never made it back this year.

Charlie Swaney says, "In March we were breaking a snow trail for wood up to Tsivii Tit [Third Tower] in the winter, when we saw a strange bird that flew off right in the middle of nowhere. It seemed like it was a bird that's only here in the summertime, 'cause we'd never seen it before."

BERRIES

The Gwich'in gatherers and berry-pickers have seen drastic changes in berries and this was covered heavily in the 2005 section. The accounts of berry scarcity and fewer clusters were common in the 2005 report, but there are new accounts. Raymond Tritt of Arctic Village says he still doesn't see salmon berries on the mountain as often as he used to. Keith James says they are having a hard time finding berries in Fort Yukon as well.

Deena Tritt is one of the main berry-pickers in Arctic Village, "Some berries are small, some of them are big, [it] depends on where the sunshine hits, but there's hardly any sunshine. Whatever is out there, they're small, but [we're] still picking them." She also says the cranberries are hard, and "it wasn't like that before." Deena said the same thing in the 2005 report; the cranberries were so hard that she had to boil them to eat them. These were new accounts in addition to her old ones.

MANAGEMENT IDEAS

The 2005 section had a section on management ideas from Gwich'in People themselves and for Gwich'in to have more inclusion and partnerships with land management. Brush-cutting was mentioned as an example of Native management. Brush-cutting was common in the old days in Arctic Village and Venetie. The Gwich'in wanted the assistance of the US Fish and Wildlife Service to reinvigorate this program. There were requests made in Arctic Village and Venetie.

Deena Tritt of Arctic Village said she wanted scientists to come up and study the plants, to "see if they are dying, or are they ok?" She wants to know why some are turning red and if new vegetation will bring new bugs too.

The Gwich'in want partnerships to investigate all the climate change effects.

GWICH'IN PREDICTIONS

The Gwich'in Elders had more predictions for the world. One Elder, Gideon James, made a prediction in the 2005 report that came true: the Coronavirus that has wreaked havoc on the world. "Because of weather, contaminants, a lot of different diseases will appear," Gideon said in the 2005 report.

Darrell Tritt of Venetie told of a prophecy by Myra Roberts of Venetie. "She said in the future everyone will have their heads down like this," he said while demonstrating someone looking down and holding something, a smartphone.

After telling of Gideon's prediction of the Coronavirus coming true, Traditional Chief Trimble Gilbert of Arctic Village said, "The next one will be food." Trimble also told of a Gwich'in prophecy that says the ozone Layer (known as Zhee Vee Luu in Gwich'in) will change, and it is changing (AMAP, 2005, p. 152).

THE OTHER GWICH'IN COMMUNITIES

There are five other Gwich'in communities aside from Arctic Village and Venetie: Fort Yukon [the hub town], Chalkyitsik, Beaver, Birch Creek, and Circle. Because of funding restraints and high travel restrictions to these communities due to Covid-19, I was not able to do interviews in these communities for the 2020 updates.

In addition, 90 percent of the Gwich'in Elders interviewed in Fort Yukon for the 2005 report have since passed away, but I was able to speak to Keith James from Fort Yukon and Paul Herbert in Chalkyitsik.

When told about my inability to interview the other Gwich'in Villages, Audrey Tritt of Arctic Village said, "No worries, the other villages are suffering all the same impacts, believe me." I believe she is right. They are probably feeling other effects more acutely, but same general effects include rapidly changing weather, dry lakes, decreased number of animals, skinny game, no birds singing, quiet forests, lowering rivers, changing river channels, warmer winters, shifting spring melts and fall freeze-ups, and overgrowth.

This ends the Arctic Village section.

CONCLUSION

The 2020 update section was very interesting. Most of the observed changes of the 2005 section remained steady the last 15 years, but there were spikes in overgrowth and weather volatility—and even the new phenomenon of destructive weather. There was more Gwich'in knowledge on meteorology and the skies such as lightning and air current behavior, which was very interesting, and there was a lot more new changes and elaborations on the 2005 report.

SUMMARY OF VENETIE CLIMATE IMPACT REPORT 2020

In this 2020 update, I was only able to interview Darrell Tritt of Venetie, because he was living in Arctic Village at the time. I was not able to go to Venetie due to an enormous funding shortage and high travel restrictions from the Coronavirus pandemic.

King Salmon

Venetie Gwich'in were surprised by the edible quality of the king salmon they were getting in 2005. The king salmon migration ended in Venetie, so its meat was traditionally inedible by the time it got there. However, the kings coming to Venetie had been edible. This has been a drastic change to the subsistence life in Venetie, and Darrell says it's still the case, "Yeah, a lot of king." Dog salmon has been a normal catch though, so I'm told. Darrell says they are seeing pike in Venetie too, which had previously never been seen there.

Weather

There are chaotic and violent weather patterns in Venetie as well, and the same strange seasonal changes. In the 2005 Climate Report from Venetie, the Gwich'in stated that the summers are colder and according to Darrell in 2020, they still are. "Winter is getting warmer than summer," Darrell laughs. He says the rapid change in weather is felt in Venetie as well.

Winds

The Elders said in the 2005 report that the winds are different now. "The winds feel different," was their statement. Darrell Tritt agreed with them and adds, "Yeah, [it's] changed, usually we get strong winds down there. Now it doesn't do that no more."

Matt Gilbert: The wind is dying down?
Darrell Tritt: Yeah.

River

The river below Venetie is the Chandalar River. Darrell says the river gets so low in the fall that you can walk across it. "The only thing that raises the water level is rain and snow," he says. Robert Frank of Venetie confirms this. "Even snow melts don't raise the river in the spring anymore, only rain." Darrell agrees with Robert. "Yeah, rain. Even this spring, the snow melted and nothing, the river didn't go up."

Long ago the Chandalar River was huge, with a lot of water, but now there are places you can "run and jump across," Matt laughs, and Darrell confirms, "Yeah!"

The rivers are so low in most Gwich'in villages that there are certain places where the Gwich'in people can no longer go. Darrell says, "Long ago, [we] used to use a prop [lower unit], [but] not anymore."

Lakes

Venetie is a land of lakes and wetlands. Big Lake, located above Venetie, has provided most of its subsistence for the village since time immemorial, but in the 2005 report, Elders claimed the lake had been drying out. Darrell confirms this. "It was drying out on the side, you could even walk out there probably about that far [indicates 6 feet]." On Darrell's measurements, the lake receded 6 feet.

MANAGEMENT

In the 2005 report, Bobby Tritt wanted the US Fish and Wildlife Service to work with Venetie to clear beaver dams from the creeks feeding Big Lake. This never occurred, and Darrell echoed Bobby's concern in the 2005 report. "Take those beaver dams out! More water back! Get fish again!"

Bobby Tritt and Darrell Tritt also advocate for US Fish and Wildlife Service to start paying Gwich'in to do harvest counts to keep track of animal populations.

Erosion

In the 2005 Venetie report, one big topic of discussion was erosion. Erosion was a bad problem in Venetie. Robert Frank says he saw whole mountainsides sliding down by plates and the mountain shrinking because of it. It was likely a mountain called Taih Tr'oo ee Mountain, north of Venetie.

Robert said in the 2005 report that the flood plain that has the Old Village on it, has receded by almost 600 feet. Darrell says this is correct.

Ducks

Ducks are a main subsistence for Venetie hunters, and they say the numbers are low. Tim Thumma has been hunting ducks since he moved to Venetie in 1983, and he said mallards and black ducks have been down in numbers. Darrell Tritt says it's still true in 2020; numbers are still low in most duck populations. They don't see flocks of ducks flying over anymore, only single ducks or a pair, occasionally, but giant flocks are a thing of the past.

Darrell says that long ago one could see huge numbers of black ducks and mallards flying into Venetie constantly, and he says they don't see that anymore. Robert Frank Sr. of Venetie says they changed their route into Venetie as well, and Darrell agrees. "They used to fly over the village from the river and fly to Big Lake. They don't do that no more. They come around, they come in from the back [now], lakeside."

There has been a lot of geese in Venetie in the spring of 2020 though. Previously there had not been many geese, but there was a lot this spring, according to Darrell.

Birds

Swallows are low in numbers and rarely seen in Venetie. Like every other Gwich'in community, Venetie no longer hears birds singing. The yellow-tail snipe (Dil'), with its ascending whistling sounds far up in the sky, has not been heard or seen in Venetie anymore either. It has not been heard in Arctic Village anymore as well, and likely all the other Gwich'in communities. "You sat around Big Lake, you always heard it, but you don't hear it no more," Darrell says.

SUMMARY OF FORT YUKON CLIMATE IMPACT REPORT 2020

In the 2020 update I was able to interview Keith James over the phone in Fort Yukon. I was not able to travel there due to funding shortages and high travel restrictions from the Coronavirus. Below are a set of questions I asked Mr. James, based on the concerns among the Fort Yukon Elders I interviewed in the 2005 report.

Sadly, most of the Fort Yukon Elders interviewed in the 2005 report have passed on. William Flitt and Doris Ward are still living, but my funding and time prevented me from reaching them. But below is my transcribed phone interview with Keith James.

FORT YUKON PHONE INTERVIEW: KEITH JAMES

Regional Gwich'in Climate Impact Report 2020 Update: Fort Yukon
OCTOBER 12, 2020

All but two of the Fort Yukon Elders interviewed for the 2005 Climate Report are deceased. These are questions based on what the Fort Yukon Elders concluded in the 2005 Gwich'in Climate Report. I interviewed Fort Yukon Elder Keith James as a replacement and had him follow up on the 2005 report.

My questions are in italics, with Keith James's answers below them in normal lettering.

Common Effects to Interior Villages: Overgrowth? Too much growth, bushes and trees, rivers are lower? Forests quiet because animals don't make sounds anymore, birds don't sing no more? Lakes are drying up? Waters are low? Winters are warm? Summers are too rainy and stormy? The skies are . . . Does all that sound true for Fort Yukon?

Yeah, that's true.

Most of the time when I was [growing] up in Birch Creek our livelihood was off the land. We [could] practically go anywhere, go into lakes for ducks. Most of the time I see little black birds on the lake, [but] we don't see that no more. Ever since that oil spill in Valdez, we never see that no more. That's the livelihood out of . . .

> 1. *Muskrats and beavers are less? The last 30 years?*
> Yeah, that's still the case. Recently, I went to Birch Creek [via boat], and I camped below a beaver house, and I didn't even see a beaver. It's not the climate change, it's the otters y'know.

Matt Gilbert: Otter is the one that's killing them or what?

Keith James: Yeah, one otter can kill a whole lake.

Matt Gilbert: I wonder what we can do about that, maybe kill that otter?

Keith James: I never did see otters on the river. It's because he kills all the beaver off on the lake and he moves to the river, I think.

2. *What about Salmon? They say first there's king, then silver then dog—first, second, third—and then the Elders in Fort Yukon said the salmon runs were longer in 2005. Is that still true? Are they longer than usual? And they said they're coming early, and they're not getting the amount of salmon they used to get.*

   Yeah, that's true. Most of it is just small, 1 foot [long], some of them. I had a wheel somewhere and I saw it.

3. *Yukon River still low? No flood in the last 25 years?*

   Yeah.

4. *River channel change?*

   Yes, quite a bit. You go down Yukon River, some islands are not even there anymore.

Matt Gilbert: Lots of changes up Yukon too?

Keith James: Yeah, every year. Lots of places I got to, you can't even go to lakes from river, because of beaver dams.

Matt Gilbert: Gwich'in people need to bust those beaver dams out.

Keith James: We used to bust them out, but on the way back, same thing, [they'd] already been rebuilt. I went out two times this fall; I never see nothing [no game].

5. *Changes to moose? Skinnier?*

   Yeah, that's true.

6. *Stanley Jonas said they're harder to find. A long time ago you could find them easy, but now it's hard to find them.*

   Yeah.

7. *Creeks? Little creeks drying up?*

   Yeah.

8. *No birds singing? Geese making no noise when flying in?*

   Yeah. Springtime, I thought I was going to listen to birds, sit outdoors for a while, no! There's lots of changes going on, but . . .

Matt Gilbert: Yeah, lots, too much, too much changes, Keith?

Keith: Yeah.

9. *Elders in 2005 said you can't drink water from river anymore? Still true?*

   Yeah.

10. *Snow melting too fast? In springtime? Still true?*

   Yeah. One night, the wind took care of it.

11. *Elders say trapping is not as good as it was a long time ago? Still true?*
    Yeah, that's true.

12. *Stanley Jonas told me something interesting. We eat lots of white-man food, but we're still hungry. Native food, we eat little bit and you're not hungry. He said a long time ago, one fish wheel can feed five families. Nowadays, you get a small bag of groceries at the store and you're still hungry.*
    Yeah, he's right.

13. *Lifestyle change is Native guys are richer compared to their grandpa and grandma. Their grandparents made less than us, my grandpa made $2 a day, but they had more than us though, even though they made less money.*
    Mm-m. That's because the prices were really down. When I was a kid. If my mother went to store with $50, son of a gun, two toboggan loads [of food].

14. *Harry Thomas said he couldn't even go up Black River for moose hunting because it's really low. He didn't want to ruin his prop.*
    Yeah, it's always been low. Same way with Birch Creek, the [sand] bar is even almost across the river.

    A long time ago, my grandpa had a big barge. They could go up Birch Creek River. Load it down with winter supplies and everybody is on that boat, no problem. They went back to Birch Creek. I even had to turn around a couple days ago. Water was dropping, I couldn't make it up there.

Matt Gilbert: Your boat is smaller than a barge?

Keith James: 24 feet long, 5 feet bottom, 5 feet across. I hit one time, even one blade is off the prop, that's how low it is. It's brand-new prop.

15. *The Elders in the 2005 report, they said everything is early? Break-up? Animal migration, birds flying south? Everything is 2 weeks early.*
    Yeah, that's still true, getting worse. I don't even see swallows. Not as much as a long time ago.

Matt Gilbert: In other Gwich'in villages, they see big flocks of swallows, hundreds of them, they don't see that no more, just a couple here and there. Same thing in Fort Yukon?

Keith James: Yeah. Going down Yukon River, you can't even see the sky with . . . so many of them. They sat on the power lines; two whole wires, nothing but swallows. You don't see that no more.

Matt Gilbert: Venetie too, I interviewed Darrell Tritt. He said it was the same with ducks. They used to see hundreds of ducks, big flocks flying over Venetie, just a couple they see here and there now. Same thing in Fort Yukon?

Keith James: Uh-huh. Just like in the fall-time, you see a *lot* of geese, not no more. We never see swans around for . . . we never see swans around here. Even black ducks, we hardly see black ducks in springtime.

16. *Rainy and cloudy all summer in Arctic Village. Same there too?*
    Yeah, same here too.

Matt Gilbert: My aunt Deena says there's not enough sunshine for the berries to grow. Is it the same there?

Keith James: Yeah. My nephew Brian took his aunt Nancy to pick berries, but they came back right away. I don't know if someone [had] been there before.

17. *Weather changing fast? It changes in 15 minutes, same there too?*
    Uh-huh.
18. *Harry Thomas said July is cold, you can see your breath in July. Still true?*
    Yeah, it's true.

Keith's own testimony on the changing climate and changing world:

Frank Ginnis, an old man, how many years ago, probably in the 1980s, he said, "You can just tell, it's changing, even the sun is changing," he said from his days.

Abel Tritt told me, "In the last days, everything is going to change according to the Bible. It says in the Bible."

Like when I was a kid, I thought my mother was a little nuts when she was telling me about today, what's going to be going on. I thought she was talking out of herself, making up stories, but to tell you the God's truth, I see it today. What she's talking about.

"People are just going to be crazy," I told her, "How in the world people just going to be crazy?" I asked her. It's going on uptown right now. My days there wasn't any drugs that's unknown. [Drugs were] not around like they are today.

[My mother] said a pound of tea is going to be $4, and in them days, son of a gun, in them days, $4 was a lot! She told me lots of things, but it's hard to explain it to people today.

Me and Clarence Alexander was working for the school district. I was working for the school district myself in Birch Creek. And we were talking, me and Clarence, talking about the days, how it's going to turn out to be? Abel Tritt came around and heard us talking. He got to talking.

My niece Faith Williams, her son was knee-high, just small kid. He told us, "When I was a kid like that, Elders were talking. When time is going really good, real good, and [all] of a sudden it's going to get [to be] hard times." Myra Roberts, the late matriarch of Venetie, had a similar prediction. I always have that in mind. I try to translate this into a new generation around here, but they don't seem to believe it. They think things . . . going on today will be going on like that every day. You could be wheeling around a wheelbarrow full of money, but [there's] nothing to buy. Nothing to buy, that's what it's going to come down to, he said. I believe that. I see it in the Bible, Matthew, chapter 24. It's inside there. What's going to be going on. I'm not a preacher, but I listen when my mother is telling [me] something.

Matt Gilbert: Mahsi cho, people need to hear this.

Keith James: This is not nonsense. I tell kids, they have more than me. You're lucky. How many times I went to school without eating. I tell kids they should be proud of who they are and the times they're living in. [There was] no welfare, no food stamps in my days. When my dad moved us to Birch Creek, we had nothing, we lived off the land, that's all. My grandpa Birch Creek Jimmie is the one who raised me up, part of my life.

BIBLIOGRAPHY

Bieniek, P. A., Bhatt, U. S., York, A., Walsh, J. E., Lader, R., Strader, H., Ziel, R., Jandt, R. R., and Thoman, R.L. (2020). Lightning variability in dynamically downscaled simulations of Alaska's present and future summer climate. *Journal of Applied Meteorology and Climatology*, 59(6), 1139–1152. https://doi.org/10.1175/JAMC-D-19-0209.1.

EPA (Environmental Protection Agency), Climate Change Adaptation Resource Center. (2021 May 26). Climate Adaptation and Erosion and Sedimentation. EPA. Climate Adaptation and Erosion & Sedimentation | US EPA.

ARCTIC VILLAGE TRANSCRIPTS
OF CLIMATE INTERVIEWS

Recorded by Matt Gilbert

Transcribed by Pam Miller

Allen Tritt 7-23-2020 Part1.mp3

[00:00:00] **Matt Gilbert:** July 23, Thursday, 2020. Allen Tritt, Part 1 recording.

[00:00:11] **Allen Tritt:** [Gwich'in *Tee chit*?] It's worse, just flying around everything, whole village, . . . all the time, all the time, everywhere, sometimes out in the . . . they just fly, all the leaves up there, grass and everything. But now there is, sometimes it's there, sometimes it's not. But nowadays we don't see too much. Because you got stuck in the house, watching TV, listening to [the] phone, and busy with phones like that. So that's why you guys didn't see nothing sounds like.

[00:00:58] **Matt Gilbert:** Ohhh.

[00:00:59] **Allen Tritt:** That's right now, even right now, watch outside, that's why I'm sitting outside all the time. That's what's going on. See what the weather looks like. [The] other day, yesterday, before you see that big red thing around the sun, you see it? That kind of stuff we watch, sometimes, we see it. So, you always have to look, see what's going on. And nowadays it's easy, in the news, anywhere in the world [that] you can see news, right in the TV, right and left, you can make a phone call and find out, you can make a phone call and find out what's going on here and there. And you, six o'clock news you can see everything [that's] going on, like that nowadays. But it's like blind, just don't know what's going on, don't know what happened.

[00:02:04] **Matt Gilbert:** Hum.

[00:02:05] **Allen Tritt:** That time we got flu, people got sick, we didn't know what was going on, meningitis, sometimes that meningitis [is] bad, people get [it] in the neck, I mean in the back, and go in the frenzy, got no way to survive. Not even more medicine, nothing. Some people . . . they survive.

[00:02:32] **Matt Gilbert:** Um hum.

[00:02:34] **Allen Tritt:** Some people know that is sickness and everything.

[00:02:39] **Matt Gilbert:** Audrey said the clouds nowadays—

[00:02:42] **Allen Tritt:** Listen.

[00:02:43] **Matt Gilbert:** OK.

[00:02:44] **Allen Tritt:** Like you said, all day, you said come on [Gwich'in ——] like this, already you nothing, but the people don't give [?] themself, they got people there. You know what I mean? They got biologists, but you know, traditional doctors, all that we got, that's why people know what's going on, what's going to be weather, they know who they're gonna ask to, [this] person's good [at] weather, this guy's good [at] hunting, and stuff like that. That's how they survive, until today, it's way different.

[00:03:23] **Allen Tritt:** [*Someone enters house*]. They you are!

[End]

Allen Tritt 7-23-2020 Part2.mp3

[00:00:00] **Allen Tritt:** Fifty years ago, when I was 16, 17 [*muffled sound*], 5 years ago people said it's gonna happen, weather's gonna change, it's gonna change, its gonna, like the way we think, even today, you listen to weather reports closely, and you watch the weather, it's gonna make a lot of difference.

[00:00:32] **Allen Tritt:** When we were . . . kids too, you know, Fort Yukon here, Venetie here, Arctic Village here, when the weather is cold, 60 below, one time Fort Yukon's warm and sometimes 60 below, and Fort Yukon, this place is hot, warm, this place is warm, sometimes this place [is] cold.

[00:00:55] **Allen Tritt:** You know what nowadays, today, the weather [is] all the same all over. The same weather, the weather the same. Now it's just like, um, you talk about tornados. You watch around, sometimes you see it, I don't know how many years ago, we sitting right here, people run out to watch the thing that's a [Gwich'in *dunlay*?].

[00:01:22] **Matt Gilbert:** Um hum.

[00:01:23] **Allen Tritt:** It went to the ground like this, went up in the air, and they're moving down, they're watching it, it's kind of small though, maybe this, smaller than this but goes up in the air. Everybody had, that time I'm fairly young, and kids, I don't even pay attention, pretty soon they told me what it looked like. But now if you see something you gonna take a picture with, so you know what to talk about. But it's coming out like that too 'round here, little by little, that tornado, what they call tornado.

[00:02:02] **Allen Tritt:** [Gwich'in ——].

[00:02:02] **Allen Tritt:** It's all over like this, anywhere. One Elder told me when the planes fly, you see the planes fly by now like this early spring, just about snow went out, when the plane's flying, you see the plane like this, like this, that wind ahead, that [Gwich'in —— (beheaded?)].

[00:02:30] **Matt Gilbert:** Ah . . . turbulence, yeah. [*Some cross talk follows*].

[00:02:33] **Allen Tritt:** [Gwich'in ——]. You can hear it, pop! [*makes sound like rifle shot*], when the plane was like this, yeah. You know, the one when the wind just goes like this, like this [*gestures*], but when it's, when flying smooth, sometimes the head [is] like this, that tornado headed, you know.

[00:02:53] **Allen Tritt:** [Gwich'in *T'sai vee*?] You see it every once in a while, like you said, you know, we do the same way, we run into it, we just play around with it, sometimes get a lot of paper up in the air.

[00:03:07] **Matt Gilbert:** Uh huh.

[00:03:09] **Allen Tritt:** Is that the end? But we have to whistle at it, to stop it. You got to whistle and stop it.

[00:03:20] **Matt Gilbert:** Some people tell me that wind is different now too, wind, it's different, they said, it feels different, like a long time ago it's different, that wind, that's what they told me.

[00:03:34] **Allen Tritt:** Um hum, that's right, it's right, you're right, that's the way it is. But I don't know, the wind is . . . really good. What's the next one?

[00:03:49] **Matt Gilbert:** Animals, you said that you don't see grouse no more, there's noise in the woods when you were small, you're right, a lot of people tell me, when you go out into the woods now it's just quiet, it's just lonely, you know.

[00:04:10] **Allen Tritt:** Yes, like your grandpa said you know up here in that pond they can just [be] singing away, wawawa, hollars away, and here and there that loon, just hollering away [*makes descending sound*]. Whoaaaaaaaaaaaaaa.
Sometimes they said [*makes loud sound*] [moose?]. ErahErah?

[00:04:33] **Matt Gilbert:** [*Laughs*].

[00:04:33] **Allen Tritt:** And that [Gwich'in *chegutti* or *ch'igiilii* (they sing?)]. [*Makes knocking sound on table*]. Knock, knock, knock, knock, knock, knock . . . knock, knock, knock, knock, ever hear that?

[00:04:37] **Matt Gilbert:** Yeah.

[00:04:38] **Allen Tritt:** Like that, in early spring, too, springtime, [Gwich'in *ah tal*?] we call it, [*ah tal*], it's down there, he's just singing away early in the morning, it's sitting in the top, some of them sitting in that [Gwich'in *nan cha*], dancing away.

[00:04:58] **Matt Gilbert:** Huh.

[00:04:58] **Allen Tritt:** That's why the Canadian people, that's why they're making noise like [Gwich'in *ah tal*?] when they do that, [*makes sound*] Huuv, huuv, huuv, huuv, that's what they say, huuv, huuv, huuv, huuv, you see when you hear them, when somebody [Gwich'in ——].

[00:05:15] **Matt Gilbert:** Yeah.

[00:05:15] **Allen Tritt:** That's why they like this.

[00:05:17] **Matt Gilbert:** Huh [*laughs*].

[00:05:19] **Allen Tritt:** He dance good but [Gwich'in *chiitsal/tsiitsal/dziitsal* (bird)], really.

[00:05:22] **Matt Gilbert:** Wow.

[00:05:23] **Allen Tritt:** That's what they sound like, that's why.

[00:05:25] **Matt Gilbert:** It's a bird, huh? Bird?

[00:05:26] **Allen Tritt:** Um uh. Really, that's the way they dance good when they dance a jig, like they dance good too, sometimes I watch them dancing away, like a jig, just like this [*moves feet on floor like jig*] in a way, beautiful.

[00:05:48] **Matt Gilbert:** That snipe, too, you don't hear that no more, it's way up there [*whistles ascending*], woo woowoowoowoowoowoowoo, woo woowoowoowoowoowoo.

[00:06:00] **Allen Tritt:** So that . . . [*cross talk for a while*].

[00:06:01] **Matt Gilbert:** Yeah, that's the way it sounds, huh? [*Bird sound*] woo woowoowoowoowoowoowoo.

[00:06:03] **Allen Tritt:** [*Bird sound*] woawoawoawoawoawoa.

[00:06:04] **Matt Gilbert:** Yeah.

[00:06:06] **Allen Tritt:** Even [Gwich'in *davil*?], that [*bird sound*], daadaadaadaaa. We don't hear that no more. When the springtime, when springtime comes, it gets warmed up, those animals come around, all kinds of noise. Sometimes you hear the ducks coming down, [*makes sound, descending*] whoooooooshooo, they land on the lake.

[00:06:31] **Matt Gilbert:** Huh.

[00:06:31] **Allen Tritt:** They make good noises like [Gwich'in *zhut*?].

[00:06:34] **Matt Gilbert:** Huh, just like an airplane landing, huh?

[00:06:36] **Allen Tritt:** Yeah, coming down, you can hear them, [*makes sound, descending*] ooooooooooooooooaaa.

[00:06:42] **Matt Gilbert:** Wow . . . Even those little swallows don't sing no more, huh? [*Starts bird sound*].

[00:06:51] **Allen Tritt:** No, there's some, but their population, not that many make noise.

[00:06:55] **Matt Gilbert:** Them, they sound like this [*bird song sound*], da da dee dd dd? Something like that? Da da dee da da?

[00:07:00] **Allen Tritt:** Yeah.

[00:07:02] **Matt Gilbert:** Yeah, they sound like that, yeah, I don't hear that no more [either].

[00:07:05] **Allen Tritt:** No . . . When the [Gwich'in *zhet*?], they're really noisy, just noisy all over. But my mom told me when they [were kids] they couldn't even hear nothing, the animals [were] hollering so bad, hollering away, sounds good, they said. The loons, ducks like that made noise all the time.

[00:07:30] **Matt Gilbert:** Next question is ducks, same thing [as] what you're saying, you said a long time ago they made big Vs up there, way up there, you don't see that no more, remember you said that?

[00:07:43] **Allen Tritt:** That's the geese, geese come out from the south, then they went north, stayed up there for summer to have eggs, little ones, that's what they're doing.

[00:07:59] **Matt Gilbert:** But you don't see them in a big V anymore, huh?

[00:08:02] **Allen Tritt:** They do that when not enough flying around. But in my day, they just keep going up like that, we kind of just lay . . . down on the ground and watch them go by. Vs, just like that, and make noise, way up there they keep going, keep going, we watch them, make noises and hear them.

[00:08:27] **Matt Gilbert:** But now you don't see that many?

[00:08:32] **Allen Tritt:** No, not that many.

[00:08:37] **Matt Gilbert:** Last question. Caribou. You said you used to know where they're at and where they go, but not no more. But it sounds like they are coming around more now though?

[00:08:50] **Allen Tritt:** Yeah, yeah, [the] reason, it's sad, because that willow grows and [they] can't see nothing, so that's why they can't even go across here. [Gwich'in ——], that's how the caribou went across here, even right by that [Gwich'in *ginzaa*?] down there. You went across the river and get shooting, we don't even have to go out, we just stay here and wait for them, shoot them away. We should take a picture of it, it's like trails, all over, just like lines all over here, all over up that way, trail, that thick in the ground. When I first came in and I asked the people here, where's the trail go to, they said, down in the flats, we know when the trail it goes to certain places, [*inaudible*] caribou [?] [*laughs*]. Yeah, they went across the river when [we] got no willows, nothing. That's why they fed the animals with [a] pack when they go through here, they run like heck in the summertime and they go across.

[00:10:11]   **Matt Gilbert:** Someone said that Elders used to cut the brush when it grew on the caribou trail a long time ago, is that true?

[00:10:19]   **Allen Tritt:** I—that I don't know, we can't cut the trail. That trail [was] already there. There's [the] same trail, but you could see that, when I was a kid, you could see the trail, [in] summertime it was like rope, like this [*points it out*], across the river, all up that way, trail, trail.

[00:10:48]   **Matt Gilbert:** Alright, that's it, I don't have anything else.

[00:10:53]   **Allen Tritt:** Yeah. In my days it's, uh, nowadays we don't know, like when we were the kids, when we were . . . kids, heck [Gwich'in ——], we were hungry all the time, next meal we got to go out [and] shoot something before we could cook it to fire, then we ate it, sometimes no salt, sometimes no sugar. No airplanes, see how far to Fort Yukon, nothing, eat meat and juice, that's what we do.

[00:11:33]   **Matt Gilbert:** Yeah, you told me that [in the] last interview about how they were a long time ago, yeah, when you go out and you shoot something and then build a fire to cook it, that takes all day, huh?

[00:11:47]   **Allen Tritt:** Yah.

[00:11:48]   **Matt Gilbert:** [*Laughs*].

[00:11:49]   **Allen Tritt:** It's not funny. It's serious.

[00:11:50]   **Matt Gilbert:** No, no, I'm laughing because you said that's—

[00:11:52]   **Allen Tritt:** That's where we build up from, we got to take it real serious, what happened. Like I told you, it's like you said, [I] don't know what's going on out there, but you don't go out. Me, every time I drive down to [the] airport [to] look at ducks and [there's] no ducks, there's not even little ones, 2 years ago there were two families [with] young ducks swimming around the lake, but now, [there's] not even nothing.

[00:12:28]   **Matt Gilbert:** No, the reason I laugh is because you told me, no, you told me kids these days just throw something in the microwave [for] 5 minutes and they got something to eat.

[00:12:37]   **Matt Gilbert:** It's like you said, maybe get one or two together, sometimes you got to keep doing that every year, you get in the canoe and go up the lake, drag the canoe, to [the] lake and . . . look around, see what's happening, see what you see. Then next year if you're gonna study like this, go around, go through that thing again and see what you see. [Gwich'in ——].

Like that Valdez oil spill, since that gets worse, a lot died, a lot of things died down, lots [?]. Never getting many ducks, many any animals they kill down there. Fires, you know all the fires down in the states for 3, 4 years ago. [*Door knock, opens the door*].

[End]

Audrey Tritt 6-21-2020.mp3 (Part 1)

[00:00:00] **Matt Gilbert:** June 21, 2020. Audrey Tritt with the climate survey 15 years later.

They want, so the environmental group, they like what you guys said 15 years ago, and they really liked it and they want, like, update, you know?

[00:00:17] **Audrey Tritt:** Okay.

[00:00:17] **Matt Gilbert:** So, I read the transcripts of your interview, I read it, and you answered a lotta stuff, and I don't think a lot of things have changed that much, um, only two things that hunters and Elders see that changed lots is, um, overgrowth . . .

[00:00:34] **Audrey Tritt:** Yeah.

[00:00:36] **Matt Gilbert:** Fifteen years, lots of growth, they said, and the weather is getting crazier, they said, that's only two things, but—

[00:00:41] **Audrey Tritt:** Um, with my understanding I noticed that the water rises fast and also drops fast, and there's a lot of [Gwich'in (*aht toe*) *t'aa*] that birch wood, we never used to have that, we're starting to get those too. I noticed it, you know, when you drive on the airstrip on this side, those trees, those branches, those never used to be around here. Just by Christian Village on down, we never—

[00:01:14] **Matt Gilbert:** Birch, cottonwood, ok [*cross talk*].

[00:01:16] **Audrey Tritt:** [Gwich'in (*aht toe*) *t'aa*], cottonwood, we never had cottonwood around here before. And we used to go a couple miles down to get wood, and now we can just go right on the timberline to get wood, we used to go a long ways to haul wood. And there's a lot of water change, I noticed that, and um—

[00:01:44] **Matt Gilbert:** Ah, the last time, in 2005, you told me that there's no more freeze-up before it snows.

[00:01:53] **Audrey Tritt:** Yeah.

[00:01:53] **Matt Gilbert:** Is that still the same?

[00:01:54] **Audrey Tritt:** Yeah.

[00:01:56] **Matt Gilbert:** Okay.

[00:01:56] **Audrey Tritt:** And it's a late breakup, a weird breakup, a lot of snow, end of May.

[00:02:03] **Matt Gilbert:** Uh huh.

[00:02:04] **Audrey Tritt:** May, usually we have no snow by May, first week of June and the ice goes out first week of May, but it went out in middle of May [this year].

[00:02:19] **Matt Gilbert:** That's what you said here, too, rivers go out fast, so same thing, nothing changed, 15 years.

[00:02:26] **Audrey Tritt:** It's shallow.

[00:02:27] **Matt Gilbert:** Shallow?

[00:02:28] **Audrey Tritt:** Really shallow.

[00:02:30] **Matt Gilbert:** So, [in the] last 15 years it got shallower?

[00:02:32] **Audrey Tritt:** Yeah.

[00:02:32] **Matt Gilbert:** Okay.

[00:02:33] **Audrey Tritt:** It really gets shallow.

[00:02:35] **Matt Gilbert:** Okay. Tell me what you're saying about fish, whitefish, the quality of meat, you said something about [that] it's skinnier, remember I saw you down there, you said it's skinnier.

[00:02:47] **Audrey Tritt:** Yeah, the fish, it's—

[00:02:47] **Matt Gilbert:** Smaller?

[00:02:47] **Audrey Tritt:** It's the, it's long, and it's really skinnier.

[00:02:53] **Matt Gilbert:** Yeah.

[00:02:55] **Audrey Tritt:** For the—

[00:02:58] **Matt Gilbert:** It almost looks like graylings [*some cross talk*].

[00:02:58] **Audrey Tritt:** Yeah, the whitefish, it almost even looks like graylings, as skinny as graylings because graylings are water fish, whitefish is lake fish, it's really rich. That's the difference I've seen in that, and this spring I caught more whitefish than any other fish, I didn't even catch that much pike, or grayling. Lush, just one lush, one sucker. Usually I'll get it all mixed, this time it's just all rich whitefish.

[00:03:37]   **Matt Gilbert:** Wow. So, how long do you keep your net in for? They'll probably want to know.

[00:03:42]   **Audrey Tritt:** Month and a half I had my fish net in, I been catching 40 whitefish a day.

[00:03:49]   **Matt Gilbert:** Wow.

[00:03:50]   **Audrey Tritt:** Yeah, that's how much I was catching, total, a day.

[00:03:53]   **Matt Gilbert:** What about ice fishing, anything change with that, or still the same?

[00:03:57]   **Audrey Tritt:** Um, no grayling, where we usually fish there was nothing. We only barely caught one or two graylings in the ice ruin, we can't fish on it.

[00:04:09]   **Matt Gilbert:** Pen [*inaudible*] said when you tried to drill a hole down there, water just gushed up.

[00:04:15]   **Audrey Tritt:** Yeah.

[00:04:15]   **Matt Gilbert:** And he said it stunk, too [*laughs*], huh?

[00:04:18]   **Audrey Tritt:** Yeah. It was weird, and like in the fall, it freezes. And [in] fall-time the ice jammed down there, that's not normal either, because when the ice freezes, it stays and it freezes. Only time it jams up is when it's springtime, 'cause I fish down there, I see it around that corner, it's just like big ice jams and it's, that's not normal.

[00:04:47]   **Matt Gilbert:** That was in the fall?

[00:04:49]   **Audrey Tritt:** Yeah, fall-time.

[00:04:51]   **Matt Gilbert:** That doesn't sound normal.

[00:04:52]   **Audrey Tritt:** Uh ha, 'cause usually in the fall-time it's just, ice will just freeze and it'll just stay frozen, it won't go up and flow, that's what it's been doing the last couple years, I noticed 'cause I fish down here many years.

[00:05:10]   **Matt Gilbert:** Yeah, [*laughs*]. I know, that's why I waited 2 days to talk to you, because I knew you'd know a lot about the river and creek.

[00:05:17]   **Audrey Tritt:** Yeah.

[00:05:18]   **Matt Gilbert:** You said something about the whitefish being small and, um, remember when I saw you down there and you were saying something about the lake or something, it wasn't supposed to be that low?

[00:05:28]   **Audrey Tritt:** Yeah.

[00:05:28]   **Matt Gilbert:** Real early in spring it's supposed to be real high, [but] it's really low.

[00:05:31] **Audrey Tritt:** You see how the river is right now? That's how it's supposed to look when the ice goes out, it was weird ice going out, the water is really shallow and the ice barely moves. And then, like right now, it looks like it's springtime out there right now, the water. That's what I noticed with it, all raining. And the other thing, I already see that, um, that willows, the cotton that floats, they usually do that in July, [but] it's June. It shouldn't be doing that.

[00:06:08] **Matt Gilbert:** What cotton?

[00:06:10] **Audrey Tritt:** Those, see it, look outside, those little white things floating around.

[00:06:15] **Matt Gilbert:** Yeah, willows.

[00:06:15] **Audrey Tritt:** We know that salmon is running with [the ones] in Fort Yukon, we know it by that cotton floating around, it's supposed to do that in July, not June, that's different.

[00:06:30] **Matt Gilbert:** Yeah, that sounds different. Huh.

[00:06:34] **Audrey Tritt:** 'Cause I'm always outside.

[00:06:38] **Matt Gilbert:** Yeah, this could go on and on, this interview. But [we] got to make it quick, um, try to. Moose, anything different about moose, dinjik, moose. Anything different about moose?

[00:06:50] **Audrey Tritt:** No, it's just skinny. It's really skinny. They say when they get it down by Christian Village area it's really rich, there's a lot of fat on it, [but] when they get it around here, around this area, it's skinny. They even say not to bother with it, that's what those Elders keep saying, they shouldn't get it, it's too skinny.

[00:07:17] **Matt Gilbert:** Plus, traditionally we're not moose people, moose just came in [a] hundred years ago [to] this Arctic Village area. That's what people are telling me.

[00:07:28] **Audrey Tritt:** Well, um, the last 10, 15 years is when we started seeing moose here, when they had that big fire in between Venetie and Arctic. Venetie, we had to make a fire line, the marten and the moose migrated up when that fire was really huge on the reservation. And that's when I noticed, when I was checking [my] fish net at Old John, I [was] just seeing a bunch of marten tracks, lots, just like a herd.

[00:08:00] **Matt Gilbert:** In 2005, they said there were a lot of marten around Arctic Village because of that 2004 fire, pushed them up here, but I guess they went back home now? Huh?

[00:08:08] **Audrey Tritt:** I don't know [*dog barks*]. I really don't know, because they said that the price of the marten went down, so they're not really trapping for it, because I always make trapping bait.

[00:08:26] **Matt Gilbert:** Now, [in] 2005 you said the spring, you said that the woods, they notice the same thing in Huslia too, I went to Orville Huntington's presentation on global warming, same thing in Huslia, the spring is quiet, the forest is quiet.

       [Darrell Tritt enters, dogs moving, barking]

[00:08:43] **Audrey Tritt:** Yeah.

[00:08:44] **Matt Gilbert:** No animals.

[00:08:45] **Audrey Tritt:** Yeah.

[00:08:45] **Matt Gilbert:** No seagulls on the sandbars.

[00:08:48] **Audrey Tritt:** Yeah.

[00:08:48] **Matt Gilbert:** Still true?

[00:08:48] **Audrey Tritt:** Yeah. [There's] hardly any seagulls, but even those little [Gwich'in *Shyahtsoo*] [*swallows*], those little birds, even those, we don't [see] . . . you remember they used to build houses on the side of our roof, they don't even do that no more, we don't even see those birds anymore. Remember we have to knock 'em down because of their bugs, we don't see those no more.

[00:09:20] **Matt Gilbert:** Rain. More rain, less rain, 15 years?

[00:09:23] **Audrey Tritt:** Different, yeah, it's really different climate.

[00:09:27] **Darrell Tritt:** Really different now, huh, different climate, different.

[00:09:31] **Matt Gilbert:** Lotta rain now, last 15 year?

[00:09:34] **Audrey Tritt:** Less.

[00:09:35] **Darrell Tritt:** Less.

[00:09:35] **Matt Gilbert:** Less.

[00:09:36] **Audrey Tritt:** Less rain, the snow is dry, we can't even make snowballs.

[00:09:41] **Matt Gilbert:** Ah, what about, everybody knows all the lakes drying out.

[00:09:48] **Darrell Tritt:** Yeah.

[00:09:48] **Audrey Tritt:** Yeah.

[00:09:50] **Darrell Tritt:** And the permafrost too, thawing out too, making all the land sink in.

[00:09:57] **Matt Gilbert:** Houses, getting harder to jack up more and more, it's just shifting.

[00:09:59] **Audrey Tritt:** Yeah, a lot of shifting.

[00:10:04]   **Matt Gilbert:** So, that dried-out lake since 2005, you think that went up, that dried-out lake, more and more dried out?

[00:10:10]   **Audrey Tritt:** Yeah, it's because of the trees.

[00:10:14]   **Matt Gilbert:** That airplane, I fly over Fort Yukon, geez, every lake is dry.

[00:10:18]   **Darrell Tritt:** Yeah.

[00:10:18]   **Matt Gilbert:** You see that, too, in the airplane?

[00:10:19]   **Darrell Tritt:** Yeah [*cross talk ... unclear*].

[00:10:20]   **Matt Gilbert:** You too, when you go to Fairbanks?

[00:10:23]   **Audrey Tritt:** Yeah, you could just see, you even see, you could even see [*cross talk*].

[00:10:27]   **Darrell Tritt:** Tell other side [of] this lake, you fly over, you always see water, now you don't see water.

[00:10:33]   **Audrey Tritt:** You just [see] dry, those lakes are really drying out.

[00:10:37]   **Matt Gilbert:** I noticed the river channel is changing too [in] some places.

[00:10:40]   **Audrey Tritt:** Yeah.

[00:10:41]   **Matt Gilbert:** Like, some are joining together, and some are just like, [a] big part of it dried out and just little skinny channel, you notice that too?

[00:10:49]   **Audrey Tritt:** Yup.

[00:10:50]   **Darrell Tritt:** Yes.

[00:10:52]   **Matt Gilbert:** Fox, any neegoo, neegoo, more or less or the same?

[00:10:57]   **Audrey Tritt:** It's the same.

[00:10:59]   **Matt Gilbert:** Small animals?

[00:11:00]   **Audrey Tritt:** Yeah, they're all the same.

[00:11:01]   **Matt Gilbert:** Yeah.

[00:11:02]   **Audrey Tritt:** The rabbits are all over the place, ground squirrels.

[00:11:05]   **Matt Gilbert:** A lot of rabbits in Arctic Village, yeah, huh ...

[00:11:12]   **Audrey Tritt:** Those tree squirrels are a nuisance, I know that. We never used to have that kind of problem in the village. Tree squirrels, dlak, never used to be around here like that. When we were growing up there was no porcupine, we used to get porcupine, we don't get that.

[00:11:29]   **Matt Gilbert:** My grandpa Trimble said there's no more porcupine.

[00:11:32]   **Darrell Tritt:** Yeah, there's no more, nowhere.

[00:11:34]   **Audrey Tritt:** There's lots in Fairbanks and Circle, they just got two.

[00:11:38]   **Matt Gilbert:** My grandpa Trimble, he said that snipes are gone too, that make a little whistling sound, way far up in the sky.

[00:11:45] **Darrell Tritt:** Whooooooooooooo, you don't even hear that no more.

[00:11:49] **Matt Gilbert:** He said it's, you think he's right?

[00:11:51] **Audrey Tritt:** Yeah, we don't hear it either. That's what I mean, we don't see certain birds, they don't come around, but we see those little yellow birds, we never used to have them [*noise in room*].

[00:12:06] **Matt Gilbert:** Wait, I'll pause it . . . never mind, I'll leave it on . . . ok [*cross talk*].

[00:12:08] **Audrey Tritt:** We never used to have those yellow birds [*noise*]. It's all right.

[00:12:19] **Darrell Tritt:** You remember those strange birds, little [*inaudible*] birds, da dee do do, you don't hear that no more.

[00:12:25] **Audrey Tritt:** That chickadee dee dee dee is in early in the morning, we don't even hear that anymore.

[00:12:31] **Darrell Tritt:** We don't hear that no more.

[00:12:32] **Audrey Tritt:** There's certain birds.

[00:12:34] **Matt Gilbert:** I noticed that the dil' [Yellowtail Snipe] was gone for a long time, [lesser] yellowlegs or something, he came back this year. It was nice to have him back again, dil', [*ding, alarm, laughing*]. You noticed that he came back?

[00:12:48] **Audrey Tritt:** Yup.

[00:12:49] **Matt Gilbert:** This year it was nice to hear him back.

[00:12:49] **Audrey Tritt:** Yup, it came back.

[00:12:52] **Matt Gilbert:** [*Laughs*] and those, um, my grandpa, those Elders were telling me that they don't see those, they came back this year too, but those swallows, they make holes in the riverbank [*cross talk*].

[00:13:04] **Darrell Tritt:** Oh yeah, holes in the bank.

[00:13:07] **Audrey Tritt:** That's what I was talking about, I don't see 'em on the side of the house, those swallows.

[00:13:10] **Matt Gilbert:** No, those ones that make the hole in the bank.

[00:13:12] **Audrey Tritt:** Ohhh.

[00:13:12] **Matt Gilbert:** Hole in the side.

[00:13:14] **Darrell Tritt:** Yeah.

[00:13:14] **Matt Gilbert:** Yeah, they got them in Venetie too. But they're back though, I see them down at that gravel pit, they made a lot of holes in the—

[00:13:20] **Audrey Tritt:** And you know what I haven't seen, those Arctic terns, they fly one place a long time.

[00:13:27]   **Darrell Tritt:** Oh, one place.

[00:13:28]   **Audrey Tritt:** Yeah, those Arctic terns they—

[00:13:30]   **Matt Gilbert:** They used to attack us when we drove by that one lake down there, they're not there no more, Darrell, those Arctic terns, they used to attack us by that lake down there.

[00:13:40]   **Darrell Tritt:** Oh yeah, those Dzeh [long-tailed jaeger] flying around, they're not there no more. They got black tails, yeah. [Note: long-tailed jaeger has a black tail, Arctic tern has a white tail, both are long tails.]

[00:13:45]   **Audrey Tritt:** They don't see those anymore. There's a lot of different birds . . .

[00:13:51]   **Matt Gilbert:** What about seagulls? You don't see those? Vyuh? You don't see them on the sandbar?

[00:13:52]   **Audrey Tritt:** Even those, it was weird though, there's a lot of . . . what do you call those?

[00:13:59]   **Darrell Tritt:** That snow was moving.

[00:14:03]   **Matt Gilbert:** She said you don't see seagulls sitting on the sandbar no more, is that true?

[00:14:07]   **Darrell Tritt:** [*Muffled*].

[00:14:08]   **Audrey Tritt:** Yeah, they sit more on telephone poles than anything [*all laugh*].

[00:14:13]   **Matt Gilbert:** What about Venetie? Same thing, they used to see them on the sandbar, sitting on the sandbar.

[00:14:17]   **Darrell Tritt:** Yeah.

[00:14:17]   **Matt Gilbert:** And you don't see that no more.

[00:14:19]   **Darrell Tritt:** No.

[00:14:21]   **Audrey Tritt:** Yeah, we noticed a lot of things have changed. Even those logs are big, you see how big they are, they never, they were the size of these ones, the size of the ones that they brought in.

[00:14:34]   **Matt Gilbert:** I noticed the mice are getting bigger, too.

[00:14:38]   **Audrey Tritt:** Yeah, there's mice up on the mountain, cripes, man, they're about this big [*shows size*].

[00:14:42]   **Matt Gilbert:** [*Laughs*] geez.

[00:14:43]   **Audrey Tritt:** I'm serious, those mice.

[00:14:45]   **Matt Gilbert:** It's about a third of a foot, she's—

[00:14:48]   **Audrey Tritt:** They're really big, that camp, those dogs, they just bring it, they look like almost as big as rats, they're that big. It's really weird.

[00:15:00]   **Darrell Tritt:** I think our climate is changing.

[00:15:06] **Matt Gilbert:** Weather's getting crazier too, like everyone said that thunder, it never used to be that loud.

[00:15:11] **Audrey Tritt:** Uh uh [negative?], and—

[00:15:13] **Matt Gilbert:** [*Laughs*]. Same thing in Venetie, too? [*Movement in room*].

[00:15:17] **Audrey Tritt:** They said that it, Sarah said it made a big red X on top of her house.

[00:15:22] **Matt Gilbert:** Wow.

[00:15:22] **Audrey Tritt:** Big red X.

[00:15:25] **Darrell Tritt:** Geez.

[00:15:26] **Audrey Tritt:** And it just started pouring while tearing down her cache, even the house shook, that's how loud it was. Those kids are just scared, a lot of them got scared.

[00:15:40] **Matt Gilbert:** I interviewed people in Venetie too, about climate change in Venetie, and some Elders in Venetie were telling me that they're seeing more and more erosion, the mountain falling.

[00:15:49] **Darrell Tritt:** Yeah.

[00:15:50] **Matt Gilbert:** You think that's true?

[00:15:52] **Darrell Tritt:** The permafrost, uh—

[00:15:54] **Matt Gilbert:** [*Interjects*] Darrell Tritt from Venetie joining the conversation here.

[00:16:00] **Audrey Tritt:** A lot of dry snow [eating?].

[00:16:04] **Darrell Tritt:** Our rivers [are] drying out too [*muffled by room noise*].

[00:16:16] **Audrey Tritt:** I forgot about this in there.

[00:16:20] **Matt Gilbert:** What about moose, anything change about moose down there?

[00:16:20] **Darrell Tritt:** Not really.

[00:16:26] **Matt Gilbert:** Ok, stabilized, yeah that's what I found out too, a lot of things stayed the same but somethings got worse, some things got better, and—

[00:16:33] **Audrey Tritt:** The other thing, too, we started to get muskrats and beavers again.

[00:16:39] **Matt Gilbert:** Wow. They were gone for a long time?

[00:16:41] **Audrey Tritt:** Yeah, they were gone for a long time.

[00:16:43] **Matt Gilbert:** What about Venetie, Darrell? Darrell, up here we used to have a lot of muskrat, don't see them no more. Just this year they started coming a little bit, same thing in Venetie?

[00:16:50] **Darrell Tritt:** No, there's lots down there.

[00:16:56] **Matt Gilbert:** I remember when I was small, I went hunting with Robert and them up in First Bend, we used to see beaver houses, I don't see it no more.

[00:17:03] **Audrey Tritt:** [*Eating*]. Just certain lakes, they see little ones. Usually make really big ones.

[00:17:13] **Matt Gilbert:** I notice mosquitos, is it just me, or do mosquitos seem like they are getting worse?

[00:17:19] **Darrell Tritt:** Ah, getting worse, uh—

[00:17:20] **Matt Gilbert:** When I was little, they weren't this bad that you want to run home, you know?

[00:17:23] **Audrey Tritt:** They just attack us.

[00:17:26] **Matt Gilbert:** It wasn't that bad when I was little, because we played around.

[00:17:28] **Audrey Tritt:** In Fairbanks, just recently, it was weird, there was this beaver dam where we had our tent, no muskrats, just beavers, and it had seven little beavers in there. Usually when a muskrat has a—I mean a beaver—has a muskrat, there's a muskrat around, nothing in Fairbanks. I didn't see none. Just beavers. They were just laughing because they know, too, those guys over there, they grew up there, how come there's no muskrats? As I noticed that too. When that beaver, like knocked on one of those big trees just right on that bridge, I mean that lady just took it down, cause there's traffic, people don't know that beavers knocked a tree down there. [*Walking in room, noise*].

[00:18:27] **Matt Gilbert:** Biggest thing that everybody talked about that I interviewed so far is that they said that overgrowth is getting crazy, they said it's starting to be jungle.

[00:18:36] **Darrell Tritt:** Yeah.

[00:18:37] **Audrey Tritt:** It is.

[00:18:38] **Matt Gilbert:** Really [*laughs*].

[00:18:40] **Audrey Tritt:** We can't even drive anywhere, we gotta break a trail. It wasn't like that before. [Gwich'in *Tr'altth'ak* (thick brush, dense, tangled)] they call it.

[00:18:51] **Matt Gilbert:** Is that true in Venetie, too, a lot of overgrowth?

[00:18:52] **Darrell Tritt:** Yeah.

[00:18:57] **Audrey Tritt:** I think that's why those little lakes are drying out.

[00:18:59] **Matt Gilbert:** They're sucking all the water?

[00:19:01] **Audrey Tritt:** Yeah.

[00:19:02] **Matt Gilbert:** You think that's true, too? That overgrowth is sucking water from the lake, the roots?

[00:19:07] **Darrell Tritt:** I think so.

[00:19:09] **Audrey Tritt:** Because [of] the permafrost.

[00:19:10] **Darrell Tritt:** Yeah, the permafrost is thawing out and drying out . . . all the lakes, that's what I think about it.

[00:19:25] **Matt Gilbert:** You think there's more and more lightning strikes too?

[00:19:30] **Audrey Tritt:** Yeah.

[00:19:33] **Matt Gilbert:** Really? Was it like that when you were little?

[00:19:35] **Audrey Tritt:** Uh na [negative].

[00:19:38] **Darrell Tritt:** Same thing.

[00:19:39] **Matt Gilbert:** Venetie too, same thing? [*Dog barks*].

[00:19:43] **Audrey Tritt:** It wasn't like that when you were growing up?

[00:19:45] **Matt Gilbert:** I know I was walking back from school and, man, there was one right by me, I was like, whoa.

[00:19:51] **Audrey Tritt:** Yeah, that's what I mean, it never used to be like that.

[00:19:52] **Matt Gilbert:** [*Laughs*] I don't remember that when I was little.

[00:19:55] **Darrell Tritt:** I don't remember that [*laughs*].

[00:19:56] **Matt Gilbert:** Deena, your sister Deena, said something interesting about that really thick lightning strike by Caitlin's house last year, big hole it made, crater, they said what she said, after that happened . . . all the blueberries died, she thinks it sent some kind of electricity in the land or something [*dog barks*].

[00:20:23] **Audrey Tritt:** Before that, down by that old generator area, the lightning hit too, and it [caused a] power outage in all that area, and then that transformer caught on fire, and then last year, I wasn't here to see that lightning strike at the transformer right outside Caitlin's house.

[00:20:47] **Matt Gilbert:** That's crazy, that never happened before when you were small?

[00:20:51] **Audrey Tritt:** No.

[00:20:52] **Matt Gilbert:** You too, you never saw that in Venetie?

[00:20:56] **Darrell Tritt:** No.

[00:20:56] **Audrey Tritt:** But we didn't even get electricity till the '80s.

[00:20:59] **Matt Gilbert:** Yeah, that's true.

[00:21:00] **Audrey Tritt:** Yeah, we didn't get electricity.

[00:21:02] **Matt Gilbert:** But still, though, you never saw lightning.

[00:21:03] **Audrey Tritt:** No, we never used to deal with lightning hitting stuff.

[00:21:07] **Matt Gilbert:** Wow.

[00:21:07] **Darrell Tritt:** [*Inaudible*]. You don't come close to the village, way out there, it comes to the village now. Hit right across the river, burnt that [*inaudible*] boom, [*inaudible*] [*all laughing, dogs, noise*].

[00:21:23] **Audrey Tritt:** I think it's that satellite.

[00:21:29] **Darrell Tritt:** No, I think it's that pollution from bombs going up this way [note: rockets launched from NASA's Poker Flat?], or something like that.

[00:21:37] **Audrey Tritt:** It's got to do some with technology, that's what I think. Because you got a lot of access, easy access with technology that comes out [of the] state of Alaska, don't know, or other states, how they play with it. It's causing an effect [in] other places.

[00:21:57] **Matt Gilbert:** So, um, you said that, they said the same thing in Huslia, what you said, [is] that in springtime that forest is just quiet, no animal sounds.

[00:22:07] **Audrey Tritt:** Nothing.

[00:22:08] **Matt Gilbert:** Same thing in Venetie? That the forest is quieter?

[00:22:11] **Darrell Tritt:** Yeah.

[00:22:11] **Matt Gilbert:** Not [many] animals up here?

[00:22:14] **Darrell Tritt:** Not since that fire, everything [*inaudible; noise in room*].

[00:22:16] **Matt Gilbert:** Audrey said when she was small it was just noisy with animals.

[00:22:25] **Darrell Tritt:** Yeah, when I was growing up.

[00:22:27] **Matt Gilbert:** Same thing with you too?

[00:22:27] **Darrell Tritt:** Yeah, every [time] you see animals, but nowadays you don't even see, like when you walk.

[00:22:34] **Matt Gilbert:** I know I went up the mountain to hunt for ptarmigan this spring, I didn't see nothing. It's just empty up there.

[00:22:41] **Audrey Tritt:** Only thing I've run into is grouse. A lot of grouse, not enough ptarmigan.

[00:22:46] **Matt Gilbert:** It's just empty and lonely up there. There's nothing up there.

[00:22:51] **Audrey Tritt:** Nothing, yeah.

[00:22:52] **Matt Gilbert:** You notice that too? A long time ago there were animals everywhere.

[00:22:54] **Audrey Tritt:** Everywhere we go we see animals.

[00:22:58] **Matt Gilbert:** You noticed that too?

[00:22:59] **Darrell Tritt:** Yeah.

[00:23:05] **Audrey Tritt:** Animals [are] being used in a weird way, maybe. First time in my life, all these years I stayed out in the woods all day, I never saw animals come up to me. Last couple years, two moose walked up to me, one and then I fish net and moose walked up to me, picking berries over here, caribou walked up to me, I've never seen it like that.

[00:23:35] **Matt Gilbert:** About that caribou, what the Elders are telling me is that they're hanging around Arctic Village more, longer, they don't go to Canada that much now.

[00:23:43] **Audrey Tritt:** Yeah, they stay around this area more than they're going across the border, I've been told.

[00:23:48] **Matt Gilbert:** That's what the Elders are saying.

[00:23:53] **Audrey Tritt:** I think it's because of that you know that routing that they have, I think it grows too much, it's too much growth, they can't go.

[00:24:06] **Matt Gilbert:** Didn't you tell me a long time ago the Elders cut the bushes so the animals could go through?

[00:24:10] **Audrey Tritt:** Yeah.

[00:24:11] **Matt Gilbert:** Did they do the same thing in Venetie, those Elders a long time ago?

[00:24:14] **Audrey Tritt:** Yeah, even if there's a beaver dam over there they'll tear out that beaver dam so the fish will run. They do that because they don't want to have that water become beaver fever or whatever they call it.

[00:24:29] **Matt Gilbert:** They did the same thing in Venetie, the Elders a long time ago, they cut the brush for the animals?

[00:24:32] **Darrell Tritt:** Yeah.

[00:24:36] **Audrey Tritt:** Yeah, stuff like that we notice, we're the ones that're here, we're the ones that're dealing with all this weird weather.

[00:24:47] **Matt Gilbert:** Yeah. Well, I got to get back home, if you want to talk more just come by my house, Audrey.

[00:24:54] **Audrey Tritt:** Yeah, if I notice anything else that I think about I'll let [you know].

[End]

Audrey Tritt (Part 2) 6-21-2020.mp3

[00:00:00] **Matt Gilbert:** What were you saying. . . . Audrey, part 2 [*cross talk*].

[00:00:00] **Audrey Tritt:** That lush, I swear it was almost as big as a salmon, that's how, it couldn't even go in my net. Some other people seen it too, said it was really long, I seen it, it [was] swimming right by, just gonna pull my fish net, it was right there, really big, I never seen lush that big before. It's just, shoosh, big splash, just took off.

[00:00:31] **Matt Gilbert:** When I was interviewing people in Venetie, Maggie told me they're starting to get salmon there, they never got salmon there.

[00:00:39] **Darrell Tritt:** Yeah, we never get salmon, just dog salmon, just dog salmon.

[00:00:41] **Matt Gilbert:** Really, just dog salmon, she was getting king salmon [*cross talk*].

[00:00:46] **Darrell Tritt:** Yeah, nowadays catching king just right below the bank.

[00:00:50] **Matt Gilbert:** [*Laughs*] geez.

[00:00:52] **Darrell Tritt:** Yeah.

[00:00:53] **Matt Gilbert:** Wow, migration changing, huh?

[00:00:56] **Audrey Tritt:** It's just that the animals, they know where it's clean, uh, so they go where it's clean water, that's what I think.

[00:01:07] **Matt Gilbert:** Maybe that's why a lotta animals are hanging around with us.

[00:01:10] **Audrey Tritt:** Because there's nothing here. Think about it.

[00:01:13] **Darrell Tritt:** Yeah.

[00:01:15] **Audrey Tritt:** How far is the next village, every which way, and we don't keep the ground, I mean, when we do stuff, we keep it clean.

[00:01:24] **Matt Gilbert:** You think that's true, the animals, they go to the cleanest land?

[00:01:26] **Darrell Tritt:** Yeah, I think so.

[00:01:29] **Audrey Tritt:** Yeah, they do, because we keep the place clean.

[00:01:34] **Matt Gilbert:** Yeah, huh, wow, interesting stuff, now you guys gave me a lot of work to do [*laughs*], I have to write it, all this.

[00:01:40] **Audrey Tritt:** Yeah, because they don't, we abandon the Styrofoam, we don't order certain things, what's affecting, you know, we don't burn trash outside, we only have one, so people, people, they don't listen. So, it's making it worse for them, for the animals, to be around, it's gotta do some with the ozone. That's what I think, because when they said that with this Coronavirus, they said they even noticed the ozone was clearer when they stop all the traffic. Certain times they gotta be in, Anchorage and Fairbanks, I been, my friends tell me that, they even feeling fresh, more fresh air, less polluted. So, they stop the traffic, you know, they're giving them tickets, they're take 'em to jail [if] they're not following the rules. So that they say even, even in notice in the air, where it's clean, clean air, because everybody just gets on the bus or the car, that's all toxic.

[00:02:54] **Matt Gilbert:** I know that before they put the sewer in over there and they messed with that bridge, ah, man that creek was really good to fish, all those little boys.

[00:03:04] **Audrey Tritt:** You can't even swim in that water now.

[00:03:05] **Matt Gilbert:** When I was little, me and Robert and Darrell and Mike and them and Danny Gemmill, we'd spear fish, and we would fish there all the time, you can't do that now.

[00:03:15] **Audrey Tritt:** No, it's too shallow, that water, that drop by that culvert, that tunnel, you could just see big rocks right there, it never used to be like that. It used to be just good flowing water, now it's just, even the tunnel sits up [and] the water stops running, that's how dry it gets down there by the culvert. When this water drops, take a picture of it, take a picture of it now while the water [is] high, and then after the water, probably by tonight or tomorrow morning, take a picture again, you'll see how fast that water channel changes.

[00:04:00] **Matt Gilbert:** It never used to change that fast? Fast when you were little? [*Cross talk*] no.

[00:04:02] **Audrey Tritt:** No . . . no, it's like one week it will be that high, now, 30 minutes, 20 minutes later we're down there at that, those logs. With just me and Mike just noticed it, we're sitting down there, looking at those logs are sitting on the ground, he just, he just tied it up when the water was high, he said. Those logs down there, and rain not even, just like a couple hours, and that water just went way up.

[00:04:35] **Matt Gilbert:** Do you see same thing in Venetie? You, that water changes fast in level?

[00:04:39] **Darrell Tritt:** Back when the water dropped, you [could] see [the] gravel bar.

[00:04:47] **Audrey Tritt:** Well, it's true.

[00:04:48] **Darrell Tritt:** You got to park your boat way down there, too.

[00:04:50] **Matt Gilbert:** Wow.

[00:04:53] **Audrey Tritt:** Remember Venetie, Old Village used to flood out.

[00:04:56] **Matt Gilbert:** Wow.

[00:04:57] **Audrey Tritt:** That water is so high all the time, we used to flood. That's why they moved the village. Because of the flood.

[00:05:05] **Matt Gilbert:** I interviewed some Elders in Fort Yukon too, and they said they had like a prophecy, like those Elders long ago, they said in the future that Yukon River's gonna be so low you could walk across it, they said . . . non, they prediction, like—

[00:05:23] **Audrey Tritt:** Yeah, they just say that, that's what, maybe what they're using with technology.

[00:05:28] **Matt Gilbert:** No, I'm saying that I think that the Elders knew that was gonna happen, the river drying up like that.

[00:05:34] **Audrey Tritt:** Yeah, because I heard a lotta stories about how the Elders had visions about TV, that you're gonna watch and it's going to teach you stuff. I mean my uncles and aunties used to tell me stories like that, that they had heard, the stories that they heard. Yeah, it's really weird.

[00:05:56] **Darrell Tritt:** Like my grandma Myra Roberts says in the, before you guys, the first thing you gotta be walking around and talking to each other. She was talking about cell phones!

[00:06:09] **Matt Gilbert:** [*Laughs*].

[00:06:09] **Darrell Tritt:** And we don't know what she meant, we didn't know what she meant [at] that time. That's what we be walking around looking like this [*pointing*], just walking down the road, talking to each other. She was talking about cell phones.

[00:06:24] **Audrey Tritt:** Yeah, they all had stories like that.

[00:06:26] **Darrell Tritt:** That's the way you ask us, that's talking about right now, that's talking about cell phones! That's how we didn't know what she was talking about.

[00:06:35] **Matt Gilbert:** And notice . . . [*cough*] that's interesting, yeah. I notice more of our mountains, like I said [Gwich'in "*Niitsitaa*" *nihts'aii*?], and the one down there. Uhm, I noted there's more crevices, you know. The Elders, there's an old word for them, they call it [Gwich'in "*go na tin*"] [Note: Gwich'in Jr. Dictionary: crevice = *gwideetakgwatsal*; crevice (in ground or ice) = *nihtr'eeltil* or *tan ahtal*]. Crevice, in the mountain, like that.

[00:06:54] **Audrey Tritt:** Yeah.

[00:06:54] **Matt Gilbert:** You know, like [the] creek is in the middle of it, like that, you know. I noted there's more of them on the mountains, you notice that too? Like on [Gwich'in "*Niitsitaa*"], the one down here.

[00:07:03] **Audrey Tritt:** Because it's warming up, it's hot out there, it's rocks, and the, just the heat.

[00:07:10] **Matt Gilbert:** Cave-in.

[00:07:11] **Audrey Tritt:** Yeah, caving it in and melting the permafrost.

[00:07:13] **Matt Gilbert:** You think the same thing is happening in Venetie too?

[00:07:17] **Audrey Tritt:** It's happening all over the place.

[00:07:18] **Darrell Tritt:** Yeah, all over the place.

[00:07:18] **Audrey Tritt:** in the state of Alaska, we notice a lot of difference because they have all these stuff that they're, like gold mining now, they never used to try to gold mine that much, they just do little gold mining stories, now they're even putting stuff for, they're really destroying those mountains, and the water, I think that's what is going on.

[00:07:47] **Matt Gilbert:** We could continue this.

[00:07:50] **Audrey Tritt:** Yeah.

[End]

Audrey Tritt (Part 3) 6-21-2020.mp3

[00:00:00] **Matt Gilbert:** This is Audrey, part 3. Tell them how you got stuck at Sarah's house, that's important right there.

[00:00:08] **Audrey Tritt:** When I went to go visit, it was nice and sunny, started doing little odds and ends chores, it was real strong lightning, rainstorm.

[00:00:20] **Matt Gilbert:** But you went up there, shorts and stuff?

[00:00:23] **Audrey Tritt:** I went up there dressed for it being warm, do little odds and ends things, but it was too cold, we even had to build a fire 'cause it was cold in her house.

[00:00:36] **Matt Gilbert:** And you said you had to spend the night there?

[00:00:37] **Audrey Tritt:** Yeah, I had to spend the night there because it was raining really hard and lightning. I wasn't going to walk home with shorts on in that rain.

[00:00:48] **Matt Gilbert:** And what [did] you say, what people are saying about kids these days, they just don't [know] what long johns are 'cause winters are warmer now?

[00:00:55] **Audrey Tritt:** Well, it don't get cold until probably end of October, end of October, first week of November, and then Christmas it snows a lot, and then we don't get the 40, 50 below until January, February, and March.

And March is when it's usually supposed to be thawing out. Fairbanks has said it's not even turning green until April. And that's not normal. They even notice it is Fairbanks. They say it's been raining for the last couple days.

[End]

Charlie Swaney 6-19-2020.mp3

[00:00:00] **Matt Gilbert:** Charlie Swaney, June 19, 2020. Doing updated climate survey because the people in DC really liked what they said, and they want an updated interview. So, I already did two people and they said not much has changed, you know, since their last interview, since '05. Some things have gotten better, some things got worse, you know. So, you in '05, you were telling a lot of good things about the caribou. [*Muffled, dog*], caribou coordinates right here. You told them, you told me lots, so, caribou, somebody said there's more or less [in] the last 15 years, since 2005? Somebody said they're hanging around the village more, you know.

[00:00:43] **Charlie Swaney:** Yeah.

[00:00:45] **Matt Gilbert:** They're not going to Canada as much, is that true? Some-one told me that.

[00:00:48] **Charlie Swaney:** Yeah, I think ah, main, or ah, one of the biggest reasons why [it's] like that is the past few years, well I'd say, the past 10 years they had a lot of fires over there and, ah, places they used to migrate through where fire is [*muffled*], when they get there they turn around and go a different direction. And, ah, another thing that I've really, ah, how would I say it, I really noticed, and also they've noticed too, is the changing of their path is willows, where willows used to be not much, right now it's even over our heads.

[00:01:44] **Matt Gilbert:** Man, it's lots, look, it, you can see here [*points to map/ photo*] it's overgrowth.

[00:01:46] **Charlie Swaney:** You look at this, you know, during this time of the year, all the way up until the time the caribou are to ready, clear their horns from their velvet, the last thing they want to do is to damage the velvet on their horns.

[00:02:02] **Matt Gilbert:** Like even from your house, I remember, we . . . like, a cou-ple of us kids used to visit Margorie here, like when she was small, we watched a movie, and I remember standing on your porch, we could see the town real well from here.

[00:02:13] **Charlie Swaney:** You could see it from here, yeah.

[00:02:13] **Matt Gilbert:** You could see it real clear, now you can't see nothing.

[00:02:15] **Charlie Swaney:** Yup, you can't see nothing now, yeah. Yeah, these trees, when I built this house, these trees were, some of them was only a foot tall, and now it's over the house, it's taller than the house.

    One thing I noticed right here though [is] that where this house is, we [didn't have] a problem last winter, but the winter before, the ground would crack a lot, and I know that had to do with the permafrost . . . thawing out and then farther down, where it's still frozen when the cold air hits it, it cracks, and that was a problem we were having here. It would even shake our house. Now it's sometimes [in the] middle of the night we wake up, it's almost like a gun going off in our house. Yeah, just like a gun, somebody shot a gun in our house, that's how loud it is.

[00:03:07] **Charlie Swaney:** When you go out in the woods, and you go places that you've gone over [the] years, you know, you see the changes happening, and it mainly all has to do with the willow, the vegetation, the way it's growing. I was mentioning to somebody yesterday that the way this vegetation is growing right now, 10 years from now, you'll go upriver and it's gonna be hard to find animals because it's going to be so thick.

[00:03:43] **Matt Gilbert:** I can't imagine how it's gonna look in 10 years, it's going to be a jungle.

[00:03:46] **Charlie Swaney:** Yeah, it is going to be a jungle. Yeah. One thing that I worry about right now, what I worry about is if it gets bad enough like that, are we gonna still see the caribou? That's the big question, I guess.

    Now for moose, they love it because that's their food.

[00:04:11] **Matt Gilbert:** What about moose, you see any changes with moose in the last 15 years, more or less?

[00:04:17] **Charlie Swaney:** The last 3 years I've never seen so many moose here than ever, ever before. I mean I, not this winter we didn't really see that many signs of moose this winter, like we did the winter before. I remember a year ago, winter, one day I went out to my wood yard [*muffled*], I never see it [there] before. Almost every day that I go out, I see fresh moose tracks going to my wood yard, last year. And you look at last fall out hunting, there's 11 people that went out and got a big bull moose last fall. We're talking about *big* bull moose. That's unheard of here, and, uh, you know, I know a lot of that has to do with vegetation thriving up here and it's . . . quieter and all that up here. But on the Canadian side around the border, they've had a lot of fires these past few years and that's chased those moose out. And they gotta go somewhere, and I'm almost sure that's why we've had a lot more moose here these past few years, I mean *way* more moose.

[00:05:39] **Charlie Swaney:** It's, you know, when lightning strikes, lightning strikes nowadays, it's more intense than before. You look at yesterday, at the lightning we had yesterday, you look at the lightning we had last year, we never see it like that.

[00:05:57] **Matt Gilbert:** You said Casey almost got hit by lightning.

[00:05:59] **Charlie Swaney:** Yeah, Casey almost got hit by lightning last night, they even caught it on video, on the camera. Gee whiz. It's way more intense than in the past. When the thunder starts roaring, your house shakes.

[00:06:19] **Matt Gilbert:** Casey was . . . right where we are standing right?

[00:06:22] **Charlie Swaney:** Right where we're standing right now.

[00:06:23] **Matt Gilbert:** Yeah, on that porch, yeah, wow.

[00:06:25] **Charlie Swaney:** Yeah, I'm really fearful of that because back in 1997 it shocked me, it hit real, real close to me and it travelled underground, and it shocked me. That's something I never forgot, that's because of that happening, that's why I really don't like lightning.

[00:06:53] **Charlie Swaney:** But, ah, another thing I notice with caribou when they started filling up here, they show up once again from different directions. All different directions.

[00:07:05] **Matt Gilbert:** Not just one direction, huh?

[00:07:08] **Charlie Swaney:** Not just one direction, like before. They're showing up from the south, they're showing up from the north, they're showing up from the east, so the reason why I say that is I'm up there and I'm watching it, I see it with my own eyes. It's different.

[00:07:27] **Charlie Swaney:** Another thing, too, that's really changing around here too is water. Water is getting less and less. Take for instance the river, there's so much bank erosion now, where the river is wider than ever before, and therefore, the wider the river, the shallower the water. So that's something that's really changed right now, erosion on the river-banks. That's all having to do with the permafrost thawing out. Once again, where is that from, it's from global warming. Yeah.

[00:08:09] **Charlie Swaney:** Another thing too, I noticed too, these past couple summers, when it rains, it doesn't just rain, it pours. And you have a little flash flood going down the road, that's how heavy it rains, even if it's only for 15, 20 minutes. You have water running down the road. Rain is really more intense now, along with the lightning and the thunder. Yeah. That's a big, bigtime change in weather for summer.

[00:08:47] **Matt Gilbert:** What about that snipe, they said it was gone for a long time, then it came back, dil'.

[00:08:52] **Charlie Swaney:** Yeah.

[00:08:53] **Matt Gilbert:** Is that true, [Rocky?]?

[00:08:54] **Charlie Swaney:** Yeah.

[00:08:56] **Matt Gilbert:** We're doing a climate survey. Dil', it was gone for a long time, but it came back this year, right?

[00:09:01] **Charlie Swaney:** Yeah, I think that has to do with their route, their route, drastic things are happening in the way they're flying, where they fly, and if it gets bad enough, they turn around. Last winter, it was in March we were way upriver at a place called [Gwich'in *Tsveedik*?], where our camp is and in the back there's a big lake back there and we were making a trail to get wood. And there was some kind of bird that took off right there, right out in the middle of nowhere, in the middle of winter. To me it seemed like it was a bird that's only here in the summertime, 'cause I'd never seen it before. The other guy that was with me [had] never seen it before. I have no idea what kind of bird that was, but I've never [seen] it in the wintertime like that before [*lots of kitchen noise*].

[00:09:55] **Matt Gilbert:** My grandpa said there's a new bird that's coming up too, like a white bird that sits [on] spruce boughs, he never saw that before.

[00:10:03] **Charlie Swaney:** That's sad, you know. Speaking of your grandpa, he's lived off this land how many years, 80 years, you know, for something to change like that . . . I, when I hear things like that nowadays and I think, down the road what's it going to be like even 10 years from now, what are we going to be seeing then? I know it's going to, if this climate change and global warming, if something's not done about it right now, it's gonna be a bigtime jungle here in the future, and when I say future I'm talking about 7, 8, 9, 10 years from now.

Like I said, it's really happening like that, when this willow gets thicker and thicker, are we gonna see the caribou anymore? I know that's one thing that's changing their route right now, is where they used to go, they can't go anymore because of the willows, they're so thick [*dogs barking*].

[00:11:22] **Matt Gilbert:** [*Points to map*]. It's like that right there, right?

[00:11:26] **Charlie Swaney:** Yeah. That's the last thing they want to walk through because they don't want to damage the velvet on their horn, if they damage the velvet on their horn enough, it stops growing and it stays like that until their horn falls off.

[00:11:40] **Matt Gilbert:** One more question. What about snowfall, everybody says not much change, but lots of change in Fairbanks, you know. But not much in Arctic Village, that's what they say.

[00:11:50] **Charlie Swaney:** Well, this past winter it was pretty much normal, but the winter before that, to tell you the truth, all the years that I've lived up here I don't think I've seen so much snow as we did the winter before [last], not this last winter but the winter before. That was something else, that snow fall.

[00:12:10] **Matt Gilbert:** Ok, thank you very much, unless you got anything else.

[00:12:18] **Charlie Swaney:** Let me think about it overnight and all that, tomorrow I might stop down and mention a few more things. Yeah.

[End]

Deena Tritt 7-23-2020

[00:00:00] **Matt Gilbert:** July 23, Thursday. Deena Tritt 2020 climate survey update. It's recording now.

[00:00:10] **Deena Tritt:** When that lightning struck last year, all the blueberries and all the birds were around, we saw different color birds, robin, and those woodpeckers, we don't see. Anyway, those, when the lightning struck, we noticed that the next day it cleared up a little bit, we went out, and then there was no blueberries anywhere. That was a big shock to us. 'Cause we could see in my neighborhood and out there, that they were green and some of them were turning blue, and then when, after the lightning struck, it seems like it was a big strike, even cut a hole by my niece Caitlin's house. It was shocking because it, the next day no blueberries, the leaves looked old, all of it, not just [in] one place, all of it. And then we realized that there [were] no more birds singing, it was quiet last year. Where usually we hear the birds singing. Even now it's quiet.

[00:01:41] **Matt Gilbert:** It didn't sound like the birds were singing this summer, too.

[00:01:45] **Deena Tritt:** I hear a few, maybe one or two. No woodpeckers, no—what they call them? The gatso [Gwich'in ——].

[00:01:58] **Matt Gilbert:** Snipe?

[00:02:00] **Deena Tritt:** Yeah, there's not any more birds that we used to see, even bugs.

[00:02:10] **Matt Gilbert:** That thunder.

[00:02:12] **Deena Tritt:** I think that thunder did something 'cause it shook everybody's house, and—

[00:02:19] **Matt Gilbert:** Even knocked out our electricity.

[00:02:21] **Deena Tritt:** Yeah.

[00:02:22] **Matt Gilbert:** I'd never seen that before.

[00:02:23] **Deena Tritt:** There were a lotta flashes, lightning, it was scary, I was there.

[00:02:31] **Matt Gilbert:** So, you think that it shocked those birds or something, or did something to the birds?

[00:02:43] **Deena Tritt:** Or something, but then they say that blue? Saw it, so maybe they left after that thunder, but I don't know what happened. We been, I been looking around, and then sometimes those birds knock on our window like they're hungry, so I get oatmeal and dump it all around. A lot of people do that, they said that sometimes the birds, you know, they tap on our window.

[00:03:17] **Matt Gilbert:** 'Cause they can't find food?

[00:03:20] **Deena Tritt:** I don't know, that's what we're thinking.

[00:03:23] **Matt Gilbert:** Robert Sam, he said that those snipes, he watches them, they do little certain things, and then when there's low-pressure weather, he said that they wait for that jet stream, it's like a river in the sky, that air, once they see it's strong from, I think, low-pressure weather, he said, or high-pressure weather when it's really windy and when air is thick, he said that stream is strong up there, and they jump in it, they just glide down, that's how they migrate, they wait for the airstream, it gets thick, then they just jump in it.

[00:04:09] **Deena Tritt:** Wow.

[00:04:10] **Matt Gilbert:** I didn't know that. See, you guys just know everything.

[00:04:16] **Deena Tritt:** Well, we live with the animals here, you know, when, like I said, when the birds tap on our window, that's when we know they're hungry. And those bees too, they don't bother us, but they're around, but we don't see [them] as much as we used to.

[00:04:35] **Matt Gilbert:** I interviewed a lot of people, there's some questions I had for you. I forgot where they're at though. The bees, yeah, they don't bother us, but they're not around like they used to [be], that's what you said?

[00:04:58] **Deena Tritt:** Um hum.

[00:05:00] **Matt Gilbert:** [*Shuffling papers*]. Shoot, I think that was it, yeah. Oh, yeah, last year you said, [in] 2005 I interviewed you, you said the blueberries, you could sit in one place, a long time ago you could sit in one place and pick them for a long time, and you said you can't do that no more, you gotta move more and more.

[00:05:40] **Deena Tritt:** Yeah, cause some of them are small, some of them are big, depends on where the sunshine hits, but there's hardly any sunshine.

[00:05:51] **Matt Gilbert:** Yeah, there's hardly any sunshine this summer.

[00:05:55] **Deena Tritt:** Um hum. So whatever is out there, they're small but they're still picking them.

[00:06:03] **Matt Gilbert:** What about cranberries, same thing?

[00:06:06] **Deena Tritt:** Yeah, they get, some of them are really hard, it wasn't like that before, and . . . what else, trees are looking different.

[00:06:19] **Matt Gilbert:** Remember, Grandma Margaret used to make that cranberry sauce all the time?

[00:06:27] **Deena Tritt:** Uh huh.

[00:06:27] **Matt Gilbert:** Nobody hardly makes that anymore, huh, because you can't find enough cranberries, yuh?

[00:06:31] **Deena Tritt:** Yeah, these days they're into blueberries 'cause they make jam and stuff like that, I like cranberries, I do both, but [there] is no time, it's cold, we didn't even see summer, we just been in the fall.

[00:06:54] **Matt Gilbert:** It's like two winters, huh?

[00:06:55] **Deena Tritt:** Yeah.

[00:07:00] **Matt Gilbert:** Those Elder stories from a long time ago, they talk about two winters too, you know, sounds like [an] ice age.

[00:07:08] **Deena Tritt:** Yeah, we're melting, too.

[00:07:13] **Matt Gilbert:** One thing, a lot of people were talking about with this update, they said there's more vegetation. Like my Grandpa Trimble, he said "I can't even look for caribou because I can't see anything, the vegetation is all high."

[00:07:28] **Deena Tritt:** Uh huh, everything growing.

[00:07:32] **Matt Gilbert:** It's starting to look like jungle, you know.

[00:07:35] **Deena Tritt:** It's scary 'cause in the village, one rain and everything grows, all these different flowers that're coming out, we don't see those purple ones, but they're around.

[00:07:55] **Matt Gilbert:** I was behind the church, I take that shortcut sometimes, and I saw a yellow bird I'd never seen before, and I was trying to take a picture, you know, but it flew away, bright yellow, I'd never seen that before.

[00:08:17] **Deena Tritt:** Yeah, we seen that around too, and there's that purple bird, I think we said it was a robin. It was purple, blue, gray. But I think they're a robin. I got a bird nest up there, that bird never came back yet. Maybe they never flew, he never made it up here 'cause of the bad weather down where they're flying from, see his bird nest up there on my porch, every year he come back and he goes in there. See it?

[00:09:05] **Matt Gilbert:** [*Gets up from table, walking*]. He never made it up.

[00:09:09] **Deena Tritt:** So, he never made it back this year.

[00:09:11] **Matt Gilbert:** Maybe the weather is too bad.

[00:09:14] **Deena Tritt:** Yeah. I want to take a picture and put it on Facebook and say my bird never came back [*laughs*]. No sunshine, that's pretty sad.

[00:09:43] **Matt Gilbert:** I know. Anyways, I hope you don't mind, but I told Kathy Tritt what you said about the lightning killing the blueberries, and she said you're right, and she said it probably killed some of the ground squirrels too.

[00:10:04] **Deena Tritt:** There's nothing up on the mountain.

[00:10:06] **Matt Gilbert:** Gee, really?

[00:10:07] **Deena Tritt:** You could see a few with their little ones, all the animals got little ones now, they're ready to fly, and some of them shoo their babies away, they're growing up now. They're little ones, all the animals got little ones, they're learning to fly, you see all those little birds, their mom shoos them away so they could be on their own. Not only birds . . . mouse, ground squirrel, rabbit.

[00:10:43] **Matt Gilbert:** Robins too?

[00:10:46] **Deena Tritt:** Wolf, yeah, but caribou, they got, they're still with their mom till August.

[00:10:54] **Matt Gilbert:** Grandpa told me something really interesting too. He said the creeks in Arctic Village were very low this year, the snow in the mountains is what feeds water to the creeks. We had a very cold spring this year, so the snow did not get to melt because there was only 1 to 2 warm days, when summer arrived, it melted everything immediately, instantly like that, 'cause [the] snow didn't have time to melt, it's just dry. So, when summer came it just evaporated like that, you know. Since the snow didn't melt, it was dry, so when it melted there was no water. See, it just evaporated because there was no water, it didn't melt, interesting.

[00:11:42]   **Deena Tritt:** Um hum, Wow . . .

[00:11:46]   **Matt Gilbert:** [*Laughs*]. I've graduated from college, and you guys are teaching me stuff, I didn't know this stuff.

[00:11:55]   **Deena Tritt:** That's why Grandma Margaret said learning never stops. We learn something every day.

[00:12:02]   **Matt Gilbert:** Wow. Um, only thing, really interesting thing Audrey told me is that, she said, weather is funny nowadays, different parts of the sky look different, like there's rolling clouds over here, then there's smooth clouds over here, she said it's not supposed to be like that, is she right?

[00:12:39]   **Deena Tritt:** Um hum. They talk about the clouds before, dark clouds and clearer clouds, I don't know, you gotta ask a scientist.

[00:12:52]   **Matt Gilbert:** No, I asked my Grandpa Trimble and he said that Gideon had said this, and then my grandpa said he's right, he said that a lotta those dark clouds from pollution, maybe that North Slope or just the pollution around the world.

[00:13:07]   **Deena Tritt:** Oh yeah.

[00:13:08]   **Matt Gilbert:** That airplane, Gideon says it's because of those airplanes going back and forth, yeah, that's why the cloud is dark.

[00:13:14]   **Deena Tritt:** That's what we were wondering, 'cause every time a jet flies up, it leaves long streaks of white, you know those white things, it comes down to us.

[00:13:26]   **Matt Gilbert:** Gideon said when he was a little boy he walked around, he said the clouds were puffy and white, and healthy, and the sky was just clear and clean.

[00:13:38]   **Deena Tritt:** That's right.

[00:13:39]   **Matt Gilbert:** [*Laughs*]. Back then he said there wasn't that many airplanes, 'cause he was a little boy in the 1950s, right? [In the] 40s, 50s there wasn't that many airplanes back then in the sky, 'specially up here, there was nothing going by, you know, but nowadays you have jets going back and forth [*laughs*].

[00:14:00]   **Deena Tritt:** Really, you're right.

[00:14:03]   **Matt Gilbert:** And I, look, I told my Grandpa Trimble that, what Gideon said, and he said that Gideon's right, because he can hardly see the stars, too, at nighttime, you know. He said a long time ago you see that star really clear.

[00:14:17]   **Deena Tritt:** That's right, we could see all the satellites, now we can see only one. How many satellites they send up there?

[00:14:35]   **Matt Gilbert:** Lots.

        Oh, another interesting thing Audrey said is, I never thought of this too, [Gwich'in *A try vee*?], those little tornados, you know, little dust balls, when we were kids we used to play with them, we used to try to jump in them, and you don't see them no more, I didn't notice that until she said, yeah, you're right I don't see them no more. 'Cause when we were small, we saw them everywhere, you know.

[00:15:15]   **Deena Tritt:** Seems that we notice things fast up here, before the whole world.

[00:15:24]   **Matt Gilbert:** That's why I said you guys know more than [Gwich'in *nangoodlit*] [*inaudible*] Western people.

[00:15:28]   **Deena Tritt:** Like that Covid now, we use spruce and pitch juice, [and] it don't affect people too much.

[00:15:36]   **Matt Gilbert:** Wow . . . what about lidiimaskit? That help?

[00:15:41]   **Deena Tritt:** That's for like, strep throat.

[00:15:45]   **Matt Gilbert:** OK, huh [*loading up woodstove*]. Notice things first up here. Anything else you want to add?

[00:16:06]   **Deena Tritt:** We need to have more scientists come up and study our plants, see if our plants are dying, or are they ok? Because some of them are turning red-like color. And more vegetation, and see what kind of bugs we're gonna expect.

[00:16:39]   **Matt Gilbert:** Or even those new—

[00:16:39]   **Deena Tritt:** I got a hole back here, that I never seen before, it's a big ditch but no one ever dug it out. I show it to people around here.

[00:16:51]   **Matt Gilbert:** Can you show it to me?

[00:16:54]   **Deena Tritt:** Yeah, it's back there. you want to go back there?

[00:16:58]   **Matt Gilbert:** Yeah, I'll take pictures.

[00:16:59]   **Deena Tritt:** We'll go out the back door.

[End]

Franklin Tritt 6.19.2020 (Part 1)

[00:00:00] **Matt Gilbert:** So, this is an updated interview for the climate interviews I did in 2005, it's now 2020, 15 years later, Friday June 19, 2020. So, it's 15 years later, you know, and they want to know if you saw any changes since last time I talked to you. Remember last [time], I read what you said in 2005, you said there was no small game except rabbits, you didn't see foxes and those small animals that much anymore, is it still the same? Or changed?

[00:00:40] **Franklin Tritt:** Still the same.

[00:00:42] **Matt Gilbert:** Still the same, OK.

[00:00:43] **Franklin Tritt:** And then I understand that when you see that cold weather, you know, like 50 below, way back [at] Christmas till that, never seen 55 below in long time, you know. We never seen that 50 or 55 below for a long time and 2019 and 2020 it went up too cold, got really cold. It was kind of weird for me.

[00:01:31] **Matt Gilbert:** It's weird. So, you didn't see 50 below for a really long time.

[00:01:34] **Franklin Tritt:** Yeah.

[00:01:34] **Matt Gilbert:** And then this winter it just shot up, wow. I know Sunny Erick in Venetie, he said those kids [are] growing up, they don't even know what long johns are [*laughs*]. Because it, um, they don't need it because winter is so warm. Do you think he's right?

[00:01:53] **Franklin Tritt:** When those young kids, they don't feel cold weather, that's why.

[00:01:57] **Matt Gilbert:** Yeah, that's what he said.

[00:02:00] **Franklin Tritt:** They don't feel cold weather because they're young.

[00:02:05] **Matt Gilbert:** Nobody's like, when I was small, we wore long johns because it was cold back then, but Sunny is saying nowadays it's so warm that those kids don't need long johns no more, do you think he's right?

[00:02:16] **Franklin Tritt:** Yeah, he's right, yeah. On top of that I understand that, you know, way back, the thunder was not that loud.

[00:02:28] **Matt Gilbert:** Geez, it was loud last night.

[00:02:30] **Franklin Tritt:** Yeah, and nowadays the thunder [is] just loud.

[00:02:34] **Matt Gilbert:** It even shakes the house little bit, huh?

[00:02:36] **Franklin Tritt:** Yeah, way back it wasn't that loud, nowadays it's just loud, you don't know, the changing weather, I guess.

[00:02:48] **Matt Gilbert:** So, the next thing you said in 2005, you said something about snowfall, there was less snow or more snow, sometimes like that, huh, one year there's lots of snow.

[00:03:04] **Franklin Tritt:** Yeah. Like Fairbanks, just recently there's no snow until November 1, that's kind of funny.

[00:03:18] **Matt Gilbert:** I think I was living there at that time, I think it was 2015, I think, there was no snow until November, I'd never seen anything like that before.

[00:03:29] **Franklin Tritt:** Yeah, same thing just happened this year, funny. It's kind of funny it snows usually September or October, but finally November, gosh.

[00:03:47] **Matt Gilbert:** What about here, snow is normal here, huh?

[00:03:50] **Franklin Tritt:** Yeah, I guess, yeah.

[00:03:55] **Matt Gilbert:** Nothing changed, yeah. Meat, you notice anything about caribou meat and fish meat?

[00:04:01] **Franklin Tritt:** No.

[00:04:03] **Matt Gilbert:** It's still OK? There's nothing?

[00:04:05] **Franklin Tritt:** It's OK. Sometimes, way back a long time ago, rack about this thick, you know, bull caribou the back, now it's just only this much [*shows*].

[00:04:20] **Matt Gilbert:** He went from 3 inches to 1 inch.

[00:04:25] **Franklin Tritt:** Yeah, used to be this thick.

[00:04:27] **Matt Gilbert:** Three inches.

[00:04:29] **Franklin Tritt:** Now it just went down to about this thick.

[00:04:32] **Matt Gilbert:** One inch, caribou fat?

[00:04:34] **Franklin Tritt:** Yeah.

[00:04:35] **Matt Gilbert:** Yeah, Audrey this spring, she was telling me whitefish is smaller now, do you think she is right?

[00:04:43] **Franklin Tritt:** No, not that I know of.

[00:04:47] **Matt Gilbert:** Her fish net, she said they're small now.

[00:04:49] **Franklin Tritt:** I don't know about that.

[00:04:51] **Matt Gilbert:** Ok, well I'm done with the questions if you had any other questions, want to say anything else about global warming.

[00:04:58] **Franklin Tritt:** Yeah, that's kind of funny for me, that thunder [is] really loud, it wasn't like that way back. You scared me, [*laughs*] just making big, suddenly—

[00:05:21] **Matt Gilbert:** I heard when that was happening, that happened in 2011 too, huh, really loud thunder.

[00:05:27] **Franklin Tritt:** Yeah, just been like that every summer.

[00:05:31] **Matt Gilbert:** I know they said some of those kids, they even hide under tables, that's what Caitlin and Towsend [?] were saying.

[00:05:39] **Franklin Tritt:** Scared too, big lightning.

[00:05:42] **Matt Gilbert:** Geez, I noticed, you think we're having more lightning? More of them now?

[00:05:50] **Franklin Tritt:** No, not really.

[00:05:52] **Matt Gilbert:** Oh, ok. So still same lightning.

[00:05:58] **Franklin Tritt:** Yeah, except that thunder is really loud, it's funny, it wasn't like that way back.

[00:06:07] **Matt Gilbert:** You think the rain is harder, too, than a long time ago?

[00:06:10] **Franklin Tritt:** No, but just about the same, I think.

[00:06:18] **Matt Gilbert:** All right.

[00:06:19] **Franklin Tritt:** That's all I got, meet me later on.

Franklin Tritt 6-19-2020 (Part 2).mp3

[00:00:00] **Matt Gilbert:** This is Franklin, part 2. You wanted to share what's going on.

[00:00:07] **Franklin Tritt:** Way back, there used to be a lotta swallows flying around, I don't see them anymore.

[00:00:15] **Matt Gilbert:** Yeah, that's what they were seeing back in 2005, so I guess nothing changed, huh?

[00:00:19] **Franklin Tritt:** Yeah, but you know the swallows, there used to be a lot of them, now [they're] not around anymore.

[00:00:25] **Matt Gilbert:** Lotta [them] flocking over.

[00:00:27] **Franklin Tritt:** Then, ah, just . . .

[00:00:28] **Matt Gilbert:** To me it seems like [they're] not flocking over.

[00:00:30] **Franklin Tritt:** Seems like the birds, seems like not too many birds, too.

[00:00:35] **Matt Gilbert:** They said for a long time that snipes disappeared, you know, snipes.

[00:00:41] **Franklin Tritt:** Yeah.

[00:00:41] **Matt Gilbert:** But he came back this year, that dil'

[00:00:44] **Franklin Tritt:** Yeah.

[00:00:44] **Matt Gilbert:** Called snipe.

[00:00:45] **Franklin Tritt:** Yeah.

[00:00:45] **Matt Gilbert:** I might be wrong, but yeah, I heard that alarm, you know, fire alarm.

[00:00:52] **Franklin Tritt:** Yeah.

[00:00:52] **Matt Gilbert:** Yeah, I was happy to hear that because he's back.

[00:00:56] **Franklin Tritt:** Yeah.

[00:00:56] **Matt Gilbert:** A lot of people said he was gone for a long time, couple a, 5 years, are they right?

[00:01:02] **Franklin Tritt:** I think they are right, yeah.

[00:01:03] **Matt Gilbert:** He just came back, just this year.

[00:01:06] **Franklin Tritt:** Yeah, there used to be a lotta muskrat too, and we hardly see any muskrat anymore.

[00:01:18] **Matt Gilbert:** Deena said they're skinny too now, she right? Muskrat?

[00:01:22] **Franklin Tritt:** I don't know, never seen.

[00:01:25] **Matt Gilbert:** She said she tried to cook one for an Elder, she said, and it was too skinny, so she just gave it to the dogs, or something.

[00:01:31] **Franklin Tritt:** She's probably right.

[00:01:32] **Matt Gilbert:** They're probably not eating good, huh?

[00:01:35] **Franklin Tritt:** I don't know what's going on, but . . .

[00:01:38] **Matt Gilbert:** Not that many, huh.

[00:01:42] **Franklin Tritt:** Yeah, there used to be a lot of muskrat, now looks like not that much.

[00:01:47] **Matt Gilbert:** What about beaver?

[00:01:48] **Franklin Tritt:** Beaver too, yeah, same, they're both the same. Okay, that's good enough now.

[00:01:58] **Matt Gilbert:** One more thing, I remember when I was small, I used to go hunting with my 410 with Robert and all of them, I used to see beaver houses on that ice, I don't see it no more.

[00:02:12] **Franklin Tritt:** Yeah, it's going, going to get worse and worse . . .

[00:02:19] **Matt Gilbert:** Yeah.

[00:02:22] **Franklin Tritt:** What you know.

[00:02:23] **Matt Gilbert:** Alright.

[00:02:24] **Franklin Tritt:** Ok, yeah.

[End]

Mike Lee 6-19-2020.mp3 *Arctic Village*

[00:00:00] **Matt Gilbert:** It's June 19, 2020. Mike Lee update interview from 2005.

[00:00:09] **Matt Gilbert:** So back then [in 2005], you'd said there was less ducks, you know, less ducks than there used to be in 2005, so that was 15 years ago, anything changes since then? Still?

[00:00:24] **Mike Lee:** Um.

[00:00:25] **Matt Gilbert:** Low number?

[00:00:25] **Mike Lee:** So, um, yeah I noticed this year I didn't see much wigeon, hardly, there's usually quite an abundance of them, but this year I saw only a few pairs, and even Alo said that, geez, there's hardly any birds. He goes, rides down to the airport every day, he looks at those lakes and usually there is those ducks in there, and there's hardly anything.

[00:00:52] **Matt Gilbert:** Geez.

[00:00:52] **Mike Lee:** We had a weird thaw this year, too, dry thaw, sort of, you should say.

[00:00:57] **Matt Gilbert:** Well, I noticed, [*music comes on*] yeah, it's on again [recorder].

[00:01:05] **Mike Lee:** Basically, just more water fowl in general is pretty low. And yeah, that's what I said, Alo said.

[00:01:14] **Matt Gilbert:** Geese are still stable?

[00:01:16] **Mike Lee:** Yeah, there's pretty a lot of geese.

[00:01:18] **Matt Gilbert:** Alo, yeah, I'm going to interview him, too. Well, I noticed dil' came back, snipe, is that the Western name? Snipe?

[00:01:25] **Mike Lee:** Yellowlegs, lesser yellowlegs, yeah . . . dil'.

[00:01:28] **Matt Gilbert:** Lesser yellowlegs, ok, it's not snipe.

[00:01:31] **Mike Lee:** Snipe is that one that [*whistles ascending call*] ooooooooooooooooooooooo, way up there, you hear him?

[00:01:38] **Matt Gilbert:** Yeah. Oh, you know those Elders back in 2005, they said snipe is gone, you don't see it no more.

[00:01:44] **Mike Lee:** Actually, I don't really hear them much, you know that, you ever notice that one you hear [them] way up there?

[00:01:50] **Matt Gilbert:** Yeah.

[00:01:50] **Mike Lee:** [*Whistles ascending*] ooooooooooooooooooooooooo.

[00:01:53] **Matt Gilbert:** Yeah, way up there.

[00:01:54] **Mike Lee:** Yeah, you don't hear that much.

[00:01:55] **Matt Gilbert:** You don't hear it anymore. And you know dil' was gone for a long time but came back this year.

[00:02:00] **Mike Lee:** Um hum . . . yeah.

[00:02:01] **Matt Gilbert:** Nice to have him back [*both laugh*].

[00:02:04] **Mike Lee:** When you're hunting, they make a lot of noise, so it's kind of irritating [*laughs*].

[00:02:07] **Matt Gilbert:** Irritating? But now that he's gone for a long time, now I'm really happy to hear his alarm sound [*both laugh*], and they said those mud, my Grandpa Trimble said mud swallows were gone too, those swallows that make holes in the mud on the bank?

[00:02:23] **Mike Lee:** Yeah.

[00:02:24] **Matt Gilbert:** But I noticed they're back, they were at that gravel pit down there.

[00:02:27] **Mike Lee:** Yeah, there's a bunch of them.

[00:02:28] **Matt Gilbert:** Yeah, there's a bunch of them there, so I'm glad some of them are back.

[00:02:30] **Mike Lee:** You notice they don't build houses on the roof no more?

[00:02:34] **Matt Gilbert:** No, I wonder why?

[00:02:34] **Mike Lee:** Probably because kids shoot them, break them down, and stuff.

[00:02:40] **Matt Gilbert:** probably. So, lakes, everybody knows they're drying up, that's common knowledge, that hasn't changed in 15 years, huh?

[00:02:46] **Mike Lee:** Well, in 15 years.

[00:02:50] **Matt Gilbert:** Sped up or slowed down?

[00:02:51] **Mike Lee:** That's about the same, I guess. But there's a couple places upriver that blew out, and even changed the channel.

[00:03:02] **Matt Gilbert:** Geez, I noticed myself the channel widening because the banks eroding.

[00:03:05] **Mike Lee:** Um hum.

[00:03:07] **Matt Gilbert:** That First Bend is wide now.

[00:03:08] **Mike Lee:** Yeah, you see it blew out that lake too, it's connected to the river now. It blew out last year.

[00:03:15] **Matt Gilbert:** The lake behind First Bend.

[00:03:16] **Mike Lee:** No, that one at First Bend, where we always used to sit?

[00:03:18] **Matt Gilbert:** Wow, I didn't go up there yet.

[00:03:19] **Mike Lee:** Yeah, if you go up there and go for a walk up there, look at it, it's totally different now [*both laugh*]. Yeah, it's no more a lake now.

[00:03:28] **Matt Gilbert:** So, moose, more or less?

[00:03:30] **Mike Lee:** I've seen quite a bit.

[00:03:31] **Matt Gilbert:** Really, that's what people are saying, too.

[00:03:32] **Mike Lee:** Yeah, there's quite a bit. I'm thinking they're moving up this way, I don't know, I guess.

[00:03:39] **Matt Gilbert:** 'Cause, I cut up one with my dad, and he shot one just like right, you know, right by the village, you could even see people's houses from where he shot [it].

[00:03:51] **Mike Lee:** Oh, really?

[00:03:51] **Matt Gilbert:** Yeah, um, oh, one more thing, you talked about warmer winters, colder summers, that's still the same, huh?

[00:04:03] **Mike Lee:** Yeah, actually, we had a pretty cold winter this year.

[00:04:07] **Matt Gilbert:** Yeah, that's what everyone said, it spiked up, I never seen 50 below for a long time.

[00:04:10] **Mike Lee:** Yeah.

[00:04:11] **Matt Gilbert:** This summer just, this winter just—

[00:04:15] **Mike Lee:** Yeah, it was a rough winter.

[00:04:17] **Matt Gilbert:** I noticed it was warm until Christmas, and then it gets cold.

[00:04:20] **Mike Lee:** Yeahhh, you notice that.

[00:04:22] **Matt Gilbert:** Yeah, I notice that.

[00:04:23] **Mike Lee:** Uh huh.

[00:04:25] **Matt Gilbert:** So, um . . .

[00:04:26] **Mike Lee:** You notice how cold this spring was too, it got cold, and everything froze up again, and I noticed that the lakes, the ice too, was still dry. Yeah, we had a weird thaw this year.

[00:04:38] **Matt Gilbert:** Weird . . . um huh.

[00:04:40] **Mike Lee:** The river took forever to go out and everything.

[00:04:44] **Matt Gilbert:** Snowfall, everyone says it's the same, stable?

[00:04:45] **Mike Lee:** Yeah.

[00:04:47] **Matt Gilbert:** In Fairbanks, like, man weird, one winter no snow until November, summertime until November . . . it was crazy.

[00:04:54] **Mike Lee:** Yeah . . . that one year, yeah, we had no snow until the beginning of September.

[00:05:01] **Matt Gilbert:** Geez.

[00:05:01] **Mike Lee:** I remember I went through two Elan frames because there was so much snow it broke up the frame.

[00:05:05]   **Matt Gilbert:** Oh no.

[00:05:05]   **Mike Lee:** Well . . .

[00:05:10]   **Matt Gilbert:** What was the last thing I wanted to talk to you about? Something to do with that . . . ugh . . . shouldn't put it away . . . I read your last interview, that's why I wrote it down.

[00:05:28]   **Mike Lee:** That's cool, you have it all saved, huh.

[00:05:31]   **Matt Gilbert:** Yeah, well, I wrote it and read it, thanks . . . emptying out, I guess what Gideon said, he said too a lot of lakes are emptying out into the river, do you think he's right?

[00:05:45]   **Mike Lee:** Yeah.

[00:05:49]   **Matt Gilbert:** Ah . . . ok, warmer winters, summers colder, oh it has something to do with, when I mentioned that, oh, 50 below, this is what I was going to say, when I interviewed hunters and Elders in Venetie and ah, Sunny Erick, John Erick, Jr. for the record, um, he said that we never have 50 below in a long, long, time, Raymond said that too, like decades, you know, he said that's why a lot of these kids nowadays, they don't even know what long johns are [*both laugh*], 'cause they don't need them since winters are so warm.

[00:06:28]   **Mike Lee:** That's funny 'cause I took out an old picture of my brother and me—

[00:06:32]   **Matt Gilbert:** And me and you.

[00:06:32]   **Mike Lee:** Wearing long johns, they're like, what are you guys wearing? Long johns [*both laugh*].

[00:06:38]   **Matt Gilbert:** Yeah, we're both 40 years old, me and Mike, when we were kids, it was normal, but kids nowadays, they never even heard of them.

[00:06:46]   **Mike Lee:** Yeah, that's right [*both laughing*].

[00:06:47]   **Matt Gilbert:** 'Cause we don't need them because winters are warm [*both laughing*].

[00:06:52]   **Matt Gilbert:** Don't need them.

[00:06:54]   **Mike Lee:** [*Laughing*] oh . . .

[00:06:58]   **Matt Gilbert:** Okay.

[00:07:02]   **Matt Gilbert:** Oh, you see anything weird, thunder, last night?

[00:07:04]   **Mike Lee:** Yeah.

[00:07:05]   **Matt Gilbert:** Geez it was loud, yeah?

[00:07:05]   **Mike Lee:** It shook the house.

[00:07:07]   **Matt Gilbert:** You never seen that, uh, all your life, living here?

[00:07:11]   **Mike Lee:** Actually, we had a big, bad thunderstorm last year.

[00:07:13] **Matt Gilbert:** Oh really?

[00:07:13] **Mike Lee:** Actually, [it] struck right by Caitlin . . . blew, lucky no one got injured our burned.

[00:07:18] **Matt Gilbert:** Oh yeah, that's right . . . do you think there's more lightning strikes than before?

[00:07:22] **Mike Lee:** Uhm.

[00:07:23] **Matt Gilbert:** When you were small?

[00:07:27] **Mike Lee:** There were some pretty bad ones, uh, but not really, but I have never heard it damaging [anything].

[00:07:37] **Matt Gilbert:** I don't think so, because when I was small, I don't remember it being dangerous.

[00:07:40] **Mike Lee:** Yeah, actually, I'll take that back, that's true.

[00:07:45] **Matt Gilbert:** Dodging lightning strikes when you're running home, we never did that.

[00:07:47] **Mike Lee:** Oh yeah, you never heard of it damaging somebody's house, you know, and that—

[00:07:51] **Matt Gilbert:** I know, oh, it damaged someone's house?

[00:07:54] **Mike Lee:** Yeah.

[00:07:55] **Matt Gilbert:** Oh, Caitlin, huh.

[00:07:56] **Mike Lee:** Yeah, it blew apart that toy house, right by the toy house, even went into the ground, under the ground and blew out of the ground.

[00:08:06] **Matt Gilbert:** You know, Deena Tritt said something really interesting, she talked a lot about blueberries and cranberries, she said after that big lightning strike at Caitlin's house, she said all the berries all over the land died immediately, it sent some kind of electrical shockwave across the land, interesting, huh?

[00:08:28] **Mike Lee:** Yeah, they weren't really getting much.

[00:08:30] **Matt Gilbert:** Really?

[00:08:31] **Mike Lee:** Yeah. Actually, some of them were getting some.

[00:08:34] **Matt Gilbert:** Oh really?

[00:08:36] **Mike Lee:** But I saw that where it struck up there.

[00:08:41] **Matt Gilbert:** Still there? crater-like?

[00:08:42] **Mike Lee:** Maybe, it's about this deep, like somebody dug up the ground with a shovel or something.

[00:08:52] **Matt Gilbert:** Is that it?

[00:08:52] **Mike Lee:** Yeah.

[End]

Raymond Tritt 6-19-2020.mp3

[00:00:00] **Matt Gilbert:** Raymond Tritt, June 19, 2020. Update interview.

[00:00:15] **Matt Gilbert:** It won't take too long, I got a question over here. Caribou, is it still the same? Caribou, it seems still the same.

[00:00:25] **Raymond Tritt:** Yeah, it's still the same. Mostly they just stay around here, you know, they don't, they just go migrate, you know ANWR [Alaska Native Wildlife Refuge], and they come back, and they don't go to Canada like they did, [they] don't go anyplace, they just come back straight down. They usually don't do that, usually scatter around, like, [on the] Canada side, and then they—

[00:00:56] **Matt Gilbert:** They hang around the Canada side; they don't do that no more?

[00:00:58] **Raymond Tritt:** It don't seem like it.

[00:01:00] **Matt Gilbert:** They're around here lots, it seems like.

[00:01:02] **Raymond Tritt:** Yeah, mostly year-round, that's something that's different.

[00:01:10] **Matt Gilbert:** What about snow, is there more or less, the same? Less?

[00:01:14] **Raymond Tritt:** Less.

[00:01:17] **Matt Gilbert:** Oh, OK. They said in Fairbanks sometimes there's no snow until November [*laughs*].

[00:01:24] **Raymond Tritt:** I know.

[00:01:25] **Matt Gilbert:** That's what's strange, huh?

[00:01:26] **Raymond Tritt:** Yeah.

[00:01:27] **Matt Gilbert:** It's summer till November sometimes [in] Fairbanks.

[00:01:31] **Raymond Tritt:** And then that one time, they had that snow over Fairbanks when [the] willows were still green, and it was snow like 2 feet deep, everybody was surprised.

[00:01:48] **Matt Gilbert:** But the snow here, it's been the same here?

[00:01:49] **Raymond Tritt:** Yeah, it's about the same.

[00:01:51] **Matt Gilbert:** Yeah. Comparatively, it's the same here.

[00:01:55] **Matt Gilbert:** Ptarmigan, I go up the mountain, I don't see them anymore.

[00:01:59] **Raymond Tritt:** No, no.

[00:02:01] **Matt Gilbert:** Ptarmigan

[00:02:02] **Raymond Tritt:** Yeah, you don't see them anymore. Just probably, yeah, I could see tracks, you know, around that glacier, yeah, about that. Not that many.

[00:02:14]   **Matt Gilbert:** You, if you went out hunting for ptarmigan, you think you would find them, or no?

[00:02:18]   **Raymond Tritt:** I'll find them all right, yeah but you might have to go real far though.

[00:02:25]   **Matt Gilbert:** In 2005, that big fire it scared that marten and lynx up here, but they went back home, huh?

[00:02:33]   **Raymond Tritt:** I don't know, I haven't shot for a long time.

[00:02:38]   **Matt Gilbert:** No, but you said they saw lynx and marten around Arctic Village, and—

[00:02:41]   **Raymond Tritt:** Yeah, there's marten around, but lynx, yeah, they've seen a couple tracks up there.

[00:02:46]   **Matt Gilbert:** When was this?

[00:02:48]   **Raymond Tritt:** That was about 4 years ago.

[00:02:51]   **Matt Gilbert:** Oh, but they haven't seen it lately?

[00:02:53]   **Raymond Tritt:** Not to there [*inaudible*].

[00:02:54]   **Matt Gilbert:** Okay. So, it sounds like they went back home, then?

[00:02:57]   **Raymond Tritt:** They probably would [*inaudible*]. They're just hanging around where there's a lot of rabbit.

[00:03:01]   **Matt Gilbert:** Geez, there's a lot a rabbit around here.

[00:03:04]   **Raymond Tritt:** Yeah, I know [*both laugh*]. So, [*inaudible*] I don't know.

[00:03:10]   **Matt Gilbert:** And, ah, in 2005 you said fish, you said there was less of them because, ah, you said [if] you stay [in] one place in the morning you could catch 30 graylings, you said it's not like that no more.

[00:03:24]   **Raymond Tritt:** No more.

[00:03:24]   **Matt Gilbert:** It's still the same, huh.

[00:03:25]   **Raymond Tritt:** Yeah, it's still the same.

[00:03:31]   **Matt Gilbert:** You said there's no salmonberry on the mountain, still no salmonberry on the mountain?

[00:03:37]   **Raymond Tritt:** I don't see any salmonberry, everything is changing.

[00:03:42]   **Matt Gilbert:** Still no salmonberry, huh?

[00:03:44]   **Raymond Tritt:** I don't know, I'll find out in August.

[00:03:48]   **Matt Gilbert:** But you never see any?

[00:03:50]   **Raymond Tritt:** No.

[00:03:53]   **Matt Gilbert:** So that's it, I guess, you have anything more you want to say about global warming?

[00:03:57]   **Raymond Tritt:** Ah, no, that's all right.

[End]

Raymond Tritt (Part 2).mp3 [6-19-2020, Arctic Village]

[00:00:00] **Matt Gilbert:** Part 2, Raymond.

[00:00:02] **Raymond Tritt:** I ran up there last night, then I [was] coming back down, it was getting windy, I get back in here. [*inaudible*] It's a big thunder [*laughs*]. Even my house was shaking [*laughs*]. I thought it was going to break a window.

[00:00:24] **Matt Gilbert:** It never used to be that loud?

[00:00:26] **Raymond Tritt:** No, just right close too, it sounded like it.

[00:00:30] **Matt Gilbert:** What about that rain, is it coming harder than when you were . . .

[00:00:35] **Raymond Tritt:** No.

[00:00:36] **Matt Gilbert:** It's same?

[00:00:36] **Raymond Tritt:** Yeah, the same.

[00:00:37] **Matt Gilbert:** Okay.

[End]

Trimble Gilbert 6-27-2020.mp3 Arctic Village

[00:00:00] **Matt Gilbert:** Trimble Gilbert, June 27, Saturday, 2020.

[00:00:10] **Matt Gilbert:** Caribou, people are saying it's hanging around the village more, they say it's hanging around the village more. Caribou.

[00:00:35] **Trimble Gilbert:** Yeah, uh hum, what's with caribou, it's way bad, for thousands of years, we had—

[00:00:52] **Matt Gilbert:** No, I meant like global warming, they said since 2005, the last time I interviewed you guys, that the caribou have been hanging around the village more, they said.

[00:01:04] **Trimble Gilbert:** Uh huh, I think they broke up that biggest herd in this part of Alaska, and so people of Arctic Village, they know a lot about the caribou, how they, migrations is ah, route is changed since, I don't know about how many years ago, it's very different and that Porcupine herd has got more land than any animal, 'cause maybe this northern part of Alaska is a big area, and . . .

[00:01:58] **Matt Gilbert:** We know all that, just that global warming effect on it, though, like anything you see different recently?

[00:02:07] **Trimble Gilbert:** Weather changed, and—

[00:02:16] **Matt Gilbert:** No, the global warming effect on the caribou, is there, are they doing anything different, that caribou?

[00:02:21] **Trimble Gilbert:** Yeah, they, that's what I'm talking about, they travel different. We're out and then the herd is coming in from the north and they usually come through here up in the Dachanlee, and all the way down to Venetie, before first of August, and then around middle of or first of August they start coming back, and they were like Gold Camp, that's where they are crossing, and up this way [Gwich'in *a Trekanjit*? (mouth), a *Trekanjit*?], that's a main trail coming back, and then all of the ridge in Dachanlee. And now it's, they come here any time and then, but not like that big [of a] herd of caribou, because that time is not [Gwich'in *tha keen*] they call them, thousands together and coming this way, and you can hear that little calf make noise, you can hear them [from a] long ways [away], there's too many of them. Sometimes they cover that [Gwich'in ——] and saw thousands of them and you could hear them. But they don't do that anymore. They just go down maybe even a little halfway, then coming back, and then they never cross the river from west [of] here. Used to be a lot of them crossing at [*inaudible list of three places*], and then all the way up to Junjik crossing towards [*inaudible*].

And then that time, [*inaudible*] hind sun, is just before October, white you can see them [from a] long ways [away], crossing the river, and but now they don't cross anymore, but sometimes they do, just not that many, now we just hunt at Dachanlee, but it's hard to get them. And even with when my boys are small, Mary and I go up with a chainsaw, that's where they're crossing but not that many, so we bring it back, some meat from there, but we don't do it for a long time, because they're not crossing.

Then around wintertime they're coming back around October, they're coming back and then they spend mostly down at [Gwich'in *Closts so*], down by Venetie, then they spend the winter up here, they go after the lichen and then some, they spend more winter around here because the other herd from the North Slope, sometimes they're kind of mixed, but they always separate. But that North Slope herd . . . spends more time in the west from here in [*inaudible*] and [*inaudible*], and they climb high mountains but the Porcupine [herd] don't do that much, but they're mixed, but they're always separate. And then the Porcupine herd is always going back to McPherson area, Old Crow area and Aklavik area. So that's where they always spend winters around Old Crow. But the Porcupine herd is pretty healthy yet, and a lot of time they're really fat. But that oil central, North Slope caribou, we know it because they're smaller and very thin, different than the Porcupine [herd], thin and very fat.

We know that, but, so that's all the change you see on the caribou with global warming.

[00:07:58] **Trimble Gilbert:** Yeah.

[00:08:01] **Matt Gilbert:** Ok. They just said that they're hanging around the village more, that's what people are saying.

[00:08:09] **Trimble Gilbert:** Uh huh, I think there's too many wolf packs, so sometimes they're hanging around, right by the school all the time, too many wolf packs, so they get close to the village feeding on the lakes and shovel snow, and more lichen around here too, in the winter too. So, after that they're heading back to the north.

[00:08:59] **Matt Gilbert:** Overgrowth, they said there's a lot of overgrowth, overgrowth, since I'm trying to update from 2005, you don't have to tell me anything that you said in 2005, just anything that happened since then, they want to know. Everybody is saying there's overgrowth, everybody can see it, so you, I don't know if you have to talk about that. Overgrowth. You know.

[00:09:34] **Trimble Gilbert:** Over . . . ?

[00:09:35] **Matt Gilbert:** Overgrowth. Lot of bushes and trees.

[00:09:38] **Trimble Gilbert:** Oh, you mean water?

[00:09:41] **Matt Gilbert:** No, the trees and bushes, a lot of it.

[00:09:46] **Trimble Gilbert:** Oh, that's part of the, this area is, when I was a kid, about 19 . . .

[00:10:02] **Matt Gilbert:** Yeah, everybody says it was nothing, yeah.

[00:10:02] **Trimble Gilbert:** Yeah, we see, and then it starts—

[00:10:07] **Matt Gilbert:** Yeah, everybody knows that, but they say it's getting worse, though, it's getting worse.

[00:10:11] **Trimble Gilbert:** Yeah, that tree is growing fast around here, the willows, maybe that's the reason they [caribou] don't go across halfway to Venetie, and too much brush, and then that on the halfway up the mountain there's trees and willows and they're kind of thick, it's kind of a barrier to caribou.

[00:10:37] **Matt Gilbert:** You said that, I read that interview.

[00:10:41] **Trimble Gilbert:** Uh huh.

[00:10:42] **Matt Gilbert:** I just want to know something new, you know, anything new.

[00:10:45] **Trimble Gilbert:** So, last 2 years, back in 1988 when I built the house here, there was a tree out there, it's smaller, maybe 7 foot, 6 foot. Now it's a big tree, I don't even see nothing from my home, and I don't use the binoculars for looking for caribou from here. That's why everything is growing fast, and that's why they lost their trail, because the older caribou, the leader caribou.

[00:11:23] **Matt Gilbert:** Yeah, yeah, you said that.

[00:11:23] **Trimble Gilbert:** They're the only ones [that] know that old trail, and then they're all gone, so that . . .

[00:11:31] **Matt Gilbert:** You said that already, I just want something new, remember, you said that, I got it written down [*door opens*].

[00:11:40] **Matt Gilbert:** What about ptarmigan? You said it was only in the mountains, but it's not in the mountains now, ptarmigan?

[00:11:47] **Trimble Gilbert:** Oh, there's nothing last 2 years. That [Gwich'in *T'al a Hi?*] is, oh towards about 20 miles, 30 miles from here to Fort Yukon trail in a clear area. There's a thousand Porcupine on that willow creek down there [Gwich'in*T'al a hi?*]. I remember when I was a kid there were a thousand of them taking off, it just like airplanes, and sounds like an airplane, so many of them.

[00:12:25] **Trimble Gilbert:** And then later on, when I was young boy, boy, maybe 20 years old, there were a lot of ptarmigans around here in springtime, making all kinds of noise, nesting, and then they, that male sitting on top of the tree, watching the nesting female. Now they don't do that anymore. Not this year, we don't even see nothing, we don't even see ptarmigan.

[00:13:01] **Matt Gilbert:** What about that snipe, that snipe, he still gone?

[00:13:05] **Trimble Gilbert:** Dil'?

[00:13:06] **Matt Gilbert:** Snipe.

[00:13:07] **Trimble Gilbert:** Uh.

[00:13:09] **Matt Gilbert:** Bird it sounds like this, aa aaaaaaaaaaaaaaaaaa. It's way up there.

[00:13:15] **Trimble Gilbert:** Zhezha Zhezha, it's a—

[00:13:21] **Matt Gilbert:** Sounds like that, [*ascending whistle*] aa aaaaaaaaaaaaaaaaaa. Way up there.

[00:13:24] **Trimble Gilbert:** Yeah, that's one, Zhe Zha, and then makes like waves like this, since we're in the Arctic, not real many, there's some this year but not very many, a lot of them are gone, dil', is nothing too.

[00:13:51] **Matt Gilbert:** He came back this year, I've heard him.

[00:13:52] **Trimble Gilbert:** But they don't make noise, though.

[00:13:55] **Matt Gilbert:** I've heard them a couple times, that alarm.

[00:13:58] **Trimble Gilbert:** Yeah, [*background noise*] birds are quiet, and they don't make noise too much anymore. Lots of them don't come back [*inaudible*] anyway.

[00:14:09] **Matt Gilbert:** What about seagull?

[00:14:10] **Trimble Gilbert:** Seagull?

[00:14:12] **Matt Gilbert:** Is it still sitting on the sand bar? Seagull?

[00:14:15] **Trimble Gilbert:** Oh, yeah. There's one right around here now.

[00:14:20] **Matt Gilbert:** No, do you still see them sitting on that sand bar?

[00:14:23] **Trimble Gilbert:** Oh, seagull, Vyuh.

[00:14:26] **Matt Gilbert:** Yeah.

[00:14:26] **Trimble Gilbert:** Nothing here too this year, a lot of them went by, but I don't know why they don't nest around here. A lot of other birds never come back here.

[00:14:48] **Matt Gilbert:** Swallows, the ones that make a hole in the bank?

[00:14:52] **Trimble Gilbert:** That's different one, too.

[00:14:56] **Matt Gilbert:** They're back, I see them down at that gravel pit.

[00:14:58] **Trimble Gilbert:** I never see that kind of swallow.

[00:15:00] **Matt Gilbert:** They're back, they're at that gravel pit, they made a lot of holes.

[00:15:03] **Trimble Gilbert:** Yeah, they're different swallows, that one got a brown head, they'll make nests around the river, brown head, and then small one is a bank swallow.

[00:15:17] **Matt Gilbert:** Yeah, they're back, they make holes in that gravel pit down there.

[00:15:20] **Trimble Gilbert:** That's a different swallow from the one I seen, really pretty swallows are here, and I see them. Other one, maybe when I was in Circle a few years back, then I saw a lot of them there, maybe that's the one that got a brown head, bank swallow.

[00:15:47] **Matt Gilbert:** And that river, it's still low, and that lake is still draining out, too?

[00:15:53] **Trimble Gilbert:** Not only here but all over. When East Fork, we don't have a problem going up a long time ago, but now is a certain place we can't go up because of the shallow, we hit the bottom. But this year, is so much rain, so I never see that much high water now, so it's really high now. But when the water is going down, then we're gonna have a problem again. And also, the lakes are going down too, even Old John Lake, we lost a lot of water. Some lakes are drained out too, a lot of 'em. Fish is still good, though, [Gwich'in *hashivan? Ah Vree Yung*?] and all that. [Gwich'in *Aliven*] is pretty low too, water.

[00:16:45]   **Matt Gilbert:** That permafrost is it still drying, coming down? Permafrost? That land is going like this?

[00:16:51]   **Trimble Gilbert:** Yeah, well, that glacier, is a [*inaudible*] normal [*inaudible*] glacier [Gwich'in *a q tan lee*?].

North Slide *q tan lee* you could see the ice all summer, I don't know about the glacier, but there may still be ice there. And [Gwich'in *Trajunjik*]. So, another thing is last year's cold weather, cold Christmas until March, and cold, and even now there's true, cold weather everywhere, nighttime it's really chilly around here. And then when the suns come out, it warms a little bit, so funny weather, changes all the time.

[00:17:51]   **Matt Gilbert:** Well, that's it, that's all I got.

[00:17:53]   **Trimble Gilbert:** Um hum.

[00:17:54]   **Matt Gilbert:** If you want to say anything more you can.

[00:18:00]   **Trimble Gilbert:** And you could get some more information from other people?

[00:18:07]   **Matt Gilbert:** I already did, that's why I don't got that many questions. They gave me a lot of information already.

[00:18:10]   **Trimble Gilbert:** Young people, they know a lot about it too, so it would be good to have young people too, they know a lot of things change too, you can ask them. That weather, climate change has really affected a lot of things we never know. Mary and I, we talk about that cold weather next year, we just worry about it.

Last year before Christmas until springtime it was just cold, so we never know. It's not only here but all over the country.

[00:19:03]   **Matt Gilbert:** Well, in 2005, I talked to all you guys about global warming, and Gideon was saying, in 2005 he said this, because of global warming we're gonna have different diseases, you know, I told him he's right because we got that Coronavirus, you know, that's why I'm wearing a mask right now.

[00:19:26]   **Trimble Gilbert:** Yup.

[00:19:28]   **Matt Gilbert:** He said we're going to have different diseases, he's right, it came through.

[00:19:32] **Trimble Gilbert:** Yeah, when I [was growing] up, we don't even know . . . nothing about disease because, when that only sore on the skin, that's all we have problems, because of the lice. Otherwise, people are very healthy people, no disease, not very many people died when I grew up, I didn't even know people who died when I was growing up. Now [this] virus came in and it changed the whole world now. World it just looks like, seems to me it's upside down now because we're losing a thousand, more than a thousand people every day we're losing. So, weather is. . . . Disease like that when they are around the people, people said, they got the weather too.

[00:20:42] **Matt Gilbert:** That's what Gideon said, he said because the weather is different, that different diseases can come in. He's right?

[00:20:49] **Trimble Gilbert:** That's what I'm saying.

[00:20:52] **Matt Gilbert:** That's why I'm wearing mask, gloves.

[00:20:53] **Trimble Gilbert:** Yeah. Dusty, again, now, is a halo [*inaudible*], different location in the double, small climate in the . . . double [*inaudible*]. That dust, you heard about that?

[00:21:09] **Matt Gilbert:** No.

[00:21:09] **Trimble Gilbert:** The dust is coming out from the clouds and now it's [in] Florida [*inaudible*], and the dust [is] now on the air. That's what they said, too. I never heard that before. That's weird, we never know, "what next," that's what we expect now.

[00:21:35] **Matt Gilbert:** Ok. All right. I'm done.

[End]

Trimble Gilbert 7-23-2020.mp3 *Arctic Village (Part 2)*

[00:00:00] **Matt Gilbert:** July 23, Thursday. Trimble Gilbert part 2. Climate survey.

[00:00:09] **Matt Gilbert:** Yeah, go ahead, it's recording.

[00:00:13] **Trimble Gilbert:** [Gwich'in *Tri Vi*] is a tornado, we got one here, but [it was] just not strong enough to pick up, damage anything around here, roofing or anything, but just pick up light stuff, papers or either some kinds of grass, and then you can see them in Tri Vi. And, uh, it does something to the earth, and I think clouds are covering a whole area sometimes, and then that time Tri Vi's come around and whip them all away, I think, that's what they said, our people. And so, they, we never had it around here no more.

[00:01:27] **Trimble Gilbert:** When I was a kid, I always saw everywhere you go that's a Tri Vi, like a baby one, always in front of you and you could see them pick up some trash sometimes, but not all the trash. Like I'm saying paper or anything light, and then Tri Vi, we call [it] that, and about 10 years ago we had one, northeast from here about 20 miles, I didn't see it myself, but Julie Hollingsworth took a picture of it, and it came down from the sky really black, a long one, but it stopped anyway up on Dachanlee about 5 mile, 2 mile, 3 mile, up northeast on Dachanlee, so I think it hit nothing.

And so that weather is, does something to the weather, and help weather not destroy the whole city like they have down [in] the south.

[00:03:00] **Trimble Gilbert:** Like another way it's, another thing is, climate change, and we settled [*inaudible*] climate change, but we're too close to the ocean now. So, every time it becomes cloudy, it never goes away. I stay at Kaktovik area sometimes, it covers a long time, all the way down to the ground. It looked like, it's getting warmed up, so that might be the way we're gonna have it.

[00:03:54] **Matt Gilbert:** It's recording again. Yeah, that, that's true, even me when I was a little boy we played around, we saw that little tornado, we even tried to jump into it and play with it, but I don't see it no more.

[00:04:09] **Trimble Gilbert:** Yeah, lots of them around here.

[00:04:11] **Matt Gilbert:** Yeah, lots of them.

[00:04:12] **Trimble Gilbert:** Ah huh.

[00:04:12] **Matt Gilbert:** I never thought of that, I never see them no more.

[00:04:18] **Trimble Gilbert:** Ah huh. Well, that's an Elder story, so it was true.

[00:04:26] **Matt Gilbert:** I didn't know that, what Audrey told me, that it goes all the way up into the cloud and blows the cloud away, makes it clearer.

[00:04:36] **Trimble Gilbert:** Maybe that's what happened. It blowed all those clouds away.

[00:04:44] **Matt Gilbert:** Yeah, that's what she said, the Elders say that.

[00:04:45] **Trimble Gilbert:** Well, that's true.

[00:04:46] **Matt Gilbert:** But she said nowadays when it comes it don't blow this cloud away, this cloud is different, now it stays even that Tri Vi, that cloud stays around, it's a different cloud, she said.

[00:05:01] **Trimble Gilbert:** Well, that's, you can see that cloud is black on the bottom, that means it's something [*room sounds*]. I keep on telling you about that same thing too, that bottom is black so like, uh, that gas was burning over north slope, it makes that cloud funny on the bottom . . .

[00:05:40] **Matt Gilbert:** She said it's really dark right now, and it's not supposed to be this dark, she said.

[00:05:39] **Trimble Gilbert:** Yeah, because that.

[00:05:46] **Matt Gilbert:** She said, "Turn my light off, I turn it off, the house is dark last night," she said, see, it's not supposed to be this dark right now.

[00:05:53] **Trimble Gilbert:** Because the bottom of the cloud is black, looks like that's oil burning.

[00:06:01] **Matt Gilbert:** From North Slope.

[00:06:02] **Trimble Gilbert:** Yeah.

[00:06:03] **Matt Gilbert:** That's what Gideon said, it's North Slope.

[00:06:03] **Trimble Gilbert:** That's true. And ah . . .

[00:06:09] **Matt Gilbert:** Audrey said electric wires, that gives us electricity, she said it's affecting the cloud, too, that clouds go like this from the electricity. You think that's true, too?

[00:06:26] **Trimble Gilbert:** I don't know, but I don't know why [we've] been hit with thunder three times [*room noise*]. Well, we been hit by thunder three times now, three, four times now, I think. First one, that's about 20 miles north of, a little more than 20 miles north of, up [Gwich'in *Nan thee tha*?]. That's where thunder hit. And then he hit that rock, that red rock ocher, so all that water is red.

[00:07:23] **Trimble Gilbert:** And then when my son Gregory was working on the Audrey house, I think, the thunder hit not too far away from that, where they work, I could see that something there hit the ground.

[00:07:38] **Trimble Gilbert:** And then later on, that Jim Hollingsworth house almost got hit, and that pretty good size hole, I never seen it, but that's what I heard, this is the third one.

[00:07:58] **Trimble Gilbert:** And then this summer, we had it again, but then he just damaged electricity and the phone, so I don't know why he keeps coming around here, and he hit that village three or four times now.

[00:08:20] **Trimble Gilbert:** So that's probably something gonna happen later on, maybe. Just like today, yesterday, down the southeast, it's a really strong one, earthquake. So, he's just doing that different thing in Alaska now, a lot of things are going on now. And another thing is, might be, something is not going right, that's why animals are getting less and less, and all the birds and other animals. Like that porcupine, 20 years ago there were a lot of them around here. Now they've been gone for a long time, and finally came back, coming back I think right now.

[00:09:21]   **Matt Gilbert:** Yeah, a lot of them come back this year, huh? . . . A lot of animals came back.

[00:09:25]   **Trimble Gilbert:** Yeah.

[00:09:27]   **Matt Gilbert:** So, you said there's less animals, you mean all over the world, there's a lot less animals? Becoming less and less animals?

[00:09:33]   **Trimble Gilbert:** Uh huh.

[00:09:34]   **Matt Gilbert:** All over Alaska? Or Canada?

[00:09:36]   **Trimble Gilbert:** When I just keep saying that, and animals are different too, they're not happy no more. You never heard that singing, not too much anymore. Some of those animals [are] really quiet, is like snipe, dil', when they see something moving around [their] nesting area, [he's just] noisy, noisy, noisy, and he was around here but he's pretty quiet. So, something is going on and so the people set up after things like that, and what next? I agree with them. Something happened, little things happened, and then the next one. So that's where we're at right now.

[00:10:39]   **Matt Gilbert:** That Coronavirus, Gideon, he predicted it too, he said—when I interviewed him in 2005, it's 2020 now—he said, because of global warming we're going to have new disease and they're going to be worse, he said. He was right, that Coronavirus came around.

[00:10:57]   **Trimble Gilbert:** Uh huh. Well, that seems like we don't know where that virus come from really, I could see that big question mark and nobody could answer it. We don't know where it come from. But it's killing all the people in the world now. And after that, what next? It seems to me that virus is just madness. They don't know what to do, a lot of them died, and [it's a] very sad thing going on. But still, a lot, I could hear a lot of people saying that they don't even talk about it, and they just talk about [the] future yet. But I don't know what kind of future we gonna have. We might [be] running out of people, that's bad. The world is for the people to live on. But if we keep losing people that's going to be a real sad thing. So, that's the next one, everybody worries about it. Next one . . . coming is food, too, there's a lot of things growing in, the fresh stuff in, all over the world, in the beef and all that, and fishing and fisheries and now a lot of people catching that virus. And then if something happens with the beef, all the food we've been eating, I think we gonna have a big problem. [*Coffee! Coffee pot's out here*].

[End]

Trimble Gilbert 7-23-2020 Part 3.mp3 Arctic Village

[00:00:00] **Matt Gilbert:** July 23, Thursday, part 3 Trimble Gilbert.

[00:00:05] **Trimble Gilbert:** One more thing, the important things I could hear from Canada, and way over [to the] northwest, Fort Good Hope, the Elder there, he called me about a week ago, he said water is rising on the river, and he said it's never, see that water's so high, it's the first time it's like that. I don't know about now, but it keeps raining. So, that's the next thing that even that . . .

[00:00:53] **Trimble Gilbert:** A lot of bad things happening now. Even king salmon. One guy called me from Fairbanks, he said he tried to get king salmon in the Yukon River, and he sent a message to them, but they said [there's] no king salmon. No more, maybe, I don't know, not many left. But I've seen the fishery, people catch more and more, and I think they might clean up everything pretty soon, I think. And that's another problem we're facing.

[00:01:38] **Matt Gilbert:** Is that it?

[00:01:49] **Trimble Gilbert:** Ah.

[End]

VENETIE TRANSCRIPTS OF CLIMATE INTERVIEWS

Interview by Matt Gilbert

Transcription by Pam Miller

Darrell Tritt 6-25-2020.mp3 Venetie [taped in Arctic Village]

[00:00:00] **Matt Gilbert:** This is June 25, Thursday 2020. It's Darrell Tritt Interview about Venetie climate change.

[00:00:13] **Matt Gilbert:** So, these are in 2005, I'm going to go down there and ask them if anything changed, you know, since recording. The first thing they're talked about was salmon; they said that there's more king salmon down there than in the past, is that true, you know?

[00:00:33] **Darrell Tritt:** Yeah, right now.

[00:00:34] **Matt Gilbert:** They still get a lot of king?

[00:00:36] **Darrell Tritt:** Yeah, a lot of king.

[00:00:37] **Matt Gilbert:** They said dog salmon, they get a lot of that too, is that true?

[00:00:40] **Darrell Tritt:** Yeah, a lot of dog salmon

[00:00:43] **Matt Gilbert:** A long time ago [it] wasn't like that?

[00:00:44] **Darrell Tritt:** No, a long time ago wasn't like that, [there weren't] no salmon, just dog salmon.

[00:00:51] **Matt Gilbert:** Huh. Anything you notice about fish in Venetie?

[00:00:54] **Darrell Tritt:** Huh?

[00:00:55] **Matt Gilbert:** Anything new about fish in Venetie?

[00:00:58] **Darrell Tritt:** Fish? I know there's, usually we don't see pikes around there, but we see pike around, huh?

[00:01:09] **Matt Gilbert:** And these interviews, a lot of them were saying that the summers are cold now . . . the summers are cold in Venetie?

[00:01:15] **Darrell Tritt:** Yeah, summers are cold.

[00:01:18] **Matt Gilbert:** Wow, just like up here.

[00:01:19] **Darrell Tritt:** Yeah, like winter is getting warmer than summer [*they laugh*].

[00:01:29] **Matt Gilbert:** They also said that the weather changed fast down there . . . is that true? Same up here in Arctic?

[00:01:37] **Darrell Tritt:** Yeah, same thing, one it's sunny, then it's raining, last time it was even snowing in July [*both laugh*].

[00:01:51] **Matt Gilbert:** Geez, so the river, in 2005 they said it was low. Is it, it's still low?

[00:01:56] **Darrell Tritt:** Yeah.

[00:01:57] **Matt Gilbert:** It's even lower, you think, now?

[00:01:57] **Darrell Tritt:** Yeah, in fall-time, you can walk across [*both laugh*].

[00:02:09] **Matt Gilbert:** Robert Frank, he said the only thing that raises the water now is rain.

[00:02:14] **Darrell Tritt:** Rain, and snow.

[00:02:17] **Matt Gilbert:** No, he said that snow used to make that river high in spring, it's not like that no more, he said now the only thing that raises [it] is rain.

[00:02:25] **Darrell Tritt:** Yeah rain, even this spring . . . the snow melted and nothing, the river didn't go up.

[00:02:35] **Matt Gilbert:** Only thing that makes it go up is rain, huh?

[00:02:37] **Darrell Tritt:** Yeah, there's a lot of rain, first time I ever seen a lot of rain around here, that's a first.

[00:02:44] **Matt Gilbert:** Wow. So, it's still low, like you can even walk across, wow.

[00:02:50] **Matt Gilbert:** So, [in] 2005 they said Big Lake was drying out.

[00:02:53] **Darrell Tritt:** Oh yeah, it was drying out on the side, you could even walk out there probably about that far [*shows*].

[00:03:02] **Matt Gilbert:** That's about 5 feet, like—

[00:03:04] **Darrell Tritt:** Yeah.

[00:03:07] **Matt Gilbert:** Geez. No, that's about 6 feet right there, you said here to the wall, huh?

[00:03:12] **Darrell Tritt:** Yeah, from here to the wall, on the shore too.

[00:03:17] **Matt Gilbert:** It never used to do that?

[00:03:17] **Darrell Tritt:** No, used to be all the way to the bank, huh.

[00:03:21] **Matt Gilbert:** Wow, so you're saying it receded 5, 6 feet, so it shrank?

[00:03:28] **Darrell Tritt:** Yeah, then the last time that, I don't know, that water came from the mountain, I guess, after the fire, came down and got a little more water.

[00:03:42] **Matt Gilbert:** Oh, OK. So, you guys used Big Lake just for ducks or for fish too, a long time ago?

[00:03:48] **Darrell Tritt:** A long time ago. But when those creeks, it's [got] too [many] beaver dams, too [many] beavers. They said that the creek . . . changed too, that [Gwich'in *go got cho* (name of a lake)], yeah . . .

[00:04:07] **Matt Gilbert:** Bobby said that, Bobby Tritt said that they should talk to Fish and Wildlife about clearing those creeks.

[00:04:14] **Darrell Tritt:** Take those beaver dams out.

[00:04:17] **Matt Gilbert:** Yeah, another thing, a lot of those Elders in Venetie were saying that they see more and more landslides and mountains chipping off. Landslides, you see that too?

[00:04:30] **Darrell Tritt:** Yeah, you know that Venetie, remember that white, right there it's just coming down, coming down. Remember that Venetie used to be way out there, that Old Village.

[00:04:41] **Matt Gilbert:** Uh huh?

[00:04:41] **Darrell Tritt:** No, it's—

[00:04:44] **Matt Gilbert:** That's what Robert Frank said, he said that Old Village, when they moved the church, caused that erosion, that was like early '80s. But he said since then that Old Village, he said that probably 400 years it eroded, just fell off.

[00:05:00] **Darrell Tritt:** It's still eroding. It's still eroding . . .

[00:05:03] **Matt Gilbert:** Is he right? Here like, here to Audrey's house it's 400 yards, he said all that is just filling in.

[00:05:10] **Darrell Tritt:** Used to be . . . yeah . . .

[00:05:12] **Matt Gilbert:** Is he right? All that's gone?

[00:05:17] **Darrell Tritt:** Still eroding, going in.

[00:05:20] **Matt Gilbert:** He said up at, I think [Gwich'in *Ticho eh*], like David Henry's cabin, he said that bank fell in like 600 feet . . .

[00:05:28] **Darrell Tritt:** Oh yeah, eroding that one too . . .

[00:05:30] **Matt Gilbert:** Same thing, like from here to Terry's house, 600 feet.

[00:05:34] **Darrell Tritt:** Yeah like . . .

[00:05:35] **Matt Gilbert:** . . . all this gone, maybe even that village might be in danger someday, huh, because those houses . . .

[00:05:46] **Darrell Tritt:** Yeah, from this side?

[00:05:49] **Matt Gilbert:** Crazy . . . so ducks, um? Eddie and Tim and them were talking about ducks, they said some ducks are low in numbers, are they right?

[00:06:00] **Darrell Tritt:** Yeah, there's a lot of time.

[00:06:02] **Matt Gilbert:** Like, Tim said when he moved to Venetie in 1983, he said there's just like waves of ducks, you don't see that no more.

[00:06:11] **Darrell Tritt:** Yeah, you don't see that no more.

[00:06:11] **Matt Gilbert:** He said just a little bit here and there.

[00:06:13] **Darrell Tritt:** Yeah.

[00:06:14] **Matt Gilbert:** Is he right?

[00:06:14] **Darrell Tritt:** Yeah.

[00:06:17] **Matt Gilbert:** Geez, that's no good. He said that [Gwich'in *Jaw* (black ducks)] black duck, [Gwich'in Dee *Tree Awh*] and [Gwich'in *Han Luk* (northern pintail)], he said they're all down in numbers.

[00:06:27] **Darrell Tritt:** Yeah, it's been down for a long time.

[00:06:31] **Matt Gilbert:** It's still true, all this?

[00:06:32] **Darrell Tritt:** Yeah.

[00:06:35] **Matt Gilbert:** Ah, so, birds, they don't hear them sing no more.

[00:06:43] **Darrell Tritt:** Yeah, it's true.

[00:06:45] **Matt Gilbert:** It's bad.

[00:06:46] **Darrell Tritt:** Yeah.

[00:06:46] **Matt Gilbert:** Even in spring you don't hear them sing that much?

[00:06:49] **Darrell Tritt:** Seems that global warming, warming must be doing something with them.

[00:06:56] **Matt Gilbert:** Must be doing something. They say that the swallows are really down, they don't see them as much.

[00:07:03] **Darrell Tritt:** Yeah, you don't see around nowhere.

[00:07:08] **Matt Gilbert:** Not many?

[00:07:07] **Darrell Tritt:** No, no.

[00:07:08] **Matt Gilbert:** So, is that true, like back in early '80s you could see a lot of big birds, lot of ducks?

[00:07:16] **Darrell Tritt:** Yeah, we used to see a lot of black ducks, a lot of hanluk ducks [Northern Pintail].

[00:07:19] **Matt Gilbert:** Wow.

[00:07:20] **Darrell Tritt:** You could see them just coming in, constantly.

[00:07:25] **Matt Gilbert:** You don't see that no more.

[00:07:27] **Darrell Tritt:** No, you don't see that no more.

[00:07:30] **Matt Gilbert:** Robert thinks it's something interesting too, he said that they're, usually they fly in this way to Venetie, but he said they changed direction some time . . . changed route.

[00:07:40] **Darrell Tritt:** Yeah, they changed route.

[00:07:41] **Matt Gilbert:** They changed route?

[00:07:42] **Darrell Tritt:** Yeah, they used to fly over the village, and from the river they just fly over the village and fly to Big Lake, they don't do that no more. They come around, they come in from the back.

[00:07:55] **Matt Gilbert:** Just like an airplane.

[00:07:56] **Darrell Tritt:** Yeah, coming from the lake side.

[00:08:01] **Matt Gilbert:** Just like that airplane route, it goes around and lands.

[00:08:02] **Darrell Tritt:** It's like they're coming from the river and go over the village, fly up to Big Lake.

[00:08:09] **Matt Gilbert:** So that flying route changed?

[00:08:11] **Darrell Tritt:** Yeah.

[00:08:14] **Matt Gilbert:** Yeah, a lot of bad changes.

[00:08:15] **Darrell Tritt:** Yeah.

[00:08:17] **Matt Gilbert:** Let's see what else he was saying. [*My stomach was growling, never eat all day.*] Oh, someone said something interesting in Venetie, they said the wind is different too, that the wind is changed, like . . . feels different, the wind?

[00:08:34] **Darrell Tritt:** Yeah, changed, usually we get strong wind down there, now it don't do that no more.

[00:08:47] **Matt Gilbert:** Like that wind is dying down?

[00:08:48] **Darrell Tritt:** Yeah.

[00:08:54] **Matt Gilbert:** Man, it's getting crazy, yeah . . . the weather?

[00:08:56] **Darrell Tritt:** Yeah.

[00:08:59] **Matt Gilbert:** Ok, we talked about that already, one Elder down there they said they saw strange birds sitting on trees, too, like [with] blue on its back, he'd never seen a bird like that before, you think that they're getting new animals, too?

[00:09:12] **Darrell Tritt:** Probably.

[00:09:18] **Matt Gilbert:** A winter ago we saw a new bird here, a white bird sat on the spruce tree branch, we'd never seen that bird before.

[00:09:27] **Darrell Tritt:** Remember those little birds that go up, [*ascending*] woo woowoowoowooowo, you don't hear them no more.

[00:09:31] **Matt Gilbert:** [*Ascending whistle*] wo wowowowowowowo, like that?

[00:09:33] **Darrell Tritt:** Yeah, wo wowowowowowowowo.

[00:09:34] **Matt Gilbert:** [*Whistle*] wo wowowowowowowo, yeah, Mike Lee said he don't hear them in Arctic Village, is it the same in Venetie too?

[00:09:39] **Darrell Tritt:** Yeah.

[00:09:40] **Matt Gilbert:** Venetie too, you don't hear them?

[00:09:43] **Darrell Tritt:** [In] Venetie you sit around the lake, Big Lake, you hear it, you always hear it, but you don't hear it no more.

[00:09:48] **Matt Gilbert:** Like if you went to Big Lake, you sat there, you won't hear it?

[00:09:51] **Darrell Tritt:** Won't hear nothing.

[00:09:54] **Matt Gilbert:** Alo [spelling?], he said here in Arctic Village, those, you see those geese making a big, giant V, said you don't see that no more. Same thing in Venetie, too?

[00:10:07] **Darrell Tritt:** They said this year was different, there was a lot of geese.

[00:10:13] **Matt Gilbert:** What about geese in Venetie, is there still lots, still low or medium or the same?

[00:10:17] **Darrell Tritt:** Last time I was [*inaudible*], we don't see them, they fly real high too.

[00:10:28] **Matt Gilbert:** Here in Arctic Village, geese came back and there was swallows that make holes in that mud, they came back 'cause I seen them down there, dil' came back too because they were gone for a long time.

[00:10:38] **Darrell Tritt:** You know what I really don't see around is porcupine . . .

[00:10:41] **Matt Gilbert:** Yeah, my grandpa said they're extinct.

[00:10:44] **Darrell Tritt:** I don't see them around, I don't see [Gwich'in *din zee*?]. Usually when you walk around in the woods you see a sign of it . . .

[00:10:51] **Matt Gilbert:** People around here, they say they don't see beaver around here no more too.

[00:10:53] **Darrell Tritt:** Around here, around this area, yeah, you don't see beaver, don't see beaver, owls.

[00:11:02] **Matt Gilbert:** What about Venetie? What about beavers?

[00:11:05] **Darrell Tritt:** There's always beavers, just porcupine I don't see. Usually, you go anywhere you see porcupine, right, not anymore.

[00:11:17] **Matt Gilbert:** So, a long time ago, like when you were like young, you know, that Chandalar by Venetie was really big?

[00:11:28] **Darrell Tritt:** Yeah, it was coming down this side, huh, cliff, it was coming down that way.

[00:11:30] **Matt Gilbert:** It was wide, and really big water?

[00:11:33] **Darrell Tritt:** Yeah.

[00:11:35] **Matt Gilbert:** But now you said you could probably even walk across it so much [*laughs*].

[00:11:39] **Darrell Tritt:** Yeah, water gone down so much.

[00:11:42] **Matt Gilbert:** Geez, like you could run and jump across, huh?

[00:11:44] **Darrell Tritt:** Yeah, and that [Negin?] River . . . gets about that wide [*shows*].

[00:11:48] **Matt Gilbert:** Geez.

[00:11:50] **Darrell Tritt:** And the water really went down.

[00:11:51] **Matt Gilbert:** Yeah, holy cow, you can't even drive a boat in that, eh?

[00:11:54] **Darrell Tritt:** Yeah, there's a longer route, you gotta go all the way around.

[00:12:00] **Matt Gilbert:** Wow. Oh, that's another thing those Elders and hunters were telling me, in all the villages. They said because the river is so low, there's a lot of places they can't get no more where they used to a long time ago . . . you think that's true?

[00:12:13] **Darrell Tritt:** Yeah, probably.

[00:12:21] **Matt Gilbert:** Yeah, they, like Robert Frank said, nowadays you need a jet unit to go anywhere because the river's too low.

[00:12:28] **Darrell Tritt:** Yeah, a long time ago [we] used to use a prop, go anywhere with a prop, not any more.

[00:12:38] **Matt Gilbert:** Prop is lower units, for people who don't know it. Alright, well, yeah, I don't have anything else. What about anything you want Fish and Wildlife to know? Or, 'cause tribal leaders, they want to work with them more on this kind of stuff, you know.

[00:12:57] **Darrell Tritt:** Just get rid of those beaver dams, like Bobby said, more water back, get fish again, and—

[00:13:14] **Matt Gilbert:** Bobby also said that Native Gwich'in people should start doing harvest counts too, to make sure animal populations is good, you know.

[00:13:23] **Darrell Tritt:** Oh yeah.

[00:13:26] **Matt Gilbert:** Fish and Wildlife could pay Native people to do that.

[00:13:29] **Darrell Tritt:** Old William used to do that, but he retired.

[00:13:30] **Matt Gilbert:** Oh really?

[00:13:31] **Darrell Tritt:** He retired of it.

[00:13:32] **Matt Gilbert:** Another thing everyone is talking about right now is over-growth, lots of villages [are] starting to look like a jungle.

[00:13:42] **Darrell Tritt:** Around here? . . . Looks like a jungle down here.

[00:13:42] **Matt Gilbert:** Yeah . . . what about Venetie? Same thing?

[00:13:47] **Darrell Tritt:** Same thing. I've never been to Venetie for 6 years, I just came up here from the street.

[00:13:58] **Matt Gilbert:** I'm sure it's same thing.

[00:14:00] **Darrell Tritt:** It is the same thing going on there.

[00:14:03] **Matt Gilbert:** What you're saying is still important though because you were there long, all your life, what you see are these changes, you're the one that knows it the best, you know. No, I was going to take the picture of Jordan's four-wheeler because it was in that water, you know.

[00:14:22] **Darrell Tritt:** Oh, yesterday?

[00:14:22] **Matt Gilbert:** Yeah, 'cause I want to tell people out there with this climate, government climate report about Gwich'in, how fast the weather changes, you know, like one day that big bank is dry, the next day it's full of water, see how fast it—

[00:14:38] **Darrell Tritt:** It's good weather, then 15 minutes later it's raining [*they laugh*].

[00:14:49] **Matt Gilbert:** I know, remember that story I told you; me and Julius got stuck at the Washeteria in Venetie in T-shirts because it was hot out, then it's pouring rain on us [*they laugh*]. Yeah, I wanted to take a picture of Jordan's four-wheeler to show people how fast it changed, cause you could even sit at that table, it's just in the water. It never used to be like that. The weather didn't change that fast a long time ago?

[00:15:22] **Darrell Tritt:** No, first I ever seen this rain.

[00:15:28] **Matt Gilbert:** Well, Mahsi, choo, yeah, anything else you want to add?

[00:15:30] **Darrell Tritt:** No

[00:15:32] **Matt Gilbert:** Ok, Mahsi choo, Darrell Tritt.

Index

Page numbers followed by *f* indicate figures

Tritt, Bobby, 19, 26–27, 50, 117, 123, 209, 272; on fishing, 32; interview of, 124–28; on rabbits, 46

Tritt, Christian: Porcupine River and, 99

Tritt, Darrell, 6, 192, 202, 203, 210, 214, 226, 229, 230, 232, 236; on Chandalar River, 208–9; clouds and, 187; on crevices, 198; interview of, 270–77; predictions by, 206; on seagulls, 204; on thunder/ lightning, 200; on winds, 208

Tritt, Deena, 147, 192, 193, 195, 214, 232, 257; on air pollution, 194; on berries, 44, 182, 206; on birds, 204, 205; interview of, 53–54, 243–48; on overgrowth, 198; on weather changes, 19

Tritt, Donald, 121, 166

Tritt, Franklin, 27, 204; on caribou, 201; interview of, 83–85, 249–51, 251–52; on moose, 39; on winter, 194

Tritt, Isaac, 99

Tritt, Julia, 9

Tritt, Kathy, 182, 191, 192, 246; on cotton balls, 188; on rabbits, 23; on snow, 196

Tritt, Raymond, 15, 23, 26, 116, 117, 178, 195, 202, 256; advice from, 82; berries and, 206; on caribou, 34–35; on dogs, 24; fish and, 41; on graylings, 203; on hunting, 10; interview of, 79–85, 258–59, 260; on lynx, 45; on moose, 39; salmon berries and, 44; on summer weather, 20

Tritt, Sarah "Ghoo," 35, 109

Tritt Creek, 122

trout, loss of, 115

Trump, Donald, 36, 186

Tsal Cho, 123

T'salvik, 116

Tsiivii tit, 60, 61, 98, 100, 123, 205

tuna, fishing for, 141

tundra, 5, 7, 14, 27, 64, 198

Tundra (book), 27

tussucks, 86

20-Mile, 15, 30, 158, 159

Tyii' troo' eeh, 144

"Ugly Clouds," 22

University of Alaska Fairbanks (UAF), 3, 7, 15, 39, 42, 184

US Fish and Wildlife Service (USFWS), 6, 7, 30, 35, 37, 45, 50, 51, 57, 89, 91, 92, 93, 135, 140, 175, 206, 209, 272; moose and, 147; Native peoples and, 277; salmon and, 124; working with, 122, 125, 126

US Geological Survey, 7, 38

USDA, Indigenous peoples and, 138

USFWS. See US Fish and Wildlife Service

Vahan stii', Steven, 77

Valdez, oil spill in, 211, 222

Vashraii Koo, 25, 28–29, 41, 63, 199

Vashraii Van, 123

Veetreegwangwaii, 113, 114

vegetation, 36, 58, 76, 119, 240; caribou and, 85, 118; changes in, 60

Venetie, 4, 6, 7, 10, 12, 15, 19, 25, 26, 27, 35, 36, 51, 61, 68, 69, 77, 82, 84, 85, 108, 114, 118; accessibility and, 33; birds in, 47, 48; climate change in, 270; Coronavirus in, 184; ducks in, 42; erosion near, 209; fish in, 74, 271; forest fire and, 73, 89; hardships for, 132; hunting near, 32; insects in, 49; lakes near, 60, 209; lynx near, 80; moose near, 38, 39, 147; rabbits in, 46; salmon and, 40, 188; snow in, 23; summers in, 20; unemployment issue and, 50; weather in, 18, 208; whitefish in, 127; Yukon River and, 28

Venetie Climate Impact Report 2005, 208

Venetie Climate Impact Report 2020, summary of, 208–9

Venetie Council, 126

Venetie Reservation, oil on, 128

Vinee Dachan Dhi'ee, 113

volcanos, 95

Vyuh, 229, 264

Vyuh Dzraii', 113

walking trails, map of, 14

Ward, Doris, 15, 17–18, 210–11; interview of, 154–57; on moose, 10

water, 167; changes in, 203; clean, 94, 138, 172, 174; rising costs of, 161, 162; warming, 40, 61

water levels, 65; drop in, 126, 135, 199, 213, 222

weather: bad, 187, 200, 246; birds and, 200; changes in, 18, 19, 25, 55, 58, 72, 81, 100, 103, 112, 116, 121, 133, 148, 160, 161, 163, 177, 183, 193–96, 207, 208, 242, 255, 265, 266, 267; clouds and, 187; cold, 160, 162, 265; effects on individuals, 25; Gwich'in on, 19–25; hot, 78, 85, 87, 162; low-pressure, 244; predictability of, 9; trusting, 163

welfare, 106, 215

wetlands, 26, 42, 209

White Eye Camp, 12

White Mountains, 7, 12

white-winged scoter, 130, 132

whitefish, 30, 63, 69, 114, 127, 199, 223, 224, 250; catching, 203; changes for, 156, 195, 200; fishing for, 143

wigeon, 203, 253

wildlife groups, partnerships with, 95–96

Williams, Faith, 215

willows, 66, 73, 81, 85, 120, 158, 239, 240, 242; caribou and, 107; cutting down, 64; growth of, 76, 127, 135; moose and, 84

Wind River, 113

winds, 87, 130; changes in, 208

winter, 84, 102, 143, 243, 261; changes in, 23–24, 87, 100, 126, 186, 194–95, 208, 255; colder, 194; warmer, 23, 54, 65, 75, 238

Wintertrail Fire, 147

wolverines, 46, 63

wolves, 63, 84, 125, 126, 142, 144, 246, 262; caribou and, 57, 89, 107, 122, 201; disappearance of, 201; moose and, 90; overpopulation of, 51; population of, 135

wood ducks, 49

woodpeckers, 201, 243

Wright, 141

Yeendaa, 9, 106

yellowtail snipe, 183, 210, 228; disappearance of, 46, 47; return of, 202; scarcity of, 202

Yukon Bridge, 141

Yukon Channel, 108

Yukon Flats, 7, 13, 26, 27, 98, 107, 108, 111, 142, 143; blueberries in, 154; changes in, 212; map of, 8; moose near, 39, 125, 157; villages in, 8f

Yukon River, 7, 11, 28, 61, 98, 143, 154, 204, 213, 237; decline of, 212; flooding of, 167; salmon and, 40

Zheh Vee Luu, 18, 207